Netaji Subhash Chandra Bose

Netaji
Subhash Chandra Bose

Series Editor
Dr. M.H. Syed

Editor
Anil Kathuria **Bharat Singh**

hbpl

Himalaya Books Pvt. Ltd.

'Ramdoot', Dr. Bhalerao Marg, Girgaon, Mumbai - 400 004
Tel : (022) 23863863, Fax : (022) 23877178
Email : himpub@vsnl.com

Edition : 2013
Edition : 2019

Published by : **H.B.P.L.**
"Pooja Apartments", 4-B, Murari Lal Street, Ansari Road,
Darya Ganj, New Delhi-110 002
Phones : 23270392, 23278631 Reliance : 30180392 to 396
Fax : 011-23256286 Email : hphdel@vsnl.com

Sole Distributers : HIMALAYA PUBLISHING HOUSE PVT. LTD.

Branch Offices

Mumbai : "Ramdoot", Dr. Bhalerao Marg, Girgaon, Mumbai-400 004.
Phones : 23860170/23863863 Fax : 022-23877178
Email : himpub@vsnl.com
Website : www.himpub.com

Nagpur : Kundanlal Chandak Industrial Estate, Ghat Road, **Nagpur - 440 018.**
Phone: 2738731, 3296733 Telefax : 0712-2721215

Bengaluru : No. 16/1 (Old 12/1), 1st Floor, Next to Hotel Highlands,
Madhava Nagar, Race Course Road, **Bengaluru - 560 001.**
Phone : 22281541, 22385461, Telefax: 080-22286611

Hyderabad : No. 3-4-184, Lingampally, Besides Raghavendra Swamy Matham,
Kachiguda, **Hyderabad - 500 027.** Phone: 040-27560041, 27550139,
Mobile:- 09848130433 Telefax: 040-27560041

Chennai : No. 85/50, Bazullah Road, T. Nagar, **Chennai - 600 017.**
Phone: 044-28344020, 32463737, 42124860

Pune : No. 527, "Laksha" Apartment, First Floor, Mehunpura, Shaniwarpeth,
(Near Prabhat Theatre), **Pune - 411 030.**
Phone: 020-24496323/24496333/32326733

Lucknow : House No. 731, Sehkhupura Colony, Near B.D. Convent School,
Lucknow - 226 024. Mobile : 09307501549

Ahmedabad : No. 114, "SHAIL", 1st Floor, Opp. Madhu Sudan House, C.G.Road,
Navrang Pura, **Ahmedabad – 380 009.**
Phone: 079-26560126, Mobiles: 09327324149, 09314679413

Ernakulam : No. 39/104 A, Lakshmi Apartment, Karikkamuri Cross Rd.,
Ernakulam, **Cochin – 682011**, Kerala.
Phone: 0484-2378012, 2378016, Mob.: 09344199799

Bhubaneswar : 5 Station Square, **Bhubaneswar (Orissa) - 751 001.**
Mobile: 9861046007, E-mail:- orissa@himpub.com

Indore : Kesardeep Avenue Extension, 73, Narayan Bagh.Flat No. 302,
IIIrd Floor, Near Humpty Dumpty School, Narayan Bagh,
Indore (M.P.) 452 007 Mobile: 09301386468

Kolkata : 108/4, Beliaghata, Main Road, Near ID Hospital, Opp. SBI Bank
Kolkata - 700 010.
Mobile: 09910440956, E-mail:- nkmitra@himpub.com

Guwahati : House No. 15, Behind Prajjyotish College, Near Sharma
Printing Press, P.O. Bharalumukh, Guwahati - 781009 (Assam)
Mobile: 07439040301; 07439040302

Printed by : Sri Prints & Sales, Delhi

Preface

Biography, is now a form of literature, very much in vogue. In fact, biography is a description or account of someone's life and the times, which is usually published in the form of a book. A biography is more than a mention of personal facts (life, education, work, relationships and death), it also portrays the subject's experience of events. Technically speaking, a work is biographical, if it covers, all of a person's life. Biography writing has a long history. A biography is real. Ancient Greeks developed the biographical tradition, which we have inherited, although until the 5th century AD, when the word 'biographia' first appeared, in Damascius' "Life of Isodorus," biographical pieces were called simply "lives". It is quite likely that the Greeks were drawing on a pre-existing eastern tradition. Certainly Herodotus' "Histories" contains more detailed biographical information on Persian kings and subjects. The earliest surviving pieces, which we would identify as biographical are Isocrates' "Life of Evagoras" and Xenophon's "Life of Agesilaos," both from the fifth century BC. "Parallel Lives" by Plutarch, a Greek writing under the Roman empire, is a series of short biographies of eminent men.

The Golden Age of English biography emerged in late eighteenth century, the century in which the terms "biography" and "autobiography" entered English lexicon. The classic works of the period were Samuel Johnson's "Critical Lives of the Poets" and James Boswell's "Massive Life of Johnson". Generally American biography followed English model. By World War I, cheap hardcover reprints had become popular. The decade of the

1920s witnessed a biographical 'boom'. Later, biographical writings developed a lot and today biographies are written and compiled in the finest form of the genre. In India too, biography, as a form of literature has been evolved, cultivated and polished over the years. Here is an effort to promote this tradition further.

This series of biographies of great men, great women and celebrities in all walks of life is an adventurous academic endeavour, in its own right. A team of researchers and compilers has worked for a good period of time to accomplish the project. For this purpose, hundreds of books by eminent authors and editors have been consulted and referred to. We have benefited from various works, liberally, in order to illustrate and enrich this effort of ours. Present book is devoted to the great personality of Netaji, Subhash Chandra Bose.

Netaji, Subhash Chandra Bose (born January 23, 1897) was a leader in the Indian independence movement. Bose was elected president of the Indian National Congress for two consecutive terms, but had to resign from the post, following ideological conflicts with Mahatma Gandhi and after openly attacking the Congress' foreign and internal policies. He established a separate political party, the All India Forward Bloc and continued to call for the full and immediate independence of India from British rule. He was imprisoned by the British authorities eleven times. With Japanese assistance, he re-organised and later led the Azad Hind Fauj or Indian National Army. He also formed the Azad Hind Government in exile and led the Indian National Army in battle against the allies at Imphal and in Burma. He is presumed to have died on 18 August 1945 in a plane crash over Taiwan. However, contradictory evidence exists regarding his death in accident.

This is a compact and comprehensive account of the above mentioned great life, which is bound to attract the attention of scholars, researchers, students and the general readers alike. Let's hope this humble effort would receive a warm welcome and due applause.

— ***Editors***

Contents

1

An Eventful Life

The Independence Movement in India, witnessed a great many leaders laying down their life for a free India. While the majority of them have faded from the public memory, it is Netaji Subhash Chandra Bose alone whose legacy continues as a legendary figure. He was a fierce patriot, a visionary leader, a great orator, flamboyant revolutionary, all rolled into one.

Subhash Chandra Bose always walked his talk and courted controversy throughout his life. Despite being elected twice as president, his strong views and firebrand politics often raised heckles within the Congress Party. But such was Bose's aura and magnetism that even those differed with him could not help but appreciate his undying love for the nation.

Great Exploits

Subhash Chandra's colourful and daring exploits in foreign lands endeared him to the millions of Indians who worshipped him as a cult figure. Bose's alleged death in mysterious circumstances has only served to augment his legend manifold. Subhash Bose had his share of detractors and critics. He was dubbed a fascist and was criticised for seeking help from Nazi Germany and imperialist Japan. All these harsh opinions notwithstanding, Subhash Chandra Bose lives in the Indian conscience a brave hero and a true patriot.

Great Beginning

Subhash Chandra Bose was born into an affluent Bengali family on January 23, 1897 in Cuttack, Orissa. Subhash's public prosecutor father ensured that his son availed the best of education in eminent institutions such as Scottish Church College, Calcutta and Fitzwilliam College at Cambridge University. In 1920, at the insistence of his parents, Bose appeared at the prestigious Indian Civil Service and secured the fourth place.

In the Arena of Freedom Struggle

During this period the Civil Disobedience Movement called by Mahatma Gandhi was sweeping across the country and Bose resigned from the ICS in April 1921 to join his fellow countrymen in the freedom struggle. He joined the youth wing of the Congress Party and soon rose up the party hierarchy by virtue of his eloquence and leadership skills. At an early stage of his life Subhash Bose accepted Deshbandhu Chittaranjan Das as his political guru. Over a span of 20 years, Bose was imprisoned eleven times by the British, the first one being in 1921. In 1924, after a brief period of incarceration, Bose was exiled to Mandalay in Burma. Subhash Bose was imprisoned again in 1930 and deported to Europe. During his stay in Europe from 1933 to 1936, Subhash Bose zealously espoused the cause of Indian freedom while meeting a number of prominent European statesmen. In 1937, Bose married Emilie Schenkl who was his secretary.

Congress to Forward Bloc

Subhash Bose was twice elected president of the Indian National Congress (1938 and 1939) but following his disagreements with Mahatma Gandhi he relinquished his post and formed a progressive group known as the Forward Block. The Second World War broke out in 1939 and Bose launched a campaign of mass civil disobedience to protest against the Viceroy's decision to declare war on India's behalf. Bose was put behind the bars but because of his hunger strike he was later placed under house arrest. Taking advantage of the laxity of the house guards and aided by his cousin Sishir Bose, Subhash managed to escape and traversing through enemy territories he reached Moscow. Bose tried to garner the help of Nazi Germany but due to the indifferent attitude of Hitler and other German leaders he left for Japan.

Soon, he assumed the leadership of Indian National Army (INA) founded by Rash Behari Bose. Bolstered by material assistance from the Japanese forces, the INA attacked the British forces in Manipur and Nagaland in northeastern India and hoisted the National Flag in the town in Moirang, in Manipur. But with the defeat of Japan, the invasion by the INA soon petered out and Netaji was forced to retreat to Malaya. Netaji Subhash Chandra Bose allegedly died in a plane crash over Taiwan, while flying to Tokyo on August 18, 1945.

Effort for Armed Revolution

The principles and the philosophy of Netaji Subhash Chandra Bose were instrumental factors in his embracing of armed revolution in the later part of his political career. Initially Bose was a follower of the Gandhian way of Freedom Movement but years of travel in European countries during exile and the ripening of mental faculties with age made him disenchanted with the ways of the Indian National Congress. Subhash Chandra's hatred for the British ran deep and he vehemently called for the immediate ouster of the colonial rulers from Indian soil. Disappointed with the leniency shown by some Congress leaders towards the British, Bose became increasingly convinced that the goal of achieving freedom would remain a pipedream as long as the British held sway over the land and peaceful protests would never be able to throw the British out.

Vision for Free India

While outlining his vision for a free India, Subhash Chandra Bose proclaimed that socialist authoritarianism would be required to eradicate poverty and social inequalities from a diverse country like India. He openly espoused for an authoritarian state on the lines of Soviet Russia and Kemal Ataturk's Turkey. Bose was also an exponent of socialism and opined that industrialisation and Soviet-style five-year plans held the key to a vibrant Indian nation.

Proclamation of an Independent Government

The Indian National Army was the manifestation of Subhash Chandra Bose's transformation from a Gandhian freedom fighter to an armed revolutionary challenging the might of the British Empire. Originally the brainchild of expatriate nationalist leader Rash Behari Bose, the INA saw Subhash Chandra assuming the leadership of the outfit as its supreme commander in 1943. With characteristic vigour and zeal, Bose set about strengthening the fledgling organisation and proclaimed the Provisional Government of Free India in Singapore on October 21, 1943. The Indian National Army was also known as the Azad Hind Fauj and it owed allegiance to the Provisional Government which was recognised by nine Axis states. The INA had a combat strength of 40,000 troops comprising mainly of Indian expatriates in South Asia and Indian prisoners of war. The INA also boasted of an exclusive women's combat unit named the Rani of Jhansi regiment.

Early Victories

As the Japanese troops launched a major offensive through Burma, the Azad Hind Fauj soldiers fought alongside them in the frontlines and contributed in many victories. Previously in December, 1943 the Azad Hind government had established its rule in the Andaman and Nicobar Islands and renamed them as *Shaheed* (Martyr) and *Swaraj* (Self-rule). On 18 April 1944, the INA troops captured the town of Moirang in Manipur and in a glorious display of patriotism, raised an Indian tricolour. However, the INA's total dependence on the Japanese troops for arms and logistics support proved to be its undoing and as the might of the Japanese began to wane, the INA too was forced to retreat. With the subsequent surrender of Japan the INA resistance collapsed and a number of officers and troops were captures by the British. The government brought these officers to the Red Fort in Delhi for court martial but eventually had to relent in the face of nationwide protests and incidents of mutiny in the ranks of British Indian Army.

Great Oratory Skills

Subhash Chandra employed his great oratory skills to inspire the troops of Indian National Army. On July 4, 1944, at a rally of

Indians in Burma, Bose famously proclaimed, "Give me blood, and I shall give you freedom." "Delhi Chalo," another phrase attributed to him, became the clarion call of the INA combatants as they marched towards Indian territory.

Gandhi and Bose

Both Netaji Subhash Chandra Bose and Mahatma Gandhi were infallibly dedicated to the cause of Indian freedom. They were loved by the masses and feared by the Raj. But between themselves, these two icons of India's Freedom Movement shared a rather frosty relationship and history is replete with instances of trenchant differences between them. Although Subhash Chandra was a follower of Gandhi during the initial days, the later part of the 1930s witnessed a growing radicalisation of his thoughts and Bose became increasingly frustrated with the lack of momentum in the Independence Movement. As Bose started to assert his bold stance in various party forums, it led to a polarisation in the Congress party ranks. Bose found himself frequently at loggerheads with Gandhi and their differences often came out in the public. All these bickering reached a climax when Subhash Chandra Bose became Congress President for a second term in 1939 defeating Gandhi-nominated candidate Pattabhi Sitaramayya. Unable to hide his displeasure, Mahatma commented "Subhash' victory is my defeat." But this unhealthy environment within the party made Bose's task all the more difficult and soon he resigned from his post.

Different Visions

Subhash Chandra Bose and Gandhi disagreed over their visions for the post-independence Indian state. Bose was influenced by the success of the five-year plans in the Soviet Union and he advocated for a socialist nation with an industrialised economy. Gandhi was opposed to the very concept of industrialisation. In spite of all the differences in ideologies, both these great men admired and respected each other. In 1942 Gandhi called Subhash Bose the "Prince among the Patriots" for his great love for the country. Bose too admired Gandhi and in a radio broadcast from Rangoon in 1944, he called Mahatma Gandhi "The Father of Our Nation."

After 65 years of his alleged death in a plane crash, the mystery over that incident and Netaji Subhash Chandra Bose's possible survival still haunts the Indian nation. The absence of any credible evidence and the subsequent inability of the government appointed committees to unravel the truth have spawned umpteen conspiracy theories with a large chuck of the population refusing to believe that their beloved leader indeed lost his life in a plane crash.

Facets of the Death Mystery

The four-member Shah Nawaz Committee was the first official endeavour to examine whether Bose actually died in a plane crash in Taihoku (Taipei) on August 18, 1945. The committee went to Japan in May, 1956 and a number of Japanese army surgeons testified that they actually conducted blood transfusion on a seriously injured Subhash Bose who later succumbed to his injuries.

The G. D. Khosla Committee, which carried on its probe from 1974-78, could not arrive on any definite conclusion. The Justice Mukherjee Committee, set up in 1999, submitted its report in 2005 and proclaimed that Netaji did not die in the plane crash. Many believe that Subhash Chandra breathed his last in Soviet custody years after the alleged crash in Taiwan. There are unconfirmed reports that in 1946 Russian strongman Josef Stalin and diplomat Vyacheslav Molotov actually discussed whether Bose should remain in the Soviet Union.

More startling is the alleged incident that (the then) Indian ambassador to Russia, Dr. S. Radhakrishnan was permitted to meet Netaji in an undisclosed location in the Soviet Union. Lt. Colonel Habibur Rehman Khan, Netaji's trusted Aide-de-Camp, is widely believed to be the sole survivor of that fateful plane crash. Rehman later enshrined Bose's ashes in the Renkoji temple Tokyo. However, despite repeated interrogations by British authorities, Rehman never substantiated Netaji's death and throughout his life maintained that he was bound by an oath of secrecy to his deceased leader. Conspiracy theories still abound regarding Netaji's death.

2

Netaji's Illustrious Journey

Netaji Subhash Chandra Bose (born January 23, 1897; presumed to have died August 18, 1945 although this is disputed), popularly known as Netaji (literally "Respected Leader"), was a leader in the Indian Independence Movement.

Bose advocated complete freedom for India at the earliest, whereas the Congress Committee wanted it in phases, through a Dominion status. Other younger leaders including Jawaharlal Nehru supported Bose and finally at the historic Lahore Congress convention, the Congress had to adopt *Purna Swaraj* (complete freedom) as its motto. Bhagat Singh's martyrdom and the inability of the Congress leaders to save his life infuriated Bose and he started a movement opposing the Gandhi-Irwin Pact. He was imprisoned and expelled from India. But defying the ban, he came back to India and was imprisoned again.

Bose was elected president of the Indian National Congress for two consecutive terms, but had to resign from the post following ideological conflicts with Mahatma Gandhi and after openly attacking the Congress' foreign and internal policies. Bose believed that Mahatma Gandhi's tactics of non-violence would never be sufficient to secure India's independence, and advocated violent resistance. He established a separate political party, the All India Forward Bloc and continued to call for the full and immediate independence of India from British rule. He was imprisoned by the British authorities eleven times. His famous motto was "Give me blood and I will give you freedom".

His stance did not change with the outbreak of the Second World War, which he saw as an opportunity to take advantage of British weakness. At the outset of the war, he left India, travelling to the Soviet Union, Germany and Japan, seeking an alliance with the aim of attacking the British in India. With Japanese assistance, he reorganised and later led the Azad Hind Fauj or Indian National Army, formed from Indian prisoners-of-war and plantation workers from British Malaya, Singapore, and other parts of South East Asia, against British forces. With Japanese monetary, political, diplomatic and military assistance, he formed the Azad Hind Government in exile, regrouped and led the Indian National Army in battle against the allies at Imphal and in Burma.

His political views and the alliances he made with Nazi and other militarist regimes at war with Britain have been the cause of arguments among historians and politicians, with some accusing him of fascist sympathies, while others in India have been more sympathetic towards the inculcation of realpolitik as a manifesto that guided his social and political choices.

He is presumed to have died on 18 August 1945 in a plane crash over Taiwan. However, contradictory evidence exists regarding his death in the accident.

Early Days

Subhash Chandra Bose was born in a Bengali Kayasth family on January 23 1897 in Cuttack (Odiya Bazar), Orissa, the ninth child among 14, of Janakinath Bose, an advocate, and Prabhavati Devi. Bose studied in an Anglo school at Cuttack until standard 6 which is now known as Stewart School and then shifted to Ravenshaw Collegiate School of Cuttack. A brilliant student, Bose topped the matriculation examination of Calcutta province in 1911 and passed his BA in 1918 in Philosophy from the Scottish Church College of the University of Calcutta.

Bose went to study in Fitzwilliam Hall of the University of Cambridge, and his high score in the Civil Service examinations meant an almost automatic appointment. He then took his first conscious step as a revolutionary and resigned the appointment on the premise that the "best way to end a government is to withdraw from it." At the time, Indian nationalists were shocked and outraged because of the Amritsar massacre and the repressive Rowlatt legislation of 1919. Returning to India, Bose wrote for the newspaper *Swaraj* and took charge of publicity for the Bengal Provincial Congress Committee. His mentor was Chittaranjan Das, spokesman for aggressive nationalism in Bengal. Bose worked for Das when the latter was elected mayor of Calcutta in 1924. In a roundup of nationalists in 1925, Bose was arrested and sent to prison in Mandalay, where he contracted tuberculosis.

He was a devout Hindu and spent much time in meditation. Strongly influenced by Swami Vivekananda's teachings, he was known for his patriotic zeal as a student.

Subhash Chandra Bose was not a political philosopher in the traditional sense. He was deeply involved in national politics of colonial India and concentrated all his energy in overthrowing British rule from the country. The achievement of freedom was thus his prime goal and hence his political ideas mainly revolved around national freedom which would pave way for a bright future for India. There is spontaneity in his political thinking which cannot be separated from his hectic political life.

Childhood

He was born on January 23, 1887 at Cuttack. As a sensitive child he perceived the subtle discrimination, Indians had to suffer at the hands of the British. A resentment developed against the British, with whom he came in contact as a pupil in his school in Orissa. This turmoil tormented teenaged Subhash and made him run away from home in quest of a Guru who could give him solace. In the meantime he studied Swami Vivekananda's philosophy which influenced him deeply and led him to identify spiritualism with social service. He wanted national construction on modern lines. After his early schooling, he joined Ravenshaw Collegiate School. From there he went to join Presidency College, Calcutta, where Indian students were extremely angry against their History teacher E. F. Oaten's arrogant behaviour. Oaten was slapped and beaten up in the college premises. Subhash Bose was suspended and rusticated for this. Later, he graduated in Philosophy from Scottish Church College. He sat in the most prestigious competitive examination of I.C.S. in England and came out with flying colours. However, love for his country made him resign this prestigious and comfortable job on 22 April 1921 and thereafter he plunged in national/freedom struggle wholeheartedly.

His Activities

In 1921, he met Gandhi after reaching India and participated in the Non-cooperation Movement. In the meantime he came in contact with C. R. Das and became his disciple. He associated with Das's political endeavour and was also jailed along with him. He took over the editorship of a news daily 'Forward' started by C. R. Das's Swaraj Party. When Das was elected Mayor of Calcutta Corporation he nominated Bose as the chief executive. He was arrested for his political activities in 1924. In 1930 he was elected Mayor of Calcutta, the same year he was elected President of AITUC. In the thirties, he was closely associated with left politics in Congress along with Jawaharlal Nehru, Congress Socialists, Communists and M. N. Roy. Because of the endeavour of the left group the Congress passed very far-reaching radical resolutions in Karachi in 1931, which declared the main Congress aim as socialisation of means of production besides guaranteeing fundamental rights. Subhash won the Congress presidential election at Haripura with the backing of leftists in 1938. Next year at Tripuri he again won the presidential election against Gandhi's candidate Pattabhi Sitararhmayya. However, his differences with Gandhi became very wide and ultimately he left the Congress. He founded a new party 'The Forward Bloc'. In 1939, the world war broke out. Subhash felt that the adversaries Nazi Germany, Fascist Italy and Japan of the main enemy of India, i.e. British imperialism, be utilised to the maximum advantage possible. He therefore jumped with full vigour in this last battle for freedom. He was arrested and put under house-detention. He, however, made a successful escape, by fooling the British authorities and reached Germany after visiting other places. Events moved fast, he reached Japan and from there to Burma and organised the Indian National

Army (INA) to fight the British and to liberate India with the help of Japan. He gave famous slogans 'Jai Hind' and 'Dilli Chalo'. He died in a plane crash before realising his dreams. Some people however still think that he is alive.

National Politics

Released from prison two years later, Bose became general secretary of the Congress party and worked with Jawaharlal Nehru for independence. Again Bose was arrested and jailed for civil disobedience; this time he emerged Mayor of Calcutta. During the mid-1930s Bose travelled in Europe, visiting Indian students and European politicians, as well as Hitler in 1936. He observed party organisation and saw communism and fascism in action. By 1938 Bose had become a leader of national stature and agreed to accept nomination as Congress president. He stood for unqualified Swaraj (independence), including the use of force against the British. This meant a confrontation with Mohandas Gandhi, who in fact opposed Bose's presidency, splitting the Congress party. Bose attempted to maintain unity, but Gandhi advised Bose to form his own cabinet. The rift also divided Bose and Nehru. Bose appeared at the 1939 Congress meeting on a stretcher. Though he was elected president again, over Gandhi's preferred candidate Pattabhi Sitaramayya, U Muthuramalingam Thevar strongly supported Bose in the intra-Congress dispute. Thevar mobilised all south India votes for Bose. However, due to the manoeuvrings of the Gandhi-led clique in the Congress Working Committee, Bose found himself forced to resign from the Congress Presidency. "I am an extremist, " Bose once said, and his uncompromising stand finally cut him off from the mainstream of Indian nationalism. Bose then organised the Forward Bloc on June 22, aimed at consolidating the political left, but its main strength was in his home state, Bengal. U Muthuramalingam Thevar, who was disillusioned by the official Congress leadership which had not revoked the CTA, joined the Forward Bloc. When Bose visited Madurai on September 6, Thevar organised a massive rally as his reception.

All India Forward Bloc

The All India Forward Bloc was a leftwing nationalist political party in India. It emerged as a faction within the Indian National

Congress in 1939, led by Subhash Chandra Bose. The party was re-established as an independent political party after the independence of India. It had its main stronghold in West Bengal.

Formation of the Forward Bloc: The Forward Bloc of the Indian National Congress was formed on 3 May 1939 by Netaji Subhash Chandra Bose, who had resigned from the presidency of the Indian National Congress on April 29 after being outmanoeuvred by Mohandas K. Gandhi. The formation of the Forward Bloc was announced to the public at a rally in Calcutta. Initially the aim of the Forward Bloc was to rally all the leftwing sections within the Congress and develop an alternative leadership inside the Congress. Bose became the president of the Forward Bloc and S. S. Cavesheer its vice-president. A Forward Bloc Conference was held in Bombay in the end of June. At that conference the constitution and programme of the Forward Bloc were approved. In July 1939 Subhash Chandra Bose announced the Committee of the Forward Bloc. It had Subhash Chandra Bose as president, S. S. Cavesheer from Punjab as its vice-president, Lal Shankarlal from Delhi, as its general secretary and Pandit B. Tripathi and Khurshed Nariman from Bombay as secretaries. Other prominent members were Annapurniah from Andhra Pradesh, Senapati Bapat, Hari Vishnu Kamnath from Bombay, Pasumpon U. Muthuramalingam Thevar from Tamil Nadu and Sheel Bhadra Yajee from Bihar. Satya Ranjan Bakshi, was appointed as the secretary of the Bengal Provincial Forward Bloc.

In August the same year Bose began publishing a newspaper titled *Forward Bloc*. He travelled around the country, rallying support for his new political project.

Nagpur Conference: The following year, on June 20-22 1940, the Forward Bloc held its first All India Conference in Nagpur. The conference declared the Forward Bloc to be a socialist political party, and the date of June 22 is considered as the founding date of the party by the Forward Bloc itself. The conference passed a resolution titled 'All Power to the Indian People', urging militant action for struggle against British colonial rule. Subhash Chandra Bose was elected as the president of the party and H. V. Kamath the general secretary.

Arrest and Exile of Bose: Soon thereafter, on July 2, Bose was arrested and detained in Presidency Jail, Calcutta. In January 1941 he escaped from house arrest, and clandestinely went into exile. He travelled to the Soviet Union via Afghanistan, seeking Soviet support for the Indian independence struggle. Stalin declined Bose's request, and he then travelled to Germany. In Berlin he set up the Free India Centre, and rallied the Indian Legion.

In August 1942 the British authorities banned the Forward Bloc. Its offices around the country were ransacked. In 1943 Bose was transported to Asia, where he took over the leadership of the Indian National Army. During the final phase of the war the INA fought alongside the Japanese against the British army.

Inside India, local activists of the Forward Bloc continued the anti-British activities without central coordination. For example, in Bihar members were involved in the Azad Dasta resistance groups, and distributed propaganda in support of Bose and INA. They did not have, however, any organic link neither with Bose nor the INA.

Indian National Army and Provisional Government

When world war II erupted in Europe, Bose was again imprisoned for civil disobedience and put under house arrest to await trial. He escaped and made his way to Berlin by way of Peshawar and Afghanistan. In Europe, Bose sought help from Germany for the liberation of India. He got Nazi permission to organise the Indian Legion of prisoners of war from Africa, but the legion remained basically German in training. Bose felt the need for stronger steps, and he turned to the Japanese embassy in Berlin, which finally made arrangements for Bose to go to Asia. In an unusual joint operation, he was transferred from a German to a Japanese submarine off the coast of Madagascar.

Bose was flown to Singapore and became commander of the INA and head of the Free India provisional government (Arzi Hukumat-e-Azad Hind).

The INA included both Indian prisoners of war from Singapore and Indian civilians in South East Asia. The strength of the INA grew to 43,000. Bose ruled Andaman Islands and Nicobar Islands as a head of India. Bose refused to be granted aid, and asked Japan for conclusion of official India-Japan loan agreements, then they concluded the agreements. The INA fought Allied forces in 1944 inside the borders of India at Imphal and in Burma, and even succeeding in capturing parts of North-East India from the Allies. Unfortunately, with Japan losing its way in the World War, aid to the INA was also reduced, and the army could not keep up its momentum. Three officers of the INA were tried at the Red Fort after the war; the trial attracted much popular sympathy, including statements by Nehru and Gandhi that the men were great patriots.

Disappearance and Alleged Demise

Bose is alleged to have died in a plane crash over Taiwan, while flying to Tokyo on 18 August 1945. It is believed that he was on route to the Soviet Union in a Japanese plane when it crashed in Taiwan, burning him fatally. However, his body was never recovered, and many theories have been put forward concerning his possible survival. One such claim is that Bose actually died later in Siberia, while in Soviet captivity. Several committees have been set up by the Government of India to probe into this matter. In May 1956, a four-man Indian team (known as the Shah Nawaz Committee) visited Japan to probe the circumstances of Bose's alleged death. However, the Indian government did not then request assistance from the government of Taiwan in the matter, citing their lack of diplomatic relations with Taiwan. However, the Enquiry Commission under Justice Mukherjee, which investigated the Bose disappearance mystery in the period 1999-2005, did approach the Taiwanese government, and obtained information from the Taiwan Government that no plane carrying Bose had ever crashed in Taipei, and there was, in fact, no plane crash in Taiwan on 18 August 1945 as alleged. The Mukherjee Commission also received a report originating from the US Department of State supporting the claim of the Taiwan Government that no such air crash took place during that time frame.

The Justice Mukherjee Commission of Enquiry submitted its report to the Indian Government on November 8, 2005. The report was tabled in Parliament on May 17, 2006. The probe said in its report that as Bose did not die in the plane crash, and that the ashes at the Renkoji Temple (said to be of Bose's) are not his. However, the Indian Government rejected the findings of the Commission, though no reasons were cited.

Several documents which could perhaps provide lead to the disappearance of Bose have not been declassified by the Government of India, the reason cited being publication of these documents could sour India's relations with some other countries.

Bose was posthumously awarded the Bharat Ratna, India's highest civilian award in 1992, but it was later withdrawn in response to a Supreme Court directive following a Public Interest Litigation filed in the Court against the "posthumous" nature of the award. The Award Committee could not give conclusive evidence on Bose's death and thus the "posthumous" award was invalidated. No headway was made on this issue however.

Bose's portrait hangs in the Indian Parliament, and a statue of him has been erected in front of the West Bengal Legislative Assembly.

The Mysterious Monk

Several people believed that the Hindu sanyasi named Bhagwanji or 'Gumnami Baba', who lived in the house Ram Bhawan in Faizabad, UP at least until 1985, was Subhash Chandra Bose in exile. There had been at least four known occasions when Gumnami Baba reportedly claimed he was Netaji Subhash Chandra Bose. The belongings of the sanyasi were taken into custody after his death, following a court order. These were later subjected to inspection by the Justice Mukherjee Commission of Enquiry. The commission came down against this belief, in the absence of any "clinching evidence".

The independent probe done by the *Hindustan Times* into the case however provided hints that the monk was Bose himself. Some people believe that Gumnami Baba died on 16 September 1985, while some dispute this. The story of Gumnami Baba came to light on his death.

It is alleged that he was cremated in the dead of night, just under the light of a motorcycle's headlamp, at Faizabad's popular picnic spot, on the bank of River Saryu, his face distorted by acid to protect his identity. Faizabad's Bengali community still pays homage at the memorial built at his cremation site on the anniversary of his birth. However, the life and activities of Bhagwanji remain a mystery even today.

Justice Mukherjee's Inadvertent Approval of Bhagwanji's Identity

Justice Manoj Kumar Mukherjee who probed into the disappearance of Netaji Subhash Chandra Bose stated in his report that the sanyasi of Faizabad (Bhagwanji) was not Bose as there was no clinching evidence to prove it. However, he inadvertently stated in a documentary shoot that he believed Bhagwanji was none other than Bose. This revelation supports the view that Bose had not died in the plane crash in 1945, and was in fact in India after that.

3

Social, Economic and Political Philosophy of Bose

An outstanding leader of the Indian National Movement Subhash Chandra Bose became a legendary figure to be almost worshipped as a great hero and a charismatic leader. A study of his biography unfolds before us his unflagging zeal, as an empiricist, in gaining a theoretical foundation for a plan of action, in his own personal life and in Indian Freedom Movement and in this respect he was influenced by his own parents, Beni Madhab Das, Headmaster, Revenshaw Collegiate School, teachings of Ramakrishna, Vivekananda and Aurobindo Ghosh, C. R. Das, Lenin, Mustafa Kemal Pasha, De Valera, Joseph Mezzini, Count Cavour, Garibaldi, and the impact of freedom movements in other countries such as American War of Independence, Italian struggle for liberation and unification, liberation struggle in Czechoslovakia and Irish struggle for freedom.

In this background his social, economic and political concepts were empirically formulated for an objective observance and ramification with the sole objective of emancipation of Mother India from the British rule of exploitation and oppression and reconstruction of Free India.

The credential of Subhash Chandra Bose as a socio-political thinker will be well traced on a careful study of his activities, letters, writings and speeches at different phases of the freedom struggle, indicating a process of evolution of his social, economic and political concepts connected with the development of his own mind responding to the shifting environment in India and the World outside. The sum of his ideas and convictions constitutes his philosophy, though he was more of an actionist.

Unique Political Ideology

While Bose's political ideology can reasonably be described as essentially "fascistic," two qualifying points need to be made here.

First, his ideology and actions were not the result of any extreme neurotic or pathological psychosocial impulses. He was not a megalomaniac, nor did he display any of the pathological traits often attributed (rightly or wrongly) to fascist leaders, such as hostile aggression, obsessive hatred or delusions. Moreover, while he was an ardent patriot and nationalist, Bose's nationalism was cultural, not racialist.

Second, his radical political ideology was shaped by a consuming frustration with the unsuccessful efforts of others to gain independence for India. His "fascist" outlook did not come from a drive for personal power or social elevation. While he was ambitious, and clearly enjoyed the devotion of his followers, his obsession was not adulation or power, but rather freedom for his beloved Motherland — a goal for which he was willing to suffer and sacrifice, even at the cost of his life.

Bose was favourably impressed with the discipline and organisational strength of fascism as early as 1930, when he first expressed support for a synthesis of fascism and socialism. During his stays in Europe during the 1930s, he was deeply moved by the dynamism of the two major "fascist" powers, Italy and Germany. After observing these regimes first-hand, he developed a political ideology of his own that, he was convinced, could bring about the liberation of India and the total reconstruction of Indian society along vaguely authoritarian-socialist lines.

Bose's lack of success in his life-long effort to liberate India from alien rule was certainly not due to any lack of effort. From

1921, when he became the first Indian to resign formally from the Indian Civil Service, until his death in 1945 as leader of an Indian government in exile, Subhash Chandra Bose struggled ceaselessly to achieve freedom and prosperity for his beloved homeland.

Social Concept

Views on Religion and Communalism

It was under the influence of his parents that Subhash Chandra Bose developed a profoundly religious and spiritual frame of mind, and love for Hindu scriptures from his early life to the last days of his glorious career in the battlefields of South East Asia in 1945. His religious and spiritual propensity was further elevated and broadened in contact with the teachings of Ramkrishna Paramahansa and Vivekananda. He always had a small copy of Bhagavat Gita in the breast pocket of his field uniform. He would plunge into deep meditation at dead hours of night even in the battlefields of South East Asia.

While in Singapore he used to drive to Ramakrishna Mission late at night, change into a priestly silk dhoti, shut himself up in the prayer room with rosary in hand and spent a couple of hours in meditation. He would display his deep devotion to God in the hours of sorrows and sufferings, weal and woe of his life.

At the time of the proclamation of the Provisional Government of Azad Hind, he took the oath, "In the name of God, I take this sacred oath that to liberate India and the thirty-eight crores of my countrymen. I, Subhash Chandra Bose, will continue the sacred war of freedom till the last breath of my life." Again, on the day of taking over direct command of the INA on 26 August 1943, he said "I pray that God may give me the necessary strength to fulfil my duty to Indians, under all circumstances, however difficult or trying they may be." Again in his address to Indian National Army at Singapore, he said, "May God now bless our Army and grant us victory in the coming fight."

Subhash Chandra Bose accepted Upanishadic concept of *'Tyaga'* and imbibed the ideal of renunciation for self-realisation and became determined to work ceaselessly for the benefit of the country and its toiling masses.

Subhash Chandra Bose, being a Secularist, had an attitude of impartiality towards all religions. According to him, the Government of Free India must have an absolutely neutral and impartial attitude towards all religions and leave it to the choice of every individual to profess or follow a particular religion of his faith; Religion is a private affair, it cannot be made an affair of the State.

It was the shrewd and subtle diplomacy of the British that the communal problems in dependent India assumed such a dangerous proportion. According to Subhash Chandra Bose, a nation-wide freedom struggle would result in psychological metamorphosis on political front. Bose was of the firm opinion that economic issues cut across communal divisions and barriers. The problems of poverty and unemployment, of illiteracy and disease, of taxation and indebtedness affected the Hindus and Muslims and other sections of the people as a whole. That the remedy lies in the solution of the political problem on the establishment of a national, popular and democratic government in which people will have direct right to participate and indirect right to criticise. Scientific propaganda was prescribed by him on the above lines to combat communalism. Shah Nawaz Khan said that, for Subhash there were no religious or provincial differences. Hindu, Muslim and Sikh soldiers in the Indian National Army were made to realise that they were sons of the same motherland. That most of ardent supporters and admirers of Netaji were found to be Muslims. Another close associate of Netaji, S. A. Ayar said that, communal harmony of a high order prevailed among the ranks.

In his unfinished autobiography, 'An Indian Pilgrim', we find, Subhash to quote "I was lucky, however, that the environment in which I grew up was on the whole conducive to the broadening of my mind." The atmosphere was on the whole liberalising. His paternal house in Oriya bazar, Cuttack was in a predominantly Muslim locality and their neighbours were mostly Muslims amongst whom his father Janakinath Bose was like a Patriarch. Janaki Babu had Muslim servants and cooks. The Bose family took part in Muslim festivals like Moharrum, Bose writes in his autobiography, "In fact I cannot remember even to have looked upon Muslims as different from ourselves in any way except that they go to pray in Mosque."

In his public speech Subhash advocated emphatically the abolition of caste system in India and introduced observance of Anti-touchability Week from April 6th to 13th. He supported intercaste marriage in India. As a true disciple of Swami Vivekananda, Bose understood that the progress of India would be possible with uplift of the down-trodden and the so-called untouchables who constitute the very essence of our society.

All Indians living in South East Asia were united in the Indian National Army irrespective of caste, race, sex and creed under the stirring leadership of Subhash Chandra Bose in a spirit of Unity, Faith and Sacrifice with the sole objective of emancipation of Mother India.

Emancipation of Women

Subhash Chandra Bose imbibed the ideals of his political mentor, Deshabandhu Chitta Ranjan and spiritual mentor, Swami Vivekananda in regard to female education and female emancipation and used to cite the examples of noble and scholarly women of ancient India like Maitreyee, Gargee, Khana and Lilabatee. Bose wanted that women should be given a very elevated position in the family and society, and believed in female emancipation in the true sense of the term and in liberating women from all shackles and artificial disabilities - social, economic and political. According to him, in the Free India, there must not be any discrimination on ground of caste, race, sex, creed or wealth.

The glorified role played by women in our national struggle, especially during the Civil Disobedience Movement, with undaunted bravery and exemplary spirit of sacrifice, shaped his attitude towards women. The love and affection and help he received from few women, especially his own mother Prabhabati Devi, C. R. Das's ideal consort Basanti Devi and Sarat Chandra Bose's wife Bibhabati Devi had enormous influence in shaping his views about women.

Subhash Chandra Bose rightly diagnosed that illiteracy and economic dependence were the root cause of serfdom of women. Bose spoke firmly in favour of removing all obstacles in the way of women's emancipation. He spoke in favour of all-round education for women for which he formulated a recipe which included literacy, physical and vocational education or training on light Cottage Industries. He was a supporter of widow remarriage and abolition of Purdah system.

When Subhash Bose in his firy speeches was advocating for all round emancipation of women, movement for women's advancement began to gather momentum, the first women organisation in India, Women's Indian Association being established in Madras in 1917. The National Council of Women in India formed in 1925 began to coordinate the work of Provincial Women's Council and other societies with the objectives of women's advancement and welfare and to connect India with international movement.

Subhash Chandra Bose in the later years commended the glorified role played by Indian women in the Freedom Movement notably in the Congress movement and Civil disobedience struggle led by Mahatma Gandhi in which they had been equal to men in addressing public meetings, conducting election campaign, taking out processions in the face of lathi charges by the brutal British Police and undergoing privation of prison life, torture and humiliation. Netaji's firm belief was that no country could really be free if her women did not enter the arena in the fight for freedom in various capacities like serving in hospitals as nurses, looking after wounded soldiers and such other auxiliary roles and they can also take up arms against enemies. So he created the Rani Jhansi Regiment and that too as it did not satisfy his faith in complete equality of women with men; he, in the Provisional Government of Azad Hind appointed one woman Cabinet Minister, giving her a position after him in the order of preference.

Education

According to Subhash Chandra Bose, education was necessary for character building and all round development of human life. Education brings forth the internal discipline in the form of control or regulation of mind and thoughts, which in its turn produces external discipline of control of action or deeds.

His spiritual mentor Vivekananda was of the view that education is the manifestation of perfection already in mind. All knowledge, secular or spiritual comes from the human soul. Thus, education helps to awaken the mind which is the store house of all knowledge. Education would boost of character, morale, virility and freedom of man. Likewise, Bose in his reconstruction plan, dreamed of an independent India where citizens would be raised to the full status of man in the true sense of the term so that they would breath a free air of social, economic and political justice and liberty. The problem of illiteracy was a fundamental problem to him.

The idea profounded by John Stuart Mill that the democracy based on universal suffrage must be preceded by universal education was well understood by Bose and therefore, he advocated elementary education for all. As a socialist and humanist he wanted mass primary education for all and as an individualist he was in favour of higher education for deserving meritorious and intelligent students. The massive educational reconstruction effected within a very short time in the USSR provided a model for Bose to support State controlled educational system for solving our educational problems.

Bose realised that education is a great force in bringing about a sense of national unity and solidarity and for that he was in favour of a common educational policy with a common script which should be 'Roman Script', the common *lingua franca* being Hindusthani.

In regard to the system of primary education, Bose was deeply influenced by the *kindergarten* system in Germany and Scandinavia, the Nursery School of England and the *Ecoles Meternelles* of France. He was in favour of visual or sensory method of education. Vivekananda's concepts of man-making and character — building elements in education influenced Bose so much so that, he wanted men of character to free India from the foreign domination. Bose firmly believed that no educational plan would be successful without a comprehensive system of teachers' training.

Economic Concept

In his presidential address at the 51st Sessions of the Indian National Congress held at Haripura in February 1938, Subhash Chandra Bose spelt out his ideas about economic planning and industrialisation of Free India, "The very first thing which our future National Government will have to do, would be to set up a Commission for drawing up a comprehensive plan of reconstruction." Bose wanted that on the advise of the National Planning Commission, State would adopt a comprehensive scheme for gradually socialising our entire agricultural and industrial system in the spheres of both production and distribution. He also spoke about abolition of landlordism and liquidation of agricultural indebtedness. Subhash Chandra Bose constituted a Planning Committee under the Chairmanship of Jawaharlal Nehru for rapid industrialisation of India on modern lines in consideration of the latter's close relationship with Mahatma Gandhi, who was not in favour of Industrialisation Programme.

According to Subhash, liberty broadly signified political, economic and social freedom. For him economic freedom was the essence of social and political freedom.

Subhash Chandra Bose bravely faught for India's independence but this independence was also an economic necessity for him. He said, "The problem of giving bread to our starving millions — the problem of clothing and educating them — the problem of improving the health and physique of the nation — all these problems cannot be solved so long as India remains in bondage. To think of economic improvement and industrial development before India is free; politically is to put the cart before the horse." According to him the appalling poverty, high incident of unemployment and low standard of living were due to the foreign domination. In view of all this he desired economic reconstruction and industrialisation on modern scientific and technological methods.

Subhash Chandra Bose said, "The moment India is free, the most important problem will be the organising of our national defence in order to safeguard our freedom in the future. For that we shall have to build up modern war industries; so that, we may produce the arms that we shall need for self-defence. This will mean a very big programme of industrialisation." He felt the necessity of modernising the backward agriculture which in turn would aggravate the problem of disguised unemployment and to remedy this development of industry would be indispensable to absorb the surplus labour from agriculture. He was much impressed by the exemplary success attained by the USSR in effecting economic development through rapid industrialisation within a very short period of time, and became a staunch protagonist for similar forced march like Soviet Union and not a gradual one as in Great Britain.

Subhash Chandra Bose classified industries into three categories, namely Large-Scale or Heavy Industries, Medium-Scale and Cottage Industries. According to him, heavy industries are important for rapid economic development. In the category of Large-Scale Industries, mother industries produce the means of production or make other industries run successfully and these are metals, heavy chemicals, machinery and tools, and communication industries like railways, telegraph, telephone and radio. He was very much in favour of large-scale industries but at the same time he never lost sight of cottage and small industries in an underdeveloped country like India.

Political Concept

The political philosophy of Subhash Chandra Bose requires an enunciation and analysis from the angles of his spiritualistic, nationalistic, secularistic, democratic and socialistic characteristics.

Nationalistic Characteristics

Subhash Chandra Bose's father was a government pleader and Public Prosecutor and became a member of the Bengal Legislative Council and earned the title of *Rai Bahadur*, but he resigned from the said post and renounced the title of *Rai Bahadur* as a protest against the repressive policies of the British Government. Moreover, he was a regular visitor to the annual sessions of the Indian National Congress and a staunch supporter of *Swadeshi*. Thus, Subhash inherited the spirit of nationalism from his father.

In his early life, as a student of the Protestant European School run by the Baptist Mission, Subhash exhibited his spirit of nationalism when discriminatory treatment was made against Indian students. His expulsion from the Presidency College for being involved in Oaten Affair in protesting against the sense of racial superiority of the British is a glaring example of his spirit of nationalism. He expressed his feeling of satisfaction, "I had rather a feeling of supreme satisfaction of joy that I had done the right thing, that I had stood up for our honour and self-respect and had sacrified for a noble cause."

Subhash's nationalistic zeal was further heightened under the influence of Swami Vivekananda. Vivekananda's call "Say brothers at the top of your voice the naked Indian, the illiterate Indian, the *Brahman* Indian, the *Pariah* Indian is my brother" had the echo in the heart of Subhash.

Aurobindo's spirit of renunciation and his sacrifice of lucrative ICS career to devote to politics impressed Subhash all the more. Aurobindo's synthesis of spiritualism and nationality had immense impact on Subhash. He resigned from the Civil Service on account of his nationalistic zeal. He writes, "It is not possible to serve one's country in the best and fullest manner if one is chained to the civil service. In short, national and spiritual aspirations are not compatible with obedience to Civil Service conditions." In his letter from Cambridge, addressed to Deshabandhu C. R. Das, he had firmly expressed his decision to resign from the Civil Service and join the Freedom Movement. On his return from Cambridge he plunged headlong into the national movement.

In order to supplement the Freedom Movement from outside India he even approached Nazi and Fascist powers to enlist their support. The *Axis* power and Japan in particular became eager to see India free. Thus, he organised the Azad Hind Fauj comprising 30,000 soldiers and officers and mobilised them on the northeastern front to give a valiant fight to the British army. There are instances galore to testify his nationalistic fervour.

Secularistic Characteristics

Secularism is not irreligion or atheism but tolerance of each-other's faith, mutual accommodation and peaceful coexistence. It involves spiritual consciousness and establishment of contact with the divine. Subhash's philosophy of nationalism acquired a spiritual tenor under the influence of his parents, Ramakrishna Paramahansa, Vivekananda and Aurobindo. When he thought of Indian nation, he thought in terms of Divine Mother, the Indian nation as God's Beloved Land. He was secular in approach to spiritualism or religion.

Subhash was brought up in a liberal and secular environment of his family which helped him to acquire a broad, non-sectarian and Catholic outlook towards people of all religions. The synthesis of various religious creeds as achieved and propounded by Ramakrishna and Vivekananda developed in Subhash faith and commitment to secularism epitomised to his concept of a broad, integral and composite nationalism. Subhash's secularism originated from his firm faith in a philosophy of synthesis of Indian culture and civilization. In his Azad Hind Government and army he had achieved miraculous success in bringing about a wonderful sense of unity among the Muslims, Hindus and Sikhs.

Socialistic Characteristics

In his Free India, Subhash Chandra Bose had the aim of creating an egalitarian society in which all members would enjoy almost equal economic benefits and social status, and there would not be any distinction between man and man on account of accident of birth, parentage, caste and creed. In his presidential address at the Maharashtra Provincial Conference held at Poone on May 3, 1928, he said, "If you want to make India really great we must build up a political democracy on the pedestal of a democratic society. Privileges based on birth, caste or creed should go, and equal opportunities should be thrown to all irrespective of caste, creed or religion."

In his Presidential Address at the Students Conference held at Lahore in October, 1929, he expounded his concept of freedom which he wanted for India. "This freedom implies not only emancipation from political bondage but also equal distribution of wealth, abolition of caste barriers and social inequalities and destruction of communalism and religious intolerance." He wanted that the privileges of landlords, capitalists and higher classes in society shall be reduced or minimised. He said, "Free India will not be a land of capitalists, landlords and castes. Free India will be a social and political democracy .... a reign of perfect equality, social, economic and political" shall prevail in Free India.

As a true Socialist, he wanted emancipation of the underdogs, i.e. peasants and workers. While stating the objectives of *Samyabadi Sangha* visualised by him, he said "The party stand for the interest groups of the masses, that is of peasants, workers, etc. and not for the vested interests that is the landlords, capitalists and moneylending classes."

In the early-20s, he became the founder President of the All Bengal Youth League of which the programme announced, "Complete Independence of India, community of interests with labours and peasants, amelioration of economic condition of the masses, reduction of working hours, a minimum scale of wages, medical leave with full pay, old age pension, compensation for infirmity or serious accidents, etc."

It was under his leadership that the labour strike in the Tata Iron and Steel Works at Jamshedpur ended in an honourable settlement in 1928. He became the President of the All India Trade Union Congress in 1931. Espousing the cause of labour, he said, "Labour today wants the right to work. It is the duty of the State to provide employment to the citizens and where the State fails to perform this duty, it should accept the responsibility of maintaining them. In other words the worker citizens cannot be at the mercy of the employer, to be thrown out on the street at his sweet will and made to starve."

Democratic Characteristics

Subhash Chandra Bose developed an ethical approach to life based on sacrifice, renunciation, self-abnegation and self sacrifice which is in a way the core of a democratic way of life. This ethical and spiritual ideals contributed to his formulation of a political philosophy in consistence with Indian culture and civilization. "The big joint family taught him love, generosity, kindness, patience, tolerance, cooperation and sympathy, the very ingredients of democracy."

That Subhash valued freedom of thought and action also in larger social context is evident from his letter dated 18.7.1915 written to his friend Hemanta Kumar Sarkar, "No body has really the right to interfere in anybody elses individual philosophy of life or speak against it but .... the basis of that philosophy has got to be sincere and true as Spencer's Theory is -'He is free to think and act so long as he does not infringe on the equal freedom of any other individual."

On the changing concept of freedom he said "The concept of human freedom has changed. In ancient times, by freedom people of India meant spiritual freedom — renunciation, freedom from lust, greed, etc. But this freedom also included freedom from political and social bondage." Subhash's emphasis on individual is dignity, and identity did never allow him to accept the totalitarian doctrine that "State is the Master, the Individual the Servant." Although in need of "a political system — a state of an authoritarian character" in place of a "So-called democratic system" he meant a State, "It will work as an organ or as the servant of the masses ... the servant of the people."

"The political foundation of democratic philosophy is the supremacy of the people as the source of authority." Due to the influence of Swami Vivekananda, Subhash had developed immense faith in the power of the people, which is evident from his letter dated 23.3.1920 written from Cambridge to his friend Charu Chandra Ganguly. "Swami Vivekananda used to say that India's progress shall be achieved only by the peasant, the washerman, the cobbler and the sweeper. These words are very true. The Western World has demonstrated what the power of the people can accomplish."

Democratic theory emphasises on the common man as the agent of change, evolution and progress, and recognises the potency and potentiality of the common man to participate in the political process. Subhash, believing in Vivekananda's view that the Brahmana, the Kshatriya and the Vaishya had their day and now, it was the turn of the Shudras, the poor and down-trodden classes to come up and be an agent of evolution and progress. He said, "The Shudras or the Untouchable Castes of India constitute the labour force, so long these people have only suffered. Their strength and their sacrifice will bring about India's progress."

Spiritualistic Characteristics

A spiritual approach of life was originally initiated under the influence of his deeply religious parents. Subsequently, his searching mind, right in his school days could explore out the meaning, significance and objectives of human life when he came in contact with the teachings, writings and philosophy of

Ramkrishna Paramahansa, Swami Vivekananda and Sri Aurobindo Ghose. Ramakrishna Paramahansa's emphasis on character building in general and spiritual approach to life. Renunciation of lust and gold and complete self-abnegation are, according to Ramkrishna, indispensable for a spiritual life. Under such influence Subhash Chandra Bose became more idealistic and spiritualistic to state, "I had a new ideal before me now which had influenced my soul to effect my own salvation and to serve humanity by abandoning all worldly desires and breaking away from all undue restraints." Meditation, sex control and Brahmacharya became matters of primary concern to him. He began to think of his future in terms of spiritual welfare and uplift of humanity.

This became the idealistic dimension of his religious and spiritual bent of mind. Subhash in his college days came in contact with Aurobindo's philosophy through his writings, "We must be dynamos of the divine electricity so that when each of us stand up, thousand around may be full of light, full of bliss and Ananda". Impressed him very deeply, Aurobindo Ghosh has written in his Bhavani Mandir, "For what is a nation? What is our mother country? It is not a piece of art nor a figure of speech, nor a fiction of mind, it is a mighty Shakti composed of all the Shaktis of all the millions of units, that make up of the nation just as Bhavani Mahisha Mardini sprang into being from the Shakti of all millions of gods assembled in our mass of force and wielded into unity.

The Shakti we call in India Bhavani Bharati is the living unity of the Shaktis of 300 million people." Subhash imbided this philosophy of Aurobindo Ghosh and thought of Indian Nation as the Divine Mother, a spiritual entity, a fragment of the universal spirit.

Thus, spiritualism became one of the principal characteristics of his political philosophy.

4

A Great Freedom Fighter

Once we talk of the Indian Independence Movement in the 1930s and early-1940s, two figures most readily come to mind: Mahatma Gandhi, the immensely popular and "saintly" frail pacifist, and his highly respected, Fabian Socialist acolyte, Jawaharlal Nehru.

Subhash Chandra Bose, was a man of comparable stature who admired Gandhi but despaired at his aims and methods, and who became a bitter rival of Nehru. Bose played a very active and prominent role in India's political life during most of the 1930s. For example, he was twice (1938 and 1939) elected President of the Indian National Congress, the country's most important political force for freedom from the Raj, or British rule.

While his memory is still held in high esteem in India, in the West Bose is much less revered, largely because of his wartime collaboration with the Axis powers. Both before and during the Second World War, Bose worked tirelessly to secure German and Japanese support in freeing his beloved homeland of foreign rule. During the final two years of the war, Bose — with considerable Japanese backing — led the forces of the Indian National Army into battle against the British.

Ideology of Fusion

As early as 1930 — in his inaugural speech as mayor of Calcutta — the fervent young Bose first expressed his support for a fusion of socialism and fascism:

> "... I would say we have here in this policy and programme a synthesis of what modern Europe calls Socialism and Fascism. We have here the justice, the equality, the love, which is the basis of Socialism, and combined with that we have the efficiency and the discipline of Fascism as it stands in Europe today."

In years that followed, the brilliant, eclectic Bengali would occasionally modify this radical doctrine, but would never abandon it entirely. For example, in late-1944 — almost a decade-and-a-half later — in a speech to students at Tokyo University, he asserted that India must have a political system "of an authoritarian character. . . To repeat once again, our philosophy should be a synthesis between National Socialism and Communism."

In the wake of the crushing defeat in 1945 of Hitler and Mussolini, "fascism" has arguably been the most despised of all political ideologies. Post-war western society recognises no fascist heroics, and even considers "fascist" traits — particularly the authoritarian, charismatic, personal style of leadership, and the positive evaluation of violence and the willingness to use it for political purposes — to be decidedly unpalatable. In India, though, Bose is regarded as a national hero, in spite of his repeated praise (as will be shown) for autocratic leadership and authoritarian government, and admiration for the European fascist regimes with which he allied himself.

Like the leaders he admired in Italy and Germany, Bose was (and still is) popularly known as Netaji, or 'revered leader'. His name, explains Mihir Bose (no relation), one of Subhash's many biographers, "is given [in India] to parks, roads, buildings, sports stadiums, artificial lakes; his statues stand in place of those of discarded British heroes and his photograph adorns thousands of calendars and millions of pan (betel-nut) shops." It is always the same portrait, continues the writer: Bose in his Indian National

Army uniform, "exhorting his countrymen forward to one last glorious struggle."

No less a figure than Gandhi paid tribute to Bose's remarkable courage and devotion. Six months after his death in an airplane crash on August 18, 1945, Gandhi declared: "The hypnotism of the Indian National Army has cast its spell upon us. Netaji's name is one to conjure with. His patriotism is second to none. . . His bravery shines through all his actions. He aimed high and failed. But who has not failed." On another occasion Gandhi eulogised: "Netaji will remain immortal for all time to come for his service to India."

Many of Bose's admirers have been inclined to downplay or even ignore the fascist elements in his ideology, and even to pretend they never existed. For example, the text of Bose's inaugural speech as mayor of Calcutta, cited above, was reprinted in a laudatory 1970 "Netaji Birthday Supplement" of the Calcutta Municipal Gazette, but with all references to fascism, including his support for a synthesis of fascism and socialism, carefully deleted. Several admiring biographers have found it easier to ignore the fascist elements in his ideology than to explain them. Their subjective accounts do not even inform the reader that Bose spoke positively about some features of fascism, or else, in an attempt to remove from their hero any possible taint, they qualify his remarks in ways that he himself did not.

'Fascist'?

During his lifetime, Bose was frequently denounced as a fascist or even a Nazi, particularly in the wake of the radical, revolutionary (as opposed to reformist) views he expressed in radio addresses broadcast to India from National Socialist Germany and, later, from quasi-fascist Japan. For example, *The Statesman*, a highly influential Calcutta periodical, charged in November 1941: "Mr. Bose's views are those of the Nazis, and he makes no secret of it," while the BBC, Britain's worldwide radio voice, frequently accused him of "Fascism" and "Nazism."

Additionally, historians and writers who do not admire Bose readily point up his "fascist" views. A. M. Nair, a historian who has written favourably of Indian revolutionary Rash Behari Bose (who had sought Japan's help during and after the First World War), found nothing to praise about Subhash Chandra Bose. After all, wrote Nair, he was clearly a fascist.

Recognised Leadership

Bose, a patriot of almost fanatical zeal, first joined the Indian National Movement in 1921, working under C. R. Das, whom he idolised. He was jailed for six months in 1921-22 because of his political activities. Immediately upon his release, the 25-year-old Bose organised (and presided over) the All-Bengal Young Men's Conference. As a result of his remarkable leadership abilities and ambition, he advanced quickly through nationalist ranks. He was soon elected General Secretary of the Bengal Provincial Congress Committee (BPCC). In 1924, at the age of 27, Bose was elected the Chief Executive Officer of the Calcutta Municipal Corporation, which effectively put him in charge of the second-largest city in the British Empire. As a result of his close ties with nationalist terrorists, in late-1924 he was detained by British authorities and held, without trial, for three years in prison. In 1928, the 31-year-old Bose was elected president of the BPCC, and, at the Calcutta meeting of the Congress party held that December, he came to national prominence by pressing (unsuccessfully) for the adoption by his provincial committee of an independence resolution.

By 1930 Bose had formulated the broad strategy that he believed India must follow to throw off the yoke of British imperialism and assume its rightful place as a leader in Asia. During his years in Mandalay prison and another short term of imprisonment in Alipore jail in 1930, he read many works on political theory, including Francesco Nitti's *Bolshevism, Fascism and Democracy* and Ivanoe Bonomi's *From Socialism to Fascism*. It is clear that these works on fascism influenced him, and caused an immediate modification of his long-held socialist views: as noted above, in his inaugural speech as mayor of Calcutta, given a day after his release from Alipore jail, he revealed his support for a seemingly contradictory ideological synthesis of socialism and fascism.

Until his death 15 years later, Bose would continue publicly to praise certain aspects of fascism and express his hope for a synthesis of that ideology and socialism. His detailed comments on the matter in his book *The Indian Struggle: 1920-34*, which was first published in 1935, accurately represent the views he held throughout most of his career. As such, the most important of them, along with Bose's own actions, will be analysed here in some detail.

Programme Outlined

Contending that the Indian National Congress was somewhat "out of date," and suffered from a lack of unity and strong leadership, Bose predicted in *The Indian Struggle* that out of a "Left-Wing revolt there will ultimately emerge a new full-fledged party with a clear ideology, programme and plan of action." The programme and plan of action of this new party would, wrote Bose, follow this basic outline:

- The party will stand for the interests of the masses, that is, of the peasants, workers, etc. and not for the vested interests, that is, the landlords, capitalists and money-lending classes.
- It will stand for the complete political and economic liberation of the Indian people.
- It will stand for a Federal Government for India as the ultimate goal, but will believe in a strong Central Government with dictatorial powers for some years to come, in order to put India on her feet.
- It will believe in a sound system of state-planning for the reorganisation of the agricultural and industrial life of the country.
- It will seek to build up a new social structure on the basis of the village communities of the past, that were ruled by the village "Panch" and will strive to break down the existing social barriers like caste.
- It will seek to establish a new monetary and credit system in the light of the theories and the experiments that have been and are current in the modern world.
- It will seek to abolish landlordism and introduce a uniform land-tenure system for the whole of India.

- It will not stand for a democracy in the Mid-Victorian sense of the term, but will believe in government by a strong party bound together by military discipline, as the only means of holding India together and preventing a chaos, when Indians are free and are thrown entirely on their own resources.
- It will not restrict itself to a campaign inside India but will resort to international propaganda also, in order to strengthen India's case for liberty, and will attempt to utilise the existing international organisations.
- It will endeavour to unite all the radical organisations under a national executive so that whenever any action is taken, there will be simultaneous activity on many fronts."

Synthesis

Bose went on to note that Nehru had said in 1933: "I dislike Fascism intensely and indeed I do not think it is anything more than a crude and brutal effort of the present capitalist order to preserve itself at any cost." There is no middle road between Fascism and Communism, said Nehru, so one "had to choose between the two and I choose the Communist ideal."

To this Bose responded:

> "The view expressed here is, according to the writer, fundamentally wrong. . . One is inclined to hold that the next phase in world- history will produce a synthesis between Communism and Fascism. And will it be a surprise if that synthesis in produced in India?... In spite of the anti-thesis between Communism and Fascism, there are certain traits in common. Both Communism and Fascism believe in the supremacy of the State over the individual. Both denounce parliamentary democracy. Both believe in party rule. Both believe in the dictatorship of the party and in the ruthless suppression of all dissenting minorities. Both believe in a planned industrial reorganisation of the country. These common traits will form the basis

> of the new synthesis. That synthesis is called by the writer "Samyavada" — an Indian word, which means literally "the doctrine of synthesis or equality." It will be India's task to work out this synthesis."

Before taking a closer look at these remarkable words, four points need to be made. First, Bose's fascist model was almost certainly Mussolini's Italy, not Hitler's Germany. In 1934 Bose made the first of several visits to Fascist Italy and found both the regime and its leader very agreeable. On that occasion he had a cordial (first) meeting with Mussolini — "a man who really counts in the politics of modern Europe." After *The Indian Struggle* appeared in print in 1935, Bose made a special stop in Rome personally to present a copy to the *Duce.*

Second, the book was completed a full year before the commencement of the Italian invasion of Ethiopia (Abyssinia), in October 1935. While Bose would, by the time he completed his book, have known about such violent incidents as "The Night of the Long Knives" — the SS killing of dozens of SA men on June 30, 1934 — he had no real reason to consider the European fascist regimes unusually violent, murderous or bellicose. "I should like to point out that when I was writing the book," he later explained:

> "Fascism had not started on its imperialistic expedition, and it appeared to me merely an aggressive form of nationalism . . . What I really meant was that we in India wanted our national freedom, and having won it, we wanted to move in the direction of Socialism. This is what I meant when I referred to a "synthesis between Communism and Fascism." Perhaps the expression I used was not a happy one."

Third, despite Bose's claim to represent the political left, and that a party supporting a fusion of fascism and socialism would be ushered in by a "Left-Wing revolt," the ideology he expounded might more appropriately be regarded as right wing. Bose's ideology was radical and contained socialist elements — such as the desire to abolish the traditional class structure and create a society of equal opportunity, and the claim to represent the peasants and workers. To that extent it can be considered left wing. It is worth noting that Hitler's "right wing" political movement — the National Socialist German Workers' Party — shared many of Bose's "socialist" goals. Nehru, a committed socialist, challenged Bose's characterisation of himself and his followers as left wing: "It seems to me that many of the so-called Leftists are more Right than the so-called Rightists. Strong language and a capacity to attack the old Congress leadership is not a test of Leftism in politics."

Lastly, it should be noted that Bose was willing to tone down his more radical political beliefs on those occasions when he considered it advantageous or necessary to do so. For example, in his February 1938 inaugural speech as President of the Indian National Congress, Bose — probably in a sincere attempt to placate the Gandhian faction — made statements that appear to represent almost an about face from the political views he had expounded in *The Indian Struggle*. In a future independent India, he said:

> "the party itself will have a democratic basis, unlike, for instance, the Nazi party which is based on the "leader principle." The existence of more than one party and the democratic basis of the Congress party will prevent the future Indian State becoming a totalitarian one. Further, the democratic basis of the party will ensure that leaders are not thrust upon the people from above, but are elected from below."

It is possible that these statements reflect a temporary change of mind, but it is more likely that they reflect Bose's efforts during this period to gain further political respectability, to prove that he was more than just a radical and revolutionary Bengali. By doing so he apparently hoped to win wider acceptance of the policies he wanted to implement in his year as Congress President: policies which were not especially radical or revolutionary.

According to Nirad Chaudhuri, his former personal secretary, Bose tried very hard during this period to seek agreement with the Gandhian faction over the direction the Congress party should move, and even "showed something like tender filial piety towards Gandhi," of whom he had been very critical in *The Indian Struggle*. It is against this political background that Bose's statements to the Congress party meeting in February 1938 should be seen.

A year later he successfully recontested the presidential election, but two months afterwards was forced to resign because of his inability to resolve his differences with Gandhi and the Gandhian faction. Probably believing that his earlier suspicions of democracy had been proven correct, and feeling that there was now no use in trying to win the favour or approval of more conservative elements in the Congress party, Bose once again proclaimed his belief in the efficacy of authoritarian government and a synthesis of fascism and socialism. Many similar examples can be cited to show how Bose outwardly (but probably not inwardly) modified his views to suit changing political contexts.

A Life Devoted to Nation

Throughout his political career, India's liberation from British rule remained Bose's foremost political goal; indeed, it was a lifelong obsession. As he explained in his most important work, *The Indian Struggle*, the political party he envisioned "will stand for the complete political and economic liberation of the Indian people." Speaking of Bose a few days after his death in August 1945, Jawaharlal Nehru said:

> "In the struggle for the cause of India's independence he has given his life and has escaped all those troubles which brave soldiers like him have to face in the end. He was not only brave but had deep love for freedom. He believed, rightly or wrongly, that whatever he did was for the independence of India... Although I personally did not agree with him in many respects, and he left us and formed the Forward Bloc, nobody can doubt his sincerity. He struggled throughout his life for the independence of India, in his own way."

Along with his abiding love for his country, Bose held an equally passionate hatred of the imperial power that ruled it: Great Britain. In a radio address broadcast from Berlin on March 1, 1943, he exclaimed that Britain's demise was near, and predicted that it would be " India's privilege to end that Satanic Empire." The fundamental principle of his foreign policy, Bose declared in a May 1945 speech in Bangkok, is that " Britain's enemy is India's friend." Although these two speeches are from his final years, they express views he had held since before his April 1921 resignation from the Indian Civil Service. It was this principle of making friends with Britain's enemies in the hope that they would assist him in liberating India that brought him in 1941 to Germany and then, in 1943, to Japan.

Violence or Non-violence?

Bose envisaged that "the complete political and economic liberation of the Indian people" would inevitably require the use of force. Just before resigning from the Indian Civil Service, he discussed with Dilip Kumar Roy, his closest friend, the subject of anti-British terrorism. "I admit is it regrettable," he said, "even ugly if you will, though it also has a terrible beauty of its own. But maybe that beauty does not unveil her face except for her devotees."

Violence was not new to Bose, even at that early stage of his career. In 1916 he had been expelled from Presidency College in Calcutta for his part in the violent assault on Professor Edward Oaten, who had allegedly insulted Indian students. Moreover, although he occasionally claimed to "detest" violence, and criticised isolated acts of terrorism (which he considered ineffective and counterproductive), he was never really committed to Gandhi's policy of non-violence. He regarded the Gandhi-supported civil disobedience campaign as an effective means of paralysing the administration, but regarded it as inadequate unless accompanied by a movement aimed at total revolution and prepared, if necessary, to use violence.

Militarism

Related to Bose's willingness to use violence to gain political objective was his belief — expressed in *The Indian Struggle,* for example — that a government by a strong party should be "bound together by military discipline." Indeed Bose was infatuated with military discipline, and later commented that his basic training in the University Unit of the India Defence Force (for which he volunteered in 1917, while a student at Scottish Church College in Calcutta) "gave me something which I needed or which I lacked. The feeling of strength and of self-confidence grew still further."

Bose was able to give much grander expression to his "militarism" when, in 1930, he volunteered to form a guard of honour during the ceremonial functions at the Calcutta session of the Congress party. Such guards of honour were not uncommon, but the one Bose formed and commanded was unlike anything previously seen. More than 2,000 volunteers were given military training and organised into battalions. About half wore uniforms, with specially designed steel-chain epaulettes for the officers. Bose, in full dress uniform (peaked cap, standing collar, ornamental breast cords, and jodhpurs) even carried a Field Marshal's baton when he reviewed his "troops." Photographs taken at the conference show him looking entirely out of place in a sea of *khadi* (traditional Indian clothing). Gandhi and several other champions of Non-violence (*Ahimsa*) were uncomfortable with this display.

The Indian National Army

A high point in Bose's "military career" came in July 1943 in Singapore. At a mass meeting there on July 4, Rash Behari Bose (no relation) handed over to him the leadership of the Indian Independence League. The next day, Subhash Bose reviewed for the first time the soldiers of the Indian National Army (INA), which then comprised 13,000 men. In his address to the troops, which is a good example of his speaking style, he cited George Washington and Giuseppi Garibaldi as examples of men who led armies that won independence for their respective countries. Bose went on:

> "Soldiers of India's army of liberation!...
>
> "Every Indian must feel proud that this Army — his own Army — has been organised entirely under Indian leadership and that, when the historic moment arrives, under Indian leadership it will go to battle...
>
> "Comrades! You have voluntarily accepted a mission that is the noblest that the human mind can conceive of. For the fulfilment of such a mission, no sacrifice is too great, not even the sacrifice of one's life...
>
> "...Today, is the proudest day of my life. For an enslaved people, there can be no greater pride, no higher honour, than to be the first soldier in the army of liberation. But this honour carries with it a

corresponding responsibility, and I am deeply conscious of it. I assure you that I shall be with you in darkness and in sunshine, in sorrow and in joy, in suffering and in victory. For the present, I can offer you nothing except hunger, thirst, privation, forced marches and death. But if you follow me in life and in death, as I am confident you will, I shall lead you to victory and freedom. It does not matter who among us will live to see India free. It is enough that India shall be free, and that we shall give our all to make her free.

"May God now bless our Army and grant us victory in the coming fight!"

This "Free India Army" (*Azad Hind Fauj*) would not only "emancipate India from the British yoke," he told the soldiers, but would, under his command, become the standing national army of the liberated nation.

Choreography for Impact

As his staging at the 1930 Calcutta session of the Congress party suggest, Bose understood early on the importance of political choreography and the aesthetics of mass meetings. After his visits to Fascist Italy and National Socialist Germany, he was even more mindful of the importance for any successful broad-based political movement of mass meetings, marches, visual symbols, and ceremonial or liturgical rituals.

For example, at the 51st session of the Congress party at Haripura in 1938, Bose made sure that his entrance as the new Congress President would be spectacular. Escorted by 51 girls in saffron saris (the number corresponding with the number of the Congress session), he was seated in an ancient chariot drawn by 51 white bullocks, and taken on a two hour procession through 51 specially-constructed gates, accompanied by 51 brass bands.

Political choreography of this type — although not to this extreme degree — was very evident at all mass rallies (which sometimes attracted crowds numbering as many as 200,000) of the Forward Bloc party that Bose formed in 1939. Carefully chosen symbols, slogans and songs, coupled with a flood of written propaganda, were used in an unsuccessful attempt to make the Forward Bloc into a mass party.

Even during the last years of the war, when he was in South East Asia heading the Provisional Government of Free India and the INA, he continued to choreograph carefully all of his rallies, meetings and ceremonies, in order to maximise their impact. He also realised that his own role in this choreography was central. Even in the hottest tropical weather, for instance, he wore an imposing military uniform, including forage cap, khaki tunic and jodhpurs, and shiny, knee-length black boots. Moreover, whenever he travelled "he demanded all the rights and privileges of a head of state. On his road travels in Malaya, for example, he insisted on a full ceremonial escort; Japanese military jeeps mounted with sub-machine guns, a fleet of cars, and motorcycle outriders." Historian Mihir Bose argues persuasively that such carefully planned actions were manifestations not of megalomania, but rather of Subhash Bose's effort to create a sense of unity transcending class, caste and origin among the large and diverse populations of Indians in South East Asia, to increase their political awareness, to arouse and inspire both them and his INA troops, and to show the world that he regarded himself as a political leader of substance and importance.

This naturally raises the question of Bose's leadership style. In the passage from *The Indian Struggle* quoted above at length, he expressed his belief in what he called "the dictatorship of the party" (the party being the governing body of a free India), but he did not specify the precise nature of the party's leadership, or whether it, too, would be dictatorial. Most importantly, he did not state whether he saw himself as the party leader, or comment directly on what role he intended for himself in a free India. Nonetheless, clues about these details can be gleaned from other sections of *The Indian Struggle* and from the speeches and statements Bose made at various times throughout his career.

Determined Leadership

Bose clearly admired strong, vigorous, military-type leaders, and in *The Indian Struggle* he listed several whom he particularly respected. These included Hitler, Mussolini, Stalin and even a former British governor of Bengal, Sir Stanley Jackson. Nowhere in this book is there any criticism of these individuals (three of them dictators) for having too much power, yet another man is chastised for this: Mahatma Gandhi. Bose admired Gandhi for many things, not least his ability to "exploit the mass psychology of the people, just as Lenin did the same thing in Russia, Mussolini in Italy and Hitler in Germany." But he accused Gandhi of accepting too much power and responsibility, of becoming a "Dictator for the whole country" who issued "decrees" to the Congress. According to Bose, Gandhi was a brilliant and gifted man, but, unlike Mussolini, Hitler and the others mentioned, a very ineffectual leader. Gandhi had failed to liberate India because of his frequent indecision and constant willingness to compromise with the Raj (something Bose said he would never do).

It is clear that Bose — who believed from his youth that he was destined for greatness — saw himself as a "strong" leader in the mold of those named above. "I ask those who have any doubts or suspicions in their minds to rely on me," he told the Indian Independence League Conference in Singapore on July 4, 1943. He continued:

> "I shall always be loyal to India alone. I will never deceive my motherland. I will live and die for India . . . The British could not bring me to submission by inflicting hardships on me. British statesmen could neither induce me nor deceive me. There is no one who can divert me from the right path."

Bose was decisive, aggressive and ambitious, and even as a university student, these features of his personality attracted many devoted followers. Dilip Kumar Roy, his companion during his days as a student at Cambridge, referred to him as "strength-inspiring," and the absolute leader of the Indian student population.

Bose's militarism, ambition and leadership traits do not necessarily indicate (contrary to popular opinion) that he was a leader in the fascist mold. If they did, one would have to consider all personalities with similar traits — Winston Churchill, for example — as "fascist." In this regard, it is worth noting that during his many years as head of various councils, committees and offices, and during 15-month tenure as President of the Indian National Congress (February 1938 to May 1939), Bose never acted in an undemocratic manner, nor did he claim powers or responsibilities to which he was not constitutionally or customarily entitled. Neither did he attempt in any way to foster a cult of his own personality (as, it could be argued, Gandhi did).

However, after he assumed control of the INA in July-August 1943, Bose's leadership style underwent a transformation. First, he allowed a cult of his personality to flourish among the two million or so Indians living in South East Asia. Prayers were regularly said on his behalf, and his birthday celebrations were — like Gandhi's in India — major festivals. He was invincible, according to one Indian myth from this period, and could not be harmed by bombs or bullets. An image of Bose that stressed his strength of character, military prowess, and willingness to sacrifice for a free India was intentionally promoted in propaganda broadcasts and printed material. With his approval, the title *Netaji* (Revered Leader) was added to his name in all articles about him appearing in the newspapers of the Indian Independence League; even his staff officers were permitted to address him with this title. By the end of the war, few Indians in south Asia still referred to him by name; he was always respectfully called *Netaji*.

Authoritarian Rule

Second, in contrast to his statement at the 1938 Haripura session of the Congress party — that leaders would be elected from below — Bose proclaimed, on October 21, 1943, the formation of the Provisional Government of Azad Hind ("Free India"). While retaining his post as Supreme Commander of the Indian National Army, he announced that he was naming himself Head of State, Prime Minister, and Minister for War and Foreign Affairs. (The most important of these positions — Head of State — he anticipated retaining in a free India). These appointments involved no democratic process or voting of any kind. Further, the authority he exercised in these posts was dictatorial and often very harsh. He demanded total obedience and loyalty from the Indians in south Asia, and any who opposed him, his army or government faced imprisonment, torture, or even execution.

Additionally, if wealthy Indians did not contribute sufficient funds to Bose's efforts, they risked confiscation of their property. Bose's threats were taken very seriously, and had the desired effect: funds did pour in. His INA troops were obliged to swear an oath of loyalty to both the Provisional Government and to him personally. He ordered the summary execution of all INA deserters, and also prepared (but was never able to implement) law codes for the entire population of India. These laws, which stipulated the death penalty for a range of offences, were to come into force when the INA, together with the Japanese Army, entered India to fight against the British.

With regard to his leadership style during this 1943-45 period, in fairness to Bose is should be pointed out that the entire world was then engulfed in a horrendous war, and political and military leaders everywhere, on all sides, adapted extraordinarily authoritarian and repressive measures. Some of the measures and policies adapted by the wartime government of the United States, for instance, were as oppressive and as severe as any planned or implemented by Bose.

A New India

Bose clearly anticipated that the British would be driven out of India in an armed struggle (under his leadership), and that a social and political revolution would begin the moment the Indian people saw British rule under attack in India itself. This revolution, he believed, would bring an end to the old caste system and traditional social hierarchy, which would be replaced by an egalitarian, casteless and classless society based on socialist models. This process would require very careful guidance, with a firm hand, to prevent anarchy and chaos.

Bose had, in fact, held these beliefs since the early-1930s, as Mrs. Kitty Kurti, a close German friend of Bose, revealed in her anecdotal memoir. At a June 1933 meeting attended by Kurti, Bose explained that:

> "Besides a plan of action which will lead up to the conquest of power, we shall require a programme for the new state when it comes into existence in India. Nothing can be left to chance. The group of men and

> women who will assume the leadership of the fight with Great Britain will also have to take up the task of controlling, guiding and developing the new state and, through the state, the entire Indian people. If our leaders are not trained for post-war leadership also there is every possibility that after the conquest of power a period of chaos will set in and incidents similar to those for the French Revolution of the 18th century may be repeated in India . . . . The generals of the war-time period in India will have to carry through the whole programme of post-war reforms in order to justify to their countrymen the hopes and aspirations that they will have to rouse during the fight. The task of these leaders will not be over till a new generation of men and women are educated and trained after the establishment of the new state and this new generation are able to take complete charge of their country's affairs."

This explains what Bose meant in *The Indian Struggle* when he wrote of the need for a strong, single-party government, "bound together by military discipline" with "dictatorial powers for some years to come, in order to put India on her feet." Only an very strong government, strict discipline, and dictatorial rule would, according to Bose, prevent the anticipated revolution from falling into chaos and anarchy. That is why the government would not — "in the first years after liberation" — "stand for a democracy in the Mid-Victorian sense of the term." It would use whatever military force was necessary to maintain law and order, and would not relinquish authority or re-establish more regular forms of government until it felt confident that "the work of post-war social reconstruction" had been completed and "a new generation of men and women in India, fully trained and equipped for the battle of life" had emerged.

Bose clearly anticipated that authoritarian rule would not last beyond the period when social reconstruction was completed, and law and order were established — when India was "on its feet," as he often wrote. As he frequently stated, Bose aimed for nothing less than the formation of "a new India and a happy India on the basis of the eternal principles of liberty, democracy and socialism." He rejected Communism (at least as it was practiced in the Soviet Union) principally because of its internationalism, and because he believed that the theoretical ideal found in the writings of Marx could not be applied, without modification, to India. Still, he maintained socialist views throughout his adult life, and, on very many occasions, expressed his hope for an egalitarian (especially classless and casteless) industrialised society in which the state would control the basic means of production.

He was opposed to liberalism, believing that greater emphasis should be placed on social goals than on the needs or desires of individuals. Individual wishes, he reasoned, must be subordinated to the needs of the state, especially during the struggle for independence and the period of reconstruction immediately following liberation. Nonetheless, having himself been imprisoned eleven times and sent into exile three times, he was fully committed to upholding the rights of minority intellectual, religious, cultural and racial groups. He hoped for an "all-round freedom for the Indian people — that is, for social, economic and political freedom," and would, he said "wage a relentless war against bondage of every kind till the people can become really free."

It could be argued that he was not as committed to the principle of democracy as he was to socialism and freedom (as he defined it). While he extolled democracy on numerous occasions, at other times his words suggest a belief that other parties would have a place, in a free India, only as long as they were "working towards the same end, in whole or in part," as his governing party. Political pluralism did not appeal to him at all. He seems to have envisioned a free India that was more authoritarian than democratic. His own actions as head of the Provisional Government of Azad Hind illustrate a lack of regard for the democratic process.

Mass Mobilisation

Bose was, nonetheless, a consistent advocate of total mobilisation: the mustering of national resources on a scale normally associated with military-like action. Realising that manpower was easily India's greatest resource (and arguably the only one available to the Independence Movement), he proclaimed that all Indians — male and female, urban and rural, rich and poor — should actively participate in the fight for freedom. From his earliest days in politics to his death in 1945, he sought to rouse the great Indian masses, and involve them directly in the political struggle. Their support for representatives at the provincial or national levels was not enough; they must themselves rise up and win independence.

During the 1930s, however, his political position was never strong enough to call for other resources than manpower, nor was India — under British control — able to offer other resources. Additionally, total mobilisation during peace-time, without an impending war or revolution in the awareness of the masses, had never been achieved (not even by the Nazis) and, arguably, never could be achieved. Bose, an astute man, no doubt realised this. With the formation of the Provisional Government of Azad Hind, he was at last in a position to appeal directly for total mobilisation to the mass of Indians — at least in South East Asia, and, less directly to those in India itself. Along with his call for mass mobilisation, he demanded that all available resources be provided for the cause of freedom. For example, he told a mass meeting in Singapore in July 9, 1943:

> "Friends! You will now realise that the time has come for the three million Indians living in East Asia to mobilise all their available resources, including money and manpower. Half-hearted measures will not do. I want Total Mobilisation and nothing less, for we have been told repeatedly, even by our enemies, that this is a total war... Out of this total mobilisation I expect at least three hundred thousand soldiers and three crores of dollars [$30,000,000]. I want also a unit of brave women to form a death-defying regiment who will wield the sword which the brave Rani of Jhansi wielded..."

Of course, Bose demanded not only the total mobilisation of Indian resources in south Asia, but of Indian resources everywhere. He called for mass mobilisation not only in support of his army, but also for his dynamic new government, the various branches of which required financing and manpower.

Women's Equality

As can be seen from the passage quoted above, Bose called on both men *and* women for total support. Unlike the German National Socialists and the Italian Fascists, who stressed the masculine in almost all spheres of social and political activity, Bose believed that women were the equals of men, and should therefore be likewise prepared to fight and sacrifice for India's liberation. Throughout the 1920s and 1930s he had campaigned in India to bring women more fully into the life of the nation. After his return to Asia in 1943, he called on women to serve as soldiers in the Indian National Army — at the time a most radical view. "When I express my confidence that you are today prepared to fight and suffer for the sake of your motherland," he told the women's section of the Independence League in July 1943:

> "I do not mean only to cajole you with empty words. I know the capabilities of our womanhood well. I can, therefore, say with certainty that there is no task which our women cannot undertake and no sacrifice and suffering which our women cannot undergo... To those who say that it will not be proper for our women to carry guns, my only request is that they look into the pages of our history. What brave deeds the Rani of Jhansi performed during the First War of Independence in 1857... Indians — both common people and members of the British Indian army — who are on the border areas of India, will, on seeing you march with guns on your shoulders, voluntarily come forward to receive the guns from you and carry on the struggle started by you."

A women's regiment was formed in 1943, and came to number about 1,000 women. It was named, appropriately, the "Rani of Jhansi Regiment," after a heroine of the Indian rebellion of 1857-58 against British rule. While those less suited to combat duties were employed as nurses and in other support roles, the majority were trained as soldiers. When the INA attacked British forces from Burma in east India in mid-1944, the women of the Jhansi Regiment fought alongside the men, suffering equally heavy casualties. When the army was forced to withdraw, the women were given no privileges. Along with the men, they marched for more than a thousand kilometres.

Commitment to Youth

Lastly, Bose was also deeply committed to the youth movement, a devotion that featured prominently in his political ideology. Convinced that young people were by nature idealistic, restless and open to new ideas — such his own radical and militant outlook — Bose accordingly devoted a great deal of time and effort to the new Youth Leagues that were formed in a number of provinces during the 1920s. Throughout his career he presided over far more youth conferences than any other all-India political figure, and his speeches to younger people he steadfastly urged a spirit of activism that contrasted sharply with the passivism preached by Gandhi and many of the older politicians. "One of the most hopeful signs of the time," he claimed at the 1928 Maharashtra Provincial Conference:

> "Is the awakening among the youth of this country... Friends! I would implore you to assist in the awakening of youth and in the organisation of the youth movement. Self-conscious youth will not only act, but will also dream; will not only destroy, but will also build. It will succeed where even you may fail; it will create for you a new India — and a free India — out of the failures, trials and experiences of the past."

India's liberation would be achieved not by Gandhi and the leading politicians of his generation, whose conservative, reformist policies bred passivity and inactivity. It would, Bose believed, be achieved only through the efforts and sacrifices of the militant, revolutionary and politically-conscious younger generation.

Economic Views

In contrast to the copious record of Bose's political ideology and actions, much less is available about other important elements of his outlook, such as his economic views and policies. For example, while he condemned capitalism and extolled socialism in the pages of *The Indian Struggle*, Bose was very vague about just what monetary or credit systems he foresaw in a free India. They would be set up, he simply wrote, "in the light of the theories and the experiments that have been and are current in the modern world." Throughout his career he never wrote or said anything more specific about such matters. He appears to have had no precise ideas about political economy, save that economics was not important in itself but must be subordinated to national political considerations.

Any discussion here of what economic systems he favoured, and when and how he intended to implement them, would thus be merely speculative.

5

Indian National Army

Azad Hind Fauj or the Indian National Army (INA) was an armed force formed by Indian nationalists in 1942 in South East Asia during World War II.

The aim of the army was to overthrow the British Raj in colonial India, with Japanese assistance. Initially composed of Indian prisoners of war captured by Japan in her Malayan campaign and at Singapore, it later drew large numbers of volunteers from Indian expatriate population in Malaya and Burma.

Initially formed in 1942 immediately after the fall of Singapore under Mohan Singh, the first INA collapsed in December that year before it was revived under the leadership of Subhash Chandra Bose in 1943 and proclaimed the army of Bose's *Arzi Hukumat-e-Azad Hind* (The Provisional Government of Free India).

This second INA fought along with the Imperial Japanese Army against the British and Commonwealth forces in the campaigns in Burma, Imphal and Kohima, and later, against the successful Burma Campaign of the Allies. The end of the war saw a large number of the troops repatriated to India where some faced trial for treason and became a galvanising point of the Indian Independence Movement.

After Indian independence, the ex-INA members, with some exceptions, were refused service in the Indian Army. However, a number of notable members later became involved in public life in India and in South East Asia.

The legacy of the INA is controversial given its associations with Imperial Japan, the course of Japanese occupations in Burma, Indonesia and other parts of South East Asia, her alliance with Nazi Germany and Fascist Italy, as well as Japanese war crimes and the alleged complicity of the troops of the INA in these. Also, its relative insignificance in military terms, its obvious propaganda value to the Japanese, as well as wartime British Intelligence propaganda of cowardice and stories that associated INA soldiers in mistreatment of captured Allied troops, to some extent mires the history of the army. However, after the war, the Red Fort trials of captured INA officers in India provoked massive public outcries in support of their efforts to fight the Raj, eventually triggering the Bombay mutiny in the British Indian forces. These events in the twilight of the Raj are accepted to have played a crucial role in its hasty end.

The Backdrop

Within the Indian Independence Movement, the origins of the concept of an armed force fighting its way into India to overthrow the Raj goes back to the First World War, when the Ghadar Party in February 1915 planned to initiate rebellion in the British Indian Army from the Punjab through Bengal to Hong Kong with German assistance. This plan failed after the information was leaked to British intelligence, but only after the Singapore garrison had rebelled.

Further German assistance in the form of arms, ammunition and trained cadres (both European and Indian) came too late to make a difference. During the Second World War, this plan found revival, with a number of different leaders, units and movements formed over the duration of the war. These included "liberation armies" formed in and with the help of Italy, Germany as well as in South East Asia. Local movements also formed within India which guerrilla tactics significantly hindered the British war effort by sabotage, civil unrest and propaganda. The South East Asian theatre saw the concept of the Indian National Army initiated by the Indian Independence League, which came to be acted out in two phases: the formation and subsequent disbandment of the Indian National Army under Captain Mohan Singh, and the formation of the Arzi Hukumat-e-Azad Hind under Subhash Chandra Bose and the reformation of the INA as its army. The concept of INA as the Azad Hind Fauj that lives in Indian public memory, and indeed as it is analysed by historians, as a fighting force is essentially the INA as the army of the Azad Hind government under Netaji Subhash Bose. Both these phases saw extensive support from the Japanese government, militarily as well as politically.

The First INA

Japan and South East Asia were major refuges for Indian nationalists living in exile before the start of World War II. They were strong proponents of militant nationalism and influenced Japanese policy significantly. Although Japanese intentions and policies with regards to India were far from concrete at the start of the war, Japan had sent intelligence missions, notably under Major I Fujiwara, into South Asia even before the start of the war to garner support from the Malayan Sultans, overseas Chinese, the Burmese resistance and the Indian Movement. These missions were successful establishing contacts with Indian nationalists in exile in Thailand and Malaya, supporting the establishment and organisation of the Indian Independence League.

At the outbreak of World War II in South East Asia, 70,000 Indian troops were stationed in Malaya. After the start of the war, Japan's spectacular Malayan Campaign had brought under her control considerable numbers of Indian prisoners of war, nearly 55,000 after the Fall of Singapore alone. The conditions of service within the British Indian Army as well as the conditions in Malaya had fed dissension among these troops. From these troops, the First Indian National Army was formed under Mohan Singh and received considerable Japanese aid and support. It was formally proclaimed in September 1942 and declared the subordinate military wing of the Indian Independence League in June that year. The unit was dissolved in December 1942 and Singh was arrested and exiled to Pulau Ubin after apprehensions of Japanese motives with regards to the INA led to disagreements, distrust and subsequently open hostility between Singh and the INA leadership on one hand, and the league's leadership, most notable Rash Behari Bose and the Japanese military command on the other. A large number of the initial volunteers chose to revert to prisoner of war Status and a large number of these were subsequently sent to work in the Death Railway or in New Guinea. From the end of December 1942 to February Rash Behari Bose struggled to hold the INA together.

The Second INA

In a series of meetings between the INA leaders and the Japanese in 1943, it was decided to cede the leadership of the IIL and the INA to Subhash Chandra Bose, since a number of the officers and troops who had returned to PoW camps, or had not volunteered in the first place, made it known that they would be willing to join the INA only on the condition that it was led by Bose. Bose had, at the start of the war in Europe, escaped from house arrest to make his way to Germany, reaching Berlin on 2 April 1941. In Germany he convinced Hitler, in a series of conferences, to support the cause of Indian Independence, forming the Free India Legion and the Azad Hind Radio By early-1943, Bose had turned his attention to South East Asia. With its large overseas Indian population, it was recognised that the region was fertile ground for establishing an anti-colonial force to fight the Raj. In January 1943, the Japanese invited Bose to lead the Indian Nationalist Movement in East Asia. He accepted and left Germany on 8 February. After a three-month journey by submarine, and a short stop in Singapore, he reached Tokyo on 11 May 1943, where he made a number of radio broadcasts to the Indian communities, exhorting them to join in the fight for India's Independence.

On 15 February 1943, the Army itself was put under the command of Lt. Col. M. Z. Kiani. The former ranks and badges were revived. A policy forming body was formed with the Director of the Military Bureau, Lt. Col. Bhonsle, in charge and clearly placed under the authority of the IIL. Under Bhonsle served Lt. Col. Shah Nawaz Khan as Chief of General Staff, Major P. K. Sahgal as Military Secretary, Major Habibur Rehman as commandant of the Officers' Training School and Lt. Col. A. C. Chatterji (later Major A. D. Jahangir) as head of enlightenment and culture.

On 4 July 1943, two days after reaching Singapore, Subhash Chandra Bose assumed the leadership of the IIL and the INA in a ceremony at Cathay Building. Bose's influence was notable. His appeal not only re-invigorated the fledgling INA, which previously consisted mainly of PoWs, his appeals also touched a chord with the Indian expatriates in South Asia as local civilians, without caste, creed and religion- ranging from barristers, traders to plantation workers, including Khudabadi Sindhi Swarankar working as shop keepers – had no military experience joined the INA, doubled its troop strength.

An Officers' Training School for INA officers, led by Habibur Rehman, and the Azad School for the civilian volunteers were set up to provide training to the recruits. A youth wing of the INA, composed of 45 Young Indians personally chosen by Bose and affectionately known as the Tokyo Boys, were also sent to Japan's Imperial Military Academy to train as fighter pilots. Also, possibly the first time in Asia, and even the only time outside the USSR, a women's regiment, the Rani of Jhansi regiment was raised as a combat force.

Troop Strength

Although there are slight variations in estimates, the INA is considered to have comprised about 40,000 troops when it was disbanded. The following is an estimate attributed to Lt. Colonel G. D. Anderson of British intelligence:

> There were 45,000 Indian troops from Malaya captured and assembled in Singapore when the Japanese captured it. Of these, about 5,000 refused to join the First INA. The INA at this time had 40,000 recruits. The Japanese were prepared to arm 16,000. When the "first INA" collapsed, about 4,000 withdrew. The Second INA, commanded by Subhash Chandra Bose, started with 12,000 troops. Further recruitment of ex-Indian army personnel added about 8,000-10,000. About 18,000 Indian civilians enlisted during this time.

In 1945, at the end of the INA, it consisted of about 40,000 soldiers.

Order of Battle

The exact organisation of the INA and its troop strength is not known, as Fay notes, since its records were destroyed by the withdrawing Azad Hind Government before Rangoon fell.

Fay's account of the INA gives the following account.

- The 1st Division was under Mohammed Zaman Kiyani. It drew a large number of ex-Indian army PoWs who had joined Mohan Singh's first INA. In addition, it also drew PoWs who had not joined in 1942. The 1st division consisted of:
  - — The 2nd Guerrilla regiment, or the Gandhi Brigade under Col. Inayat Kiani, consisting of two infantry battalions.
  - — The 3rd Guerrilla regiment, or the Azad Brigade under Col. Gulzara Singh, consisting of three battalions.
  - — The 4th Guerrilla regiment, or the Nehru Brigade. This unit was later under the command of Lt. Col. G. S. Dhillon.
  - — The 1st Guerrilla regiment, or the Subhash Brigade under Col. Shah Nawaz Khan, consisting of three infantry battalions. This unit was the first and the major commitment of the INA to the U Go Offensive.

  The 1st Division was lightly armed. Each battalion was composed of five Companies of infantry. The individual companies were armed with six anti-tank rifles, six Bren guns and six Vickers machine guns. Some NCOs carried hand grenades, while men going forward on duty were issued British stocks of hand grenades by senior officer of the Bahadur groups attached to each unit. Mortars were available, but Fay points out these were not available at battalion level.

- The 2nd Division under Aziz Ahmed. The 2nd division was formed to a large extent after the Imphal offensive had started, and drew a large remnant of the Hindustan Field Force of the First INA. The 2nd Division consisted of:

— The 1st Infantry Regiment, later to be merged with the 5th Guerrilla regiment to form the 2nd Infantry Regiment. The 1st Infantry drew a large number of civilian volunteers from Burma and Malaya, and came to have equipped with the lions share of the heavy armament that the INA possessed.

— The 5th Guerilla regiment, later to be renamed the 2nd Infantry Regiment under Col. Prem Sahgal. This unit drew a large number of the remnants of the Hindustan Field Force.

- An additional 3rd Division of the INA was composed chiefly of local volunteers in Malaya and Singapore. This unit disbanded before Japan Surrendered. There was also a motor transport division, but this did not have a significant capability or resources.
- The Rani of Jhansi Regiment, under Lakshmi Sahgal, composed of female volunteers from Malaya and Burma.

The INA in Operation

As the Japanese offensive opened, the INA sent its first forces into battle. The INA's own strategy was to avoid set-piece battles for which it lacked arms, armament as well as manpower. Initially, it sought to obtain arms as well as increase its ranks from British Indian soldiers expected to defect to patriotic cause. Once the Japanese forces were able to break the British defences at Imphal, the INA would cross the hills of North-East India into the Gangetic plain, where it was to work as a guerrilla army and expected to live off the land, garner support, supplies, and ranks from amongst the local populace to ultimately touch off a revolution.

Prem Kumar Sahgal, an officer of the INA once Military secretary to Subhash Bose and later tried in the first Red Fort trials, explained that although the war itself hung in balance and nobody was sure if the Japanese would win, initiating a popular revolution with grass-root support within India would ensure that even if Japan lost the war ultimately, Britain would not be in a position to reassert its colonial authority, which was ultimately the aim of the INA and Azad Hind.

1944

The plans decided between Bose and Kawabe envisaged the INA was to be assigned an independent sector of its own in the U Go offensive and no INA unit was to operate less than a battalion strength. For operational purposes, the Subhash Brigade was assigned under the command of the Japanese general Head Quarters in Burma.

Advance parties of the Bahadur Group also went forward with the advanced Japanese units early during the offensive. As Japan opened its offensive towards India, the INA's first division, consisting of four Guerrilla regiments, was divided between the diversionary Ha Go offensive in Arakan 1944, with one battalion reaching as far as Mowdok in Chittagong. A Bahadur group unit, led by Shaukat Malik, took the border enclave of Moirang in early-April.

The main body of the first division was however committed to the U Go Offensive directed towards Manipur, initially successfully protecting the Japanese flanks against Chin and Kashin guerrillas as the Mutaguchi's three divisions crossed the Chindwin river and the Naga Hills, and later directed towards the main offensive through Tamu in the direction of Imphal and Kohima. However, by the time Khan's forces left Tamu, the offensive had been held, and the troops were redirected to Kohima. By the time Khan's forces reached Ukhrul in the vicinity of Kohima, Japanese forces had begun their withdrawal from Kohima.

The first division suffered the same fate as did Mutaguchi's Army when the siege of Imphal was broken. With little or no supplies and supply lines deluged by the Monsoon, harassed by Allied air-dominance and local Burmese irregulars, the INA began withdrawing when the 15th Army and Burma Area Army began withdrawing, and suffer the same terrible fate as wounded, starved and diseased men succumbed during the hasty withdrawal into Burma. The INA lost a substantial amount of men and material in the retreat, and a number of units were disbanded or used to feed the newly formed units of the second division.

1945

As the allied Burma campaign began the following year, however, the INA remained committed to the defence of Burma, and was a part of the Japanese defensive deployments. The second division, tasked with the defence of Irrawaddy and the adjoining areas around Nangyu, was instrumental in opposing Messervy's 7th Indian Division when it attempted to cross the river at Pagan and Nyangyu during Irrawaddy operations.

Later, during the Battles of Meiktila and Mandalay, the 2nd division was instrumental in denying the British 17th Division the area around Mount Popa that would have exposed the Flank of Kimura's forces attempting to retake Meiktila and Nyangyu. Ultimately however, the division was obliterated. As the Japanese situation became precarious, Azad Hind withdrew from Rangoon with Ba Maw's government and the Japanese forces for Singapore along with the remnants of the first division and the Rani of Jhansi Regiment. Nearly 6,000 troops amongst the surviving units of the Army remained in Rangoon under A. D Loganathan surrendered as Rangoon fell, and helped keep order till the allied forces entered the city.

The only Indian territory that the Azad Hind govt. controlled were the Indian territories that fell during the Imphal offensive, and the islands of Andaman and Nicobar. However, the latter two were bases for the Japanese Navy, and the navy never really fully relinquished control. Enraged with the lack of administrative control, the Azad Hind Governor, Lt. Col. Loganathan later relinquished his authority to return to the Government's head quarters in Rangoon. The Japanese forces is said to have carried out torture on thousands of local inhabitants during the occupation, and some historians inexplicably apportion the blame to Subhash Bose's provisional government.

INA and the War of India's Liberation

Indian National Army of Liberation in the East

On 15 February 1942, Singapore fell to the Japanese army advancing southward from the Malayan peninsula. Two days later, in an impressive ceremony held at Farrar Park in the heart of the town, [British] Indian troops were handed over to the Japanese as prisoners-of-war by their commanding officer, Colonel Hunt.

Major Fujiwara took them over on behalf of the victorious Japanese, and then announced that he was handing them over to Captain Mohan Singh of the Indian contingents, who should be obeyed by them as their Supreme Commander. Mohan Singh then spoke to the Indian PoWs, expressing his intention of raising an Indian national army out of them to fight for India's freedom. He held a preliminary discussion with some prominent Indians in Malay and Burma in a meeting in Singapore on 9 and 10 March, which was attended by Rashbehari Bose, a veteran Indian revolutionary exile living in Japan for the last quarter of a century. Bose then called a conference in Tokyo, which was held 28-30 March. The delegates representing several East and South East Asian countries present at the conference decided to form the Indian Independence League to organise an Indian Independence Movement in East Asia.

Bose was recognised as head of the organisation. The conference further resolved that "military action against the British in India will be taken only by the INA and under Indian command, together with such military, naval and air cooperation and assistance as may be requested from the Japanese by the Council of Action" and further, "after the liberation of India, the framing of the future Constitution of India will be left entirely to the representatives of the people of India."

On 15 June 1942, a conference opened in Bangkok with over a hundred delegates of the IIL (Indian Independence League) attending from all over Asia. By the close of the nine-day conference a resolution was unanimously adopted setting forth the policies of the Independence Movement in East Asia. The IIL was proclaimed the organisation to work for India's freedom; the Indian National Army was declared the military arm of the movement with Mohan Singh as the commander-in-chief and Rashbehari Bose was elected president of the Council of Action. It was further decided that Singapore would be the headquarters of the IIL. Netaji had stated in a message to the conference that his personal experience had convinced him that Japan, Italy and Germany were sworn enemies of British imperialism; yet, independence could come only through the efforts of Indians themselves. India's freedom would mean the rout of British imperialism. The Indian National Army was officially inaugurated in September 1942.

Unfortunately, at this point distrust began to grow within the Indian group against Rashbehari Bose's leadership. Some thought that having been long associated with Japan, he gave precedence to the Japanese interests over Indian interests. According to Japanese records:

> Some even thought that he was just the protege of the Japanese, and that the latter were exploiting Indians for their own ends. Such resentment finally resulted in a revolt of a group of leaders headed by Captain Mohan Singh within the INA in November 1942. As a consequence, Mohan Singh and his associate, Colonel Gill, were both arrested by the Japanese and the Indian Army was disbanded. However, in 1943 a new Indian Army was organised, put under the command of Lt. Col. Bhonsle, who held this post until the final dissolution of the army.

Describing the revived INA, Joyce Lebra writes:

> On 15 February 1943, the INA was reorganised and former ranks and badges revived. The Director of the Military Bureau, Lieutenant-Colonel Bhonsle, was clearly placed under the authority of the IIL to avoid any repetition of IIL-ANA rivalry. Under Bhonsle was Lt. Col. Shah Nawaz Khan as Chief of General Staff, Major P. K. Sahgal as Military Secretary; Major Habibur Rehman as commandant of the Officers' Training School; and Lt. Col. A. C. Chatterji, and later Major A. D. Jahangir, as head of enlightenment and culture. Apart from this policy-forming body was the Army itself, under the command of Lt. Col. M. Z. Kiani. This was the organisation which held the INA together until the arrival of Subhash Chandra Bose from Berlin, six months later.

In February, the Japanese military officer Iwakuro had called a meeting of about three hundred officers of the INA at Bidadri camp in Singapore and spoke to them about the advisability of joining the army, but with no effect. According to Ghosh, "Later on, in a 'heart-to-heart talk' with some officers, it emerged that a large number of officers and men would be willing to continue in the INA on the express condition that Netaji would be coming to Singapore."

The story of Netaji's exploits in Germany and the history of the Indian Legion was known to Indian revolutionaries of the IIL in East Asia for some time now, and they awaited his arrival eagerly. As the first INA wavered, faltered and was finally disbanded, and as its successor merely continued to exist, the need for Netaji's leadership began to be felt more keenly. Mohan Singh had mentioned his name to General Fujiwara as early as 1941. In all conferences the need of his guidance had been emphasised by the delegates.

While Netaji and Abid Hasan continued to push towards the East making a wide sweep out into the Atlantic, by pre-arrangement, a Japanese submarine left Penang Island on 20 April for the tip of Africa, under strict orders not to attack or risk detection. The two submarines had a rendevous four hundred miles south-southwest of Madagascar on 26 April. After sighting each other and confirming their identity, the submarines waited for a day for the sea to become calm. Then on 28 April, in what was known to be the only known submarine-to-submarine transfer of passengers (in the annals of World War II) in an area dominated by the enemy's air and naval strength, Netaji and Abid Hasan were transhipped into the Japanese submarine via a rubber raft.

Travelling across the ocean, the Japanese 1-29 reached Sabang on 6 May, 1943. It was an isolated offshore islet north of Sumatra. There, Netaji was welcomed by Colonel Yamamoto, who was the head of the Hikari Kikan, the Japanese-Indian liaison group. From Sabang, Netaji and Yamamoto left for Tokyo by plane, stopping *en route* at Penang, Manila, Saigon and Taiwan. The plane landed in Tokyo on 16 May. All throughout his submarine voyage from Germany and for about a month after his arrival in Tokyo, Netaji's identity and presence was kept a secret. He was supposed to be a Japanese VIP named Matsuda.

Although he remained incognito during the first few weeks in Japan, Netaji did not waste any time by just waiting. From 17 May onwards, he met Japanese Army and Navy Chiefs-of-Staff, Navy Minister and Foreign Minister in rapid succession. However, he had to wait for nearly three weeks before Japanese Prime Minister Tojo granted him an interview. But Tojo was so impressed with Netaji's personality that he offered to meet him again after four days. Two days later, on 16 June, Netaji was invited to visit the Diet where Tojo surprised him with his historic declaration on India:

> We are indignant about the fact that India is still under the ruthless suppression of Britain and are in full sympathy with her desperate struggle for independence. We are determined to extend every possible assistance to the cause of India's independence. It is our belief that the day is not far off when India will enjoy freedom and prosperity after winning independence.

It was not until 18 June that Tokyo Radio announced Netaji's arrival. The news was reported in the Tokyo press the following day. At this announcement, the atmosphere was electrified overnight. The Axis press and radio stressed the significance of the event. The INA and the Indian Independence Movement suddenly assumed far greater importance in the eyes of all. On 19 June, Netaji held a press conference. This was followed by two broadcasts to publicise further his presence in East Asia, and during the course of these he unfolded his plan of action. Bose's plan stood for the coordination of the nationalist forces within India and abroad to make it a gigantic movement powerful enough to overthrow the British rulers of India. The assumption on which Bose seemed to have based his grand scheme was that the internal conditions in India were ripe for a revolt. The Non-cooperation Movement must turn into an active revolt.

And to quote Netaji's own words during the press conference: "Civil disobedience must develop into armed struggle. And only when the Indian people have received the baptism of fire on a large scale would they be qualified to achieve freedom." Netaji then embarked upon a series of meetings, press conferences, radio broadcasts and lectures in order to explain his immediate task to the people concerned, and the world.

Accompanied by Rashbehari Bose, Netaji arrived at Singapore from Tokyo on 27 June. He was given a tumultuous welcome by the resident Indians and was profusely 'garlanded' wherever he went. His speeches kept the listeners spellbound. By now, a legend had grown around him, and its magic infected his audiences. Addressing representatives of the Indian communities in East Asia on 4 July he said: Not content with a civil disobedience campaign, Indian people are now morally prepared to employ other means for achieving their liberation. The time has therefore come to pass on to the next stage of our campaign. All organisations, whether inside India or outside, must now transform themselves into a disciplined fighting organisation under one leadership. The aim and purpose of this organisation should be to take up arms against British imperialism when the time is ripe and signal is given.

At a public meeting where Netaji spoke these words, Rashbehari Bose formally handed over to Subhash Chandra Bose the leadership of the IIL and command of the INA. The hall was packed to capacity. In his last speech as leader of the movement Rashbehari Bose said:

> Friends! This is one of the happiest moments in my life. I have brought you one of the most outstanding personalities of our great Motherland to participate in our campaign. In your presence today, I resign my office as president of the Indian Independence League in East Asia. From now on, Subhash Chandra Bose is your president, your leader in the fight for India's independence, and I am confident that under his leadership, you will march on to battle and to victory.

In that meeting Netaji announced his plan to organise a Provisional Government of Free India.

It will be the task of this provisional government to lead the Indian Revolution to its successful conclusion ... The Provisional Government will have to prepare the Indian people, inside and outside India, for an armed struggle which will be the culmination of all our national efforts since 1883. We have a grim fight ahead of us. In this final march to freedom, you will have to face danger, thirst, privation, forced marches — and death. Only when you pass this test will freedom be yours.

The next day, on 5 July, Netaji took over the command of the Indian National Army, now christened Azad Hind Fauj (Free India Army). Tojo arrived from Manila in time to review the parade of troops standing alongside with Bose. Addressing the soldiers, Netaji said:

> Throughout my pubic career, I have always felt that, though India is otherwise ripe for independence in every way, she has lacked one thing, namely, an army of liberation. George Washington of America could fight and win freedom, because he had his army. Garibaldi could liberate Italy because he had his armed volunteers behind him. It is your privilege and honour to be the first to come forward and organise India's national army. By doing so you have removed the last obstacle in our path to freedom ... When France declared war on Germany in 1939 and the campaign began, there was but one cry which rose from the lips of German soldiers — "To Paris! To Paris!" When the brave soldiers of Nippon set out on their march in December 1941, there was but one cry which rose from their lips — "To Singapore! To Singapore!" Comrades! My soldiers! Let your battle-cry be — "To Delhi! To Delhi!" How many of us will individually survive this war of freedom, I do not know. But I do know this, that we shall ultimately win and our task will not end until our surviving heroes hold the victory parade on another graveyard of the British Empire — Lal Qila or the Red Fortress of ancient Delhi.

On 27 July, Netaji left Singapore for a 17-day tour of the East Asian and South East Asian countries. The prime objective of this tour was to enlist moral and monetary support for his movement from other countries, as well as the resident Indian communities. He was given a rousing reception in Rangoon, where he attended the Burmese independence on 1 August; from Rangoon Netaji went to Bangkok and met Thai Prime Minister Pilbulsongram. He won the moral support of Thailand and tumultuous ovation from the Indian community. He then flew to Saigon and addressed Indians there. Returning to Singapore for a brief rest, he flew to Penang to address a rally of 15,000 Indians. Everywhere, he held his audience spellbound for hours with his superb oratory, and at the conclusion of his speech the people raced to reach the platform and pile up all they had before him — a total of two million dollars. This scene was repeated over and over in towns and cities all over South East Asia, when Netaji stood before thousands of people like a prophet, addressing them for the cause of India's freedom. Merchants, traders, businessmen and women came forward everywhere and donated their wealth and ornaments in abundance, to enable their leader to fulfil his mission.

In his plan for total mobilisation, Netaji had outlined a grandiose scheme for an army of three million men. However, the immediate target was set at 50,000. The major part of this number would be from the Indian PoWs and the rest from civilian volunteers. According to Bose's plan there would be three divisions from thirty thousand regulars and another unit of twenty thousand mainly from civilian volunteers. The Japanese authorities informed Netaji at that time that it could provide arms for thirty thousand men only. However, by 1945 it was authoritatively known that the actual strength of the INA rose to not less than 45,000 men. After completing the task of reorganising the Indian Independence League and launching preparations for revolutionising the army, and after conducting a successful campaign to mobilise the support of the Indian communities throughout South East Asia — a phase which lasted from July to October — Netaji turned towards formation of the Provisional Government of Azad Hind (Free India). This had to be done before the army could be sent for action in the battlefield. This government was officially proclaimed in Singapore at a mass rally on 21 October 1943 where Netaji was unanimously elected as the Head of the State and the Supreme Commander of the Indian National Army. While taking the oath he said:

> In the name of God, I take this sacred oath that to liberate India and the three hundred eighty million of my countrymen. I, Subhash Chandra Bose, will

> continue the sacred war of freedom till the last breath of my life. I shall remain always a servant of India, and to look after the welfare of three hundred eighty million of Indian brothers and sisters shall be for me my highest duty. Even after winning freedom, I will always be prepared to shed even the last drop of my blood for the preservation of India's freedom.

The Provisional Government of Free India had five Ministers with Netaji as the Head of the State, Prime Minister and Minister for War and advisers representing the Indian communities in East Asia. The first momentous decision which the new government took was its declaration of war on Britain and the United States, which was decided on the night of 22-23 October. Toye writes: "The Cabinet had not been unanimous about the inclusion of the USA. Bose had shown impatience and displeasure — there was never any question then or later of his absolute authority: the Cabinet had no responsibility and could only tender advice." Recognition of the Provisional Government came quickly from nine countries — the Axis powers and their allies. They were: Japan, Burma, Croatia, Germany, the Philippines, Nanking China, Manchuto, Italy and Siam (Thailand), but for some unknown reasons, Vichy France withheld its recognition. The Japanese Army promised all-out support for the provisional government.

Towards the end of October, Netaji flew to Tokyo again to meet Tojo and to attend the greater East Asia Conference. Since India technically did not fall within this sphere, he attended as an observer. He made an impressive speech at the conference, stressing the creation of a new Asia where all vestiges of colonialism and imperialism would be eliminated. The Japanese navy had captured the Andaman and Nicobar islands in the Bay of Bengal during the early months of war. As a result of Netaji's requests, Prime Minister Tojo announced at the conference that Japan had decided to place the two islands under the jurisdiction of the Provisional Government of Free India, thereby giving it its first sovereignty over a territory.

The ceremonial transfer took place in December, and Netaji named Lieutenant-Colonel Loganathan, an officer in the Medical Services, as the chief commissioner in charge of the civil administration of the islands. Soon thereafter preparations began for sending the army to the front and moving the provisional government headquarters to Rangoon, in Burma. In the meantime, Netaji announced the formation of a women's brigade within the INA and named it "Rani of Jhansi Regiment," after the celebrated Queen of Jhansi, Laxmibai, who had led her soldiers against the British in an uprising during the First War of Independence in 1857. Coincidentially, another Laxmi, Lieutenant-Col. Laxmi, was placed in charge of this regiment by Netaji. In November it was agreed between Netaji and the Japanese military headquarters that the INA first division and the civil and military headquarters would move to Burma in January 1944.

The Imphal Campaign

The Imphal Campaign, including the battle of Kohima — the first major town to be captured by the INA inside India — will perhaps go down as one of the most daring and disastrous campaigns in the annals of world military history. General Mutaguchi, commander of the Japanese forces in North Burma since 1943, had been convinced that Imphal should be attacked. The objects of such an offensive were to forestall any invasion of Burma in 1944 and to establish the Japanese defences on the frontier mountains. The idea would be first to overwhelm the British in Arakan, involving all their reserves in battle for Chittagong and the gateway to eastern Bengal. Then, by April, Kohima and Imphal could be conquered at leisure, without danger of their being reinforced. The monsoon, beginning in May, would postpone operations, and after the rains were over, in the absence of a new British defence posture east of the river Brahmaputra, the entire Assam and East Bengal would lie open to the Indian National Army and the Japanese.

Imphal, the capital of the state of Manipur, lay on a flat, nearly treeless plateau just inside the Indian border. Its elevation was about 3,000 feet, surrounded on all sides by impassable mountains. The mountain range in the east with 2,000-4,000 foot peaks above the plateau stretches some five hundred miles. To the West and South are the Chin hills of the Arakan range, a formidable stretch of inhospitable terrain. The jungle surrounding this basin is hostile to human habitation. The northern access to the plain from India and Assam lay through Dimapur and the steep Kohima Road. From Dimapur, a single track railway swept through Assam and Bengal and was an important military objective to both armies. For the INA the importance of the Imphal campaign was that it was the only major battle in which it would participate with the object of achieving freedom for India. As Salto and Hayashida write:

> The Imphal Operation was the final offensive of the East Asia War, mounted by three Burma-based Japanese divisions, and one INA division. The campaign lasted from 15 March to 9 July 1944. The operation has often been compared to the operation Wacht am Rhein or the Battle of the Bulge, which was the final all-out drive launched by Germany towards Ardennes on the Western Front, from December 1944 to January 1945. Both operations almost succeeded and both are termed "gambles" by historians today. If the German push towards Ardennes was Wacht am Rhein, the Japanese-Indian thrust against Imphal might be called "Wacht am Chindwin" although the official Japanese code-name for the action was most prosaic: Operation "U".

River Chindwin lay across the Indo-Burmese border, and its crossing from the east by an army would signal an invasion of India.

Execution orders for Operation U became operative on 7 January 1944, coinciding with completion of the shifting of the Provisional Government headquarters in Rangoon. In the evening of the same day, Lt. General Masakazy Kawabe, commanding the overall Burma headquarters, held a welcome party in honour of Netaji and his staff officers. Netaji spoke, and concluded his speech with these words: "My only prayer to the Almighty at this moment is that we may be given the earliest opportunity to pay for our freedom with our own blood." One INA Division, named after Netaji as Subhash Regiment, was readied for action at the front with the Japanese. Toye writes:

> ... He spent the whole days ... with the Subhash Regiment, reviewing, watching it at exercises and on

> parade, talking to its officers, exerting his magic on it in a way that he had not attempted before. These were his comrades, the men by whose means he would uphold the rights and honour of India. Everything depended on their achievement in battle; they must absorb all his feelings of confidence, feel the whole of his personal force. On 3 February he bade them farewell: "Blood is calling for blood. Arise! We have no time to lose. Take up your arms. There in front of you is the road, our pioneers have built. We shall march along that road. We shall carve our way through enemy's ranks, or, if God wills, we shall die a martyr's death. And in our last sleep we shall kiss the road which will bring our Army to Delhi. The road to Delhi is the road to Freedom. On to Delhi!"

Mutaguchi set 15 March as the D-day for the beginning of the Imphal campaign. The deployment of well over 120,000 troops along the Chindwin river, a front of some 200 kilometres, went on smoothly and undetected by British spies planted in the area. In the meantime, Netaji received some good news. The Arakan offensive, launched on 4 February, had cut off the 7th Indian Division of the British Army in Mayu valley. Contributing to this success was the reconnaissance and subversion of an Indian outpost position by Major Misra, the INA Commander in Arakan. At the same time, he received messages from the underground network working inside India under his direction, whose selected trained spies had been sent by submarine. On D-day, Mutaguchi assembled the war correspondents at his headquarters in central Burma and declared: "I am firmly convinced that my three divisions will reduce Imphal in one month. In order that they can march fast, they carry the lightest possible equipment and food enough for three weeks. They will get everything from the British supplies and dumps. Boys! See you again in Imphal at the celebration of the Emperor's birthday on 29 April."

The Japanese-Indian offensive took the British by complete surprise. The Japanese and INA troops literally galloped through mountains and jungles routing the enemy on the way. Prior to the Imphal offensive, an INA detachment under Colonel Saligal had created a breach through the British lines in the Arakan sector.

Now the INA's deployment was extended to the Imphal sector. As the INA under Netaji's command set foot on the Indian soil, the main Japanese force also defeated the obstinate resistance of the enemy on 22 March, broke through the India-Burma border, and advanced from the north and west to encircle Imphal. The initial success of the INA at the Arakan front generated much enthusiasm. In a Special Order of the Day, Netaji referred to the "Glorious and brilliant actions of the brave forces of the Azad Hind Fauj."

On 8 April, Japanese Imperial Headquarters issued a communique which said: "Japanese troops, fighting side by side with the Indian National Army, captured Kohima early on 6 April." A jubilant Netaji at this time started talking with the Japanese about the administration of the liberated and soon-to-be-liberated territories in India. In response to a call by Netaji, Prime Minister Tojo made an announcement clarifying that all areas of India occupied as a result of Japanese advance would be placed under the jurisdiction of the Provisional Government. This was followed by Netaji's announcement that he was appointing the Finance Minister of his Cabinet, Major-General A. C. Chatterjee, as the governor of the newly liberated areas. Netaji described the march of the INA into India as the event of the century. He had also just declared the Legion in Europe to be part of the INA and had appointed Nambiar to be a Minister in the Provisional Government; his Chief Commissioner had been installed in the Andamans, his first heroes from the Arakan front had been decorated, and the INA troops had raised the national standard of free India in Kohima; and now, the fall of Imphal seemed very near.

Did the Imphal Campaign come almost two years too late? What would have happened if Netaji had arrived in East Asia a year earlier? By the, end of 1942, the Axis had scored successes everywhere:

> Rommel was in Egypt, the German invasion of Russia had gone smoothly, Nationalist China was on her knees, and India and Australia were expecting a Japanese invasion. Prospects for the Allies were dark in the Pacific and the Rising Sun was at its zenith from Japan to the Bay of Bengal ... Britain was unable

> to dispute with the Japanese Navy, and there were not enough British and Indian troops in India to assure its defence. Even air protection was inadequte ... Japanese forces had not pursued retreating British troops beyond the Chindwin river in Burma in May 1942, allegedly because "an invasion was likely to arouse ill-feelings amongst the Indian masses." ... So the Japanese remained east of the Chindwin river, leaving British Indian forces to build up their strength in the Imphal plain.

But above all, in that moment of a golden opportunity, the towering leadership of Netaji, a provisional government, and an Indian national army worthy of its name was readied for action at the all these were non-existent in East Asia. Japan by itself simply lacked the motivation for extending war into India, let alone think of its independence. The fact remains, however, that the Imphal campaign was indeed first conceived in 1942, right after the conquest of Burma. According to the official history of the British Armed Forces in the Second World War:

> Soon after the completion of the Japanese conquest of Burma in June 1942, a certain Lt. Col. Hayashi had advocated an attack on Imphal. He considered that the Japanese should strike against India without giving time to the defenders to recuperate from their disastrous retreat, and Imphal's capture would rob them of the best base for launching a counter-offensive against Burma ... 18th division argued that the jungles of Burma were impassable for large bodies of operational troops and that any attack on Indian territory would provoke anti-Japanese feelings in India. About December 1942, therefore, the plan was abandoned.

Lieutenant-General Kuroda Shigetoku, Southern Army Chief of Staff, stated later that if the operation had been carried out in 1942 when first conceived, rather than in 1944, it would have succeeded. According to Lebra, "General Tojo stated in the spring of 1945 that he regretted Japan had missed the opportunity in 1942."

As the INA and the Japanese forces continued to lay siege on Imphal, the Allied air superiority gained strength and the enemy was preparing for counterattack. Shah Nawaz, commanding two battalions of the Subhash Regiment in the Chin Hills, told of the hardships his men were suffering as a result of disease and of supply and transport difficulties. However, owing to communication problems, the news of difficulties his men were undergoing at the front did not reach Netaji in detail. While there was a stalemate in the front and the offensive came to a halt, there were meetings and jubilations at Rangoon where Netaji collected money and donations in other forms for the conduct of his campaign. He offered to send additional INA regiments to the Front and more troops were despatched. For about a month Operation U went according to plan. Enemy forces were successfully encircled in the Imphal area.

Suddenly, in the middle of April, the military balance began to shift against Japan and the INA. Wingate's airborne unit had already been attacking from the air over the Burmese supply routes. British forces were being supplied by airlift into the besieged Imphal, and reinforcements began to flow in.

British forces were being sent to Kohima to the north by both rail and air. Japan had no matching air power to strike back at enemy air operations. By the end of April the battle strength of Japanese and INA divisions was decreased forty per cent. Time for success by surprise attack had already passed and gradually the offensive turned into a defensive battle.

The monsoon that followed brought the ultimate disaster. As roads became impassable, all supply routes were cut off. Muddy streams flooded roads and valleys, and rivers swelled to sweep away tanks and ammunition. In the wake of the monsoon, disease became rampant. Cholera, malaria, dysentery, beriberi and jungle sores began to take their toll. The INA and the Japanese started living on rations consisting of rice mixed with jungle grass. The 33rd Division had fought desperately for forty days without being able to penetrate the British lines at Imphal. And now that vast amounts of military supplies were reaching the beleaguered garrison at Imphal, there was virtually no hope for a renewed offensive. On 8 July, on the recommendation of top-ranking Generals including Kawabe and Mutaguchi, Prime Minister Tajo issued the order to halt the operation.

The story of the retreat from Imphal is one of the greatest tragedies of World War II. It is a story of misery, hunger and death. Japanese and INA troops, bottled up in the Kawab valley between the Chin Hills in the west and the Chindwin river in the west, began their long trek back through jungles and mountains, headed by division commanders and guards in jeeps and horses. Officers, supply, communication and medical units followed. Behind them marched thousands of stragglers: rain-soaked, emaciated with fever and malnutrition. Soon, corpses began accumulating along the trek, and they had to be left unburied. Of the 220,000 Japanese troops who began the Imphal Campaign, only 130,000 survived, and of these only 70,000 remained at the front to retreat. INA casualties were over fifty per cent. It was a disaster equal in magnitude to Dunkirk and Stalingrad. Lebra writes:

> When Bose heard the order to retreat he was stunned. He drew himself up and said to Kawabe in ringing tones: "Though the Japanese Army has given up the operation, we will continue it. We will not repent even if the advance of our revolutionary army to attain independence of our homeland is completely defeated. Increase in casualties, cessation of supplies, and famine are not reasons enough to stop marching. Even if the whole army becomes only spirit we will not stop advancing towards our homeland. This is the spirit of our revolutionary army." In an article in Azad Hind on 6 November 1944, after the retreat from Imphal, Bose was reported to have "reiterated his firm conviction that final victory in this war would belong to Japan and Germany ... that a new phase of war was approaching in which the initiative would again lie in the hands of the Japanese."

Each Japanese commander gave his own analysis of the causes of the failure of Operation U, like the problem of the chain of command, lack of air power, or dispersal rather than concentration of forces. However, Netaji thought it was timing, with respect to the monsoon. He felt that the only chance to take Imphal was before the rains came, and most strategists agreed on this point. From the historic perspective, however, Fujiwara perhaps was the most correct. According to him, the Imphal disaster could have been avoided had the operation been undertaken a year earlier, at a time when the British power in the region was weak. The delay in launching the Imphal offensive was no doubt due to Netaji's late arrival from Europe to East Asia. The Imphal campaign should have been undertaken at a time when the Axis victories had reached their zenith and the Allied forces were on retreat everywhere.

During the last three months of 1944, Japanese forces had withdrawn to the banks of the Irrawaddy in Burma, where they intended to make a stand. Netaji enthusiastically offered the reorganised INA First Division, when the Japanese 15th division was ordered to oppose the British. Subsquently, the 2nd Division was also readied for action. In February 1945, the INA held some positions in the region of Mandalay in Burma, giving battle to the advancing enemy. This was the second campaign of Netaji's army, and it held out tenaciously at Nyaungu for some time. However, Allied troops later crossed the Irrawaddy at several points and the Japanese and INA units were surrounded. There were some desertions. Despite unique examples of heroism and Netaji's presence in the battlefields, risking his own life in the face of enemy attacks, the second campaign of the INA (which was purely a defensive one) finally had to give way to the gradual reconquest of Burma by the British.

The end of this campaign was followed by a chain of events that included the final Japanese defeat, an alleged plane crash in Formosa in which Netaji reportedly perished, the surrender of the INA to the Allied forces and the trial of their leaders at the Red Fort in Delhi, staged by the British. However, all these fateful events, occurring during the final phase of World War II and its aftermath, should be considered parts of an altogether different episode relating to Subhash Chandra Bose and the Indian National Army. In the present episode we have examined the historical tasks fulfilled by Netaji and his army in Europe and Asia during World War II, and their significance. In recognition of Netaji's historically significant role as a war leader, Guy Wint pays him a rare tribute with these words: "He played ... an extraordinarily decisive part. By accident, and by seizing an exceptional opportunity, he was able to cut a figure which made him outstanding among the comparatively small number of men who influenced the course of the war by their individual qualities."

A Great Commander

Subhash Chandra Bose, (January 23, 1897 - August 18, 1945?), also known as Netaji, was one of the most prominent leaders of the Indian Independence Movement against the British Raj. He is immortalised in Indian History for having formed the Azad Hind Government in exile, and regrouping and leading the Indian National Army to battle against the allies in Imphal and Burma during the World War II. Bose was elected president of the Indian National Congress for two consecutive terms. However, he had to resign from the post in the face of a motion of no-confidence, stemming from ideological conflicts with Mahatma Gandhi. Bose felt that Mahatma Gandhi's tactics of non-violence would never be sufficient to secure India's independence, and advocated violent resistance. He established a separate political party, the All India Forward Bloc and continued to call for the full and immediate independence of India from British rule. His stance did not change with the outbreak of War, which he saw as an opportunity to take advantage of British weakness.

He was imprisoned by the British authorities 11 times. At the outset of World War II, in a daring act of escape from the eyes of the British, he fled from India, and reached Germany by a lengthy and dangerous route. His political views and the alliances he made with Nazi and other militarist regimes opposed to the British Empire have been the cause of arguments among historians and politicians, with some accusing him of Fascism. He is believed to have died on 18 August 1945 in a plane crash over Taiwan, however, contradicting evidence exists regarding his death in the accident.

Bose was born to an affluent family in Cuttack, Orissa. Bose was educated at Cambridge University. In 1920, Bose took the Indian Civil Service entrance examination and was placed fourth with highest marks in English. However, he resigned from the prestigious Indian Civil Service in April 1921 despite his high ranking in the merit list, and went on to become an active member of India's Independence Movement. He joined the Indian National

Congress, and was particularly active in its youth wing. However, Bose's ideals did not match with that of Mahatma Gandhi's belief in non-violence. He therefore returned to Calcutta to work under Chittaranjan Das, the Bengali freedom fighter and co-founder (with Motilal Nehru) of the Swaraj Party. In 1921, Bose organised a boycott of the celebrations to mark the visit of the Prince of Wales to India, which led to his imprisonment. In April 1924, Bose was elected to the post of Chief Executive Officer of the newly constituted Calcutta Corporation wherein C R Das was mayor. Though Subhash was entitled to Rs. 3,000/month as salary but he decided to take half of that amount, i.e. Rs. 1,500/month, still a very generous amount, considering a schoolteacher earned Rs. 50/month in those days. Later, in October that year, Bose was arrested as a suspected terrorist. At first, he was kept in Alipore jail and later he was exiled to Mandalay in Burma (where earlier Tilak spent 6 years in prison). On January 23 1930, Bose was once again arrested for leading an "independence procession", protesting against British rule in India. After his release from jail on September 25, he was elected as the Mayor of the City of Calcutta.

Over a span of 20 years, Bose was incarcerated eleven times by the British, either in India or in Rangoon. He spent many years in various capacities as the Chief Executive Officer of the Calcutta Municipal Corporation, and later as Mayor himself. Along with Jawaharlal Nehru, he was one of the radical left wing leaders of the Congress Party. He was exiled from India by the British during the mid-1930s to Europe, where he championed India's cause for self-rule before gatherings and conferences. In 1934 he met the love of his life, Emilie Schenkl, in Vienna, and they were married in 1937 in Bad Gastein.

After his father's death, the British authorities allowed him to land at Calcutta's airport only for the religious rites, which would be followed by his swift departure. During this time he travelled extensively in India and in Europe before stating his political opposition to Gandhi. He became the president of the Haripura Indian National Congress in 1938, against Gandhi's wishes. He was elected for a second term in 1939 in Tripuri Congress Session; Gandhi had supported Pattabhi Sitaramayya and commented "Pattabhi's defeat is my defeat" after learning the election results. Although Bose won the election, Gandhi's continued opposition led to the latter's resignation from the Working Committee, and the possibility that the rest of the CWC would resign. In the face of this gesture of no-confidence, Bose himself resigned, and was left with no alternative but to form an independent party, the All India Forward Bloc. Bose also initiated the concept of the *National Planning Committee* in 1938.

Actions during the Second World War

Bose advocated the approach that the political instability of war-time Britain should be taken advantage of — rather than simply wait for the British to grant independence after the end of the war (which was the view of Gandhi, Nehru and a section of the Congress leadership at the time). In this, he was influenced by the examples of Italian statesmen Giuseppe Garibaldi and Giuseppe Mazzini.

During his stay in Europe from 1933 to 1936, he met several European leaders and thinkers, including Benito Mussolini, Edvard Benes, Karl Seitz, Eamon de Valera, Romain Rolland and Alfred Rosenberg. He came to believe that India could achieve political freedom only if it had political, military and diplomatic support from outside, and that an independent nation necessitated the creation of a national army to secure its sovereignty. His correspondence reveals that despite his clear dislike for British subjugation, he was deeply impressed by their methodical and systematic approach and their steadfastly disciplinarian outlook towards life. In England, he exchanged ideas with British Labour Party leaders and political thinkers like Lord Halifax, George Lansbury, Clement Attlee, Arthur Greenwood, Harold Laski, J. B. S. Haldane, Ivor Jennings, G. D. H. Cole, Gilbert Murray and Sir Stafford Cripps on the future of India. He came to believe that a free India needed Socialist authoritarianism, on the lines of Turkey's Kemal Ataturk, for at least two decades.

The Great Escape

On the outbreak of war, Bose advocated a campaign of mass civil disobedience to protest against the Viceroy, Lord Linlithgow's decision to declare war on India's behalf without consulting the Congress leadership. Having failed to persuade Gandhi of the necessity of this, Bose organised mass protests in Calcutta calling for the 'Holwell Monument' commemorating the Black Hole of Calcutta, which then stood at the corner of Dalhousie Square, to be removed. He was thrown in jail by the British, but was released following a seven-day hunger strike. Bose's house in Calcutta was kept under surveillance by the CBI, but their vigilance left a good deal to be desired. With two court cases pending, he felt the British would not let him leave the country before the end of the war — it has been suggested that he was desperate to see his wife, who was in Berlin This set the scene for Bose's "Great Escape" to Germany, via Afghanistan and the Soviet Union.

Bose had never been to Afghanistan, and could not speak the local tribal language (Pashto). Bose escaped from under British surveillance at his house in Calcutta On January 19, 1941, accompanied by his nephew Sisir K. Bose, Bose gave his watchers the slip and journeyed to Peshawar with the assistance of the Abwehr (Wehrmacht Military Intelligence) he made his way to Peshawar where he was met at Peshawar Cantonment station by Akbar Shah, Mohammed Shah and Bhagat Ram Talwar.

Bose was taken to the home of Abad Khan, a trusted friend of Akbar Shah's. On the 26th January, 1941, Bose began his journey to reach Russia through India's North West frontier with Afghanistan. For this reason, he enlisted the help of Mian Akbar Shah, then a Forward Bloc leader in the North West Frontier Province. Shah had been out of India *en route* to the Soviet Union, and suggested a novel disguise for Bose to assume. Since Bose could not speak one word of Pashto, it would make him an easy target of Pashto speakers working for the British. For this reason, Shah suggested that Bose act deaf and dumb, and let his beard grow to mimic those of the tribesmen.

Supporters of the Aga Khan helped him across the border into Afghanistan where he was met by an Abwehr unit posing as a party of road construction engineers from the Organisation Todt who then aided his passage across Afghanistan via Kabul to the border with Soviet Russia. Once in Russia the NKVD transported Bose to Moscow where he hoped that Russia's traditional enmity to British rule in India would result in support for his plans for a popular rising in India. However, Bose found the Soviets' response disappointing and was rapidly passed over to the German Ambassador in Moscow, Count von der Schulenberg. He had Bose flown on to Berlin in a special courier aircraft at the beginning of April where he was to receive a more favourable hearing from von Rippentrop and the Foreign Ministry officials at the Wilhelmstrasse.

In Germany

Having escaped incarceration at home by assuming the guise of a Pathan insurance agent (Ziauddin) to reach Afghanistan, Bose travelled to Moscow on the passport of an Italian nobleman "Count Orlando Mazzotta". From Moscow, he reached Rome, and from there he travelled to Germany, where he instituted the Special Bureau for India under Adam von Trott zu Solz, broadcasting on the German-sponsored Azad Hind Radio. He founded the *Free India Centre* in Berlin, and created the Indian Legion (consisting of some 4500 soldiers) out of Indian prisoners of war who had previously fought for the British in North Africa prior to their capture by Axis forces. The Indian Legion was attached to the Wehrmacht, and later transferred to the Waffen SS; its members swore their allegiance to both Hitler and Bose to secure India's independence. At a time, when no one in Germany dared criticise Hitler, Bose was openly critical of Hitler's treatment of Jews, the destruction of democratic institutions in Germany and the Nazi invasion of the Soviet Union. He was also, however, prepared to envisage an invasion of India via the USSR by Nazi troops, spearheaded by the Azad Hind Legion; many have questioned his judgement here, as it seems unlikely that the Germans could have been easily persuaded to leave after such an invasion, which would also have resulted in an Axis victory in the War.

The lack of interest shown by Hitler in the cause of Indian independence eventually caused Bose to become disillusioned with Hitler and he decided to leave Nazi Germany in 1943. He travelled by the German submarine *U-180* around the Cape of Good Hope to Imperial Japan (via Japanese submarine *I-29*), which helped him raise his army in Singapore. This was the only civilian transfer across two submarines of two different navies in World War II.

In Japan and South East Asia

The Indian National Army (INA) was originally founded by the expatriate nationalist leader Rash Behari Bose, who handed over control of the organisation to Subhash Chandra Bose after his arrival in the Far East in 1943. At its height it consisted of some 85,000 regular troops, including a separate women's army unit named after Rani Lakshmi Bai (the women's combat army unit was the first of its kind in Asia). These troops were under the aegis of a provisional government, with its own currency, court and civil code, called the Provisional Government of Free India (or, the Arzi Hukumat-e-Azad Hind), and recognised by nine Axis states — Germany, Japan, Italy, the Independent State of Croatia, Wang Jingwei's Government in Nanjing, Thailand, a provisional government of Burma, Manchukuo and Japanese-controlled Philippines. Of those countries, five were puppet states established by Axis occupation. This government participated as a delegate or observer in the so-called Greater East Asia Co-Prosperity Sphere.

As the Japanese pressed forward through Burma towards India, some of the INA's troops assisted in the Japanese victory over the British in the battles of Arakan and Meiktila, along with the Burmese National Army led by Ba Maw and Aung San. A year after the islands were taken by the Japanese, the Provisional Government and the INA were established in the Andaman and Nicobar Islands in the Bay of Bengal, part of the British Indian Empire under Japanese occupation, which he renamed Shaheed (Martyr) and Swaraj (Self-rule). Bose visited the islands on just one occasion late in 1943, when he was carefully screened from the local population by the Japanese authorities, who at that time were torturing the leader of the Indian Independence League on the Islands, Dr. Diwan Singh (who later died of his injuries, in the Cellular Jail). The islanders made several attempts to alert Bose to their plight, but apparently without success.

On the Indian mainland, an Indian Tricolour, modelled after that of the Indian National Congress, was raised for the first time in the town in Moirang, in Manipur, in northeastern India. The towns of Kohima and Imphal were placed under siege by divisions of the Japanese, Burmese and the Gandhi and Nehru Brigades of INA. At the time of the Great Bengal Famine of 1943, during which millions died of starvation as a consequence of British inefficiency and indifference, Bose had offered (through radio) to provide Burmese rice to the victims of the famine. The British authorities in India (and in the UK) refused the offer, arguing that it was made for propaganda purposes.

Bose had hoped that large numbers of soldiers would desert from the Indian Army when they would discover that INA soldiers were attacking British India from the outside. However, this did not materialise on a sufficient scale. Instead, as the war situation worsened for the Japanese, troops began to desert from the INA. At the same time Japanese funding for the army diminished, and Bose was forced to raise taxes on the Indian populations of Malaysia and Singapore, sometimes extracting money by force. When the Japanese were defeated at the battles of Kohima and Imphal, the Provisional Government's aim of establishing a base in mainland India was lost forever. The INA was forced to pull back, along with the defeated Japanese Army. Japan's surrender also led to the eventual surrender of the Indian National Army.

Political Views

Bose advocated complete freedom for India at the earliest, whereas most of the Congress Committee wanted it in phases, through a Dominion status. Even though Bose and Gandhi had differing ideologies, the latter called Bose the "Patriot of Patriots" in 1942. Bose admired Gandhi, recognising his importance as a symbol of Indian Nationalism; he called him "The Father of Our Nation" in a radio broadcast from Rangoon in 1944, in which he stated that "I am convinced that if we do desire freedom we must be prepared to wade through blood", a statement somewhat at odds with Gandhi's philosophy of non-violence.

Thus, although they shared the goal of an Independent India, by 1939 the two had become divided over the tactics which should be used to achieve Indian Independence, and to some degree the form which the post-independence state should take: Gandhi was hostile to industrialisation, whilst Bose saw it as the only route to making India strong and self-sufficient (in this he may have been influenced, like many other Indian intellectuals of the time, by reports of the success of the Soviet five-year plans). Nehru disagreed with Gandhi on this point as well, though not over the tactics of protest.

At the time the Second World War began, great divisions existed in the Indian Independence Movement about whether to exploit the weakness of the British to achieve independence. Some felt that any distinctions between the political allegiances and ideologies of the warring factions of Europe were inconsequential in the face of the possibility of Indian independence, given the fact that the British themselves showed so little respect for democracy or democratic reforms in India. Others felt that it was inappropriate to seek concessions when Britain itself was in peril, or else that pressure was better applied within India and in peaceful fashion, and found that their distaste for Nazi Germany and Japan outweighed any possibility that an alliance with them would bring India's independence closer.

Bose, in particular, was accused of 'collaborating' with the Axis, after he fled to Germany in 1941 and offered Hitler an alliance. He criticised the British during World War II, saying that while Britain was allegedly fighting for the freedom of the European nations under Nazi control, it would not grant independence to its own colonies, including India. It may be observed that along with Nehru, Bose had organised and led protest marches against the Japanese invasion of Manchuria in 1931, and of China itself in 1938, when he was Congress president.

In 1937 he published an article attacking Japanese Imperialism in the Far East, although he betrayed some admiration for other aspects of the Japanese regime . Bose's earlier correspondence (prior to 1939) also reflects his deep disapproval of the racist practices of, and annulment of democratic institutions in Nazi Germany . He also, however, expressed admiration for the authoritarian methods (though not the racial ideologies) which he saw in Italy and Germany during the 1930s, and thought they could be used in building an independent India Nevertheless, Bose's tenure as Congress Party President (1938-39) did not reflect any particular anti-democratic or authoritarian attributes .Rather, his role then was more that of a negotiator, and a consensus-builder within the ranks of the senior Congress leadership (led by Mahatma Gandhi, Sardar Patel and Jawaharlal Nehru and others) on the one hand, and the Muslim League (led by Mohammed Ali Jinnah) on the other. Nirad C. Chaudhuri, Anton Pelinka and Leonard Gordon have remarked that Bose's skills were best illustrated at the negotiating table, rather than on the battlefield.

That Bose eventually changed his political stance (which initially was that of Gandhi and Nehru) reflects his deep discontent with the nature of the British rule, and a growing belief that the formation of an Indian free state was too far into the future on the British political roadmap to be acceptable. At the Tripuri Congress session of 1939, he made his views quite explicit — he demanded for a programme of immediately giving the British Government a six-months ultimatum to grant the national demand of independence and of launching a mass Civil Disobedience Movement if it failed to do so. He believed that "... the country was internally more ripe for a revolution than ever before and that the coming international crisis would give India an opportunity for achieving her emancipation, which is rare in human history."

Bose's judgement in allying with the Japanese has been questioned, as many argue that he would have been unable to ensure an independent India had he ridden to power on Japanese bayonets, and was in danger of being turned into a puppet ruler like Pu-yi, the last Chinese Emperor in Manchukuo. In 1943 Rash Behari Bose had urged this on him during his last visit to Subhash Bose in Singapore, pointing out that the Japanese had claimed right of conquest in Manchuria and would do so in India, whilst Quit India had shown that this would not be accepted by the Indian Nation.

Bose may have believed that the people of India would be with him, and that therefore he would be able to resist Japanese demands. He knew that India was a long way from Japan, and that the Japanese were already at the limits of their capabilities. He also pointed out that the American revolutionaries had accepted assistance from France, and this didn't make the US a French colony. Nevertheless, given the INA's overwhelming dependence on Japanese military support, he would have been in a very weak position. Bose also seems to have ignored the appalling treatment meted out by the Japanese to the Asian inhabitants of the lands they conquered as part of the Greater East Asian Co-prosperity sphere, which included the forcible recruitment of labour from the overseas Indian population to build projects such as the Burma Railway, and massacres of Malayan Chinese in Singapore where he spent most of the War.

Bose has been branded as a fascist in some quarters. Others believe that Bose had clearly expressed his belief that democracy was the best option for India. The pro-Bose thinkers believe that his authoritarian control of the Indian National Army was based on political pragmatism and a post-colonial recovery doctrine rather than any anti-democratic belief..

However, during the war (and possibly as early as the 1930s) Bose seems to have decided that no democratic system could be adequate to overcome India's poverty and social inequalities, and he wrote that an authoritarian state, similar to that of Soviet Russia (which he had also seen and admired) would be needed for the process of national rebuilding. Accordingly some suggest that Bose's alliance with the Axis during the war was based on more than just pragmatism, and that Bose may have been a Fascist, though not a Nazi; alternatively, others consider he might have been using populist methods of mobilisation common to many post-colonial leaders. Had either of the alliances he forged during the war resulted in Indian independence in the manner he envisaged, it would have been at the cost of an Allied defeat in the Second World War, a price that some Indians would argue is too high: Gandhi himself, in the immediate aftermath of the war, said that Bose had been "foolish in imagining, that by allying himself with the Japanese and the Germans, who were not only aggressive Powers, but also dangerous Powers, he could get Indian freedom". The alternative of non-violent protest within India espoused by Gandhi and the rest of Congress ultimately led to British withdrawal, albeit at the expense of the partition of the country along communal lines.

Even before 1939, Congress had secured political concessions from the British in the form of elected Provincial Assemblies, and an agreement that the British taxpayer would foot the bill for Indian rearmament . Although it was rejected by Congress at the time, the 1942 Cripps mission's offer of full independence after the war could be considered the point at which the British departure became inevitable. Britain's weakness after the war, and domestic political pressure on the Labour Government also made British withdrawal more likely. Publicly at least, Bose never believed that this would happen unless they were driven out by force: as late as 1944 he announced that "I am honestly convinced that the British Government will never recognise India's demand for independence" . In this he was mistaken.

Yet it may be equally true that he would never have accepted the partition of India as true independence, just as Gandhi always refused to accept that the people of India were two separate nations. Some would also argue that it was the activities and spectre of the INA and what Bose represented which convinced the British imperial administration to hand over a divided India to the Congress and the Muslim League. They also consider it a backhanded tribute to Bose that the Congress tricolour and the Muslim League green flag flew together for the last time during the mutiny of the Indian navy in Bombay unleashed in 1946 by popular fury at the trial of INA officers by the British. This view is popular in India and among Indian Historians today, but finds little support amongst historians. With hindsight, however, it is admissible that Bose's original goal of starting mass militant revolution among the Indians once his army reached India was certainly the way history acted out, with the stories of the INA inspiring the British Indian Armed forces into increasingly rebellious resentment. There is no doubt that Bose was a great patriot, and was considered as such even by his rivals in the Congress. Gandhi himself wrote that Bose's "... patriotism is second to none", and he was moved to proclaim after Bose's disappearance that he was a "prince among patriots"— a reference to Bose's achievement in integrating women and men from all the regions and religions of India in the Indian National Army. Bose wanted freedom for India at the earliest opportunity, and to some extent, he didn't care who he had to approach for assistance . It is thus quite understandable that he remains a controversial figure to this day.

Government in Exile

Arzi Hukumat-e-Azad Hind

Arzi Hukumat-e-Azad Hind (the Provisional Government of Free India), or simply Azad Hind, was an Indian Government-in-Exile established in Singapore in 1943.

It was a part of a political movement originating in the 1940s outside of India with the purpose of allying with Axis powers to free India from British Rule. Established by Indian nationalists-in-exile during the latter part of the second world war in Singapore with monetary, military and political assistance from Imperial Japan, to fight against British Rule in India. Founded on October 21, 1943, the government was inspired by the concepts of Netaji Subhash Chandra Bose who was also the leader of the government and the Head of State of this Provisional Indian Government in Exile. The government proclaimed authority over Indian civilian and military personnel in South East Asian British colonial territory and prospective authority over Indian territory to fall to the Japanese forces and the Indian National Army during the Japanese thrust towards India during the Second World War. The government of Azad Hind had its own currency, court and civil code, and in the eyes of many Indians its existence gave a greater legitimacy to the independence struggle against the British.

However, while it possessed all the nominal requisites of a legitimate government, it lacked large and definite areas of sovereign territory until the government assumed control of the Andaman and Nicobar Islands from Japan in 1943 and the occupation of parts of Manipur and Nagaland. Throughout its existence, it remained heavily dependent on Japanese support.

Immediately after the formation of the government-in-exile, Azad Hind declared war against the Anglo-American allied forces on the Indo-Burma Front. Its army, the "Azad Hind Fauj", (Indian National Army or the *INA*) went into action against the British Indian Army and the allied forces alongside the Imperial Japanese Army in the Imphal-Kohima sector. The INA was to make its mark in the battle of Imphal where along with the Japanese 15th Army it breached the British defences in Kohima, reaching the salient of Moirang before Allied air dominance and compromised supply lines forced both the Japanese and the INA to lift the siege.

The existence of Azad Hind was essentially coterminous with the existence of the Indian National Army. While the government itself continued until the civil administration of the Andaman Islands was returned to the jurisdiction of the British towards the end of the war, the limited power of Azad Hind was effectively ended with the surrender of the last major contingent of INA troops in Rangoon. The supposed death of Bose is seen as the end of the entire Azad Hind Movement.

The Allies at the time, as well as some post-war historians, regarded the Government as a puppet state. The government was not recognised by Allied governments or Vichy France.

The legacy of Azad Hind is, however, open to judgement. After the war, the Raj observed with alarm the transformation of the perception of Azad Hind from traitors and collaborators to "the greatest among the patriots". Given the tide of militant nationalism that swept through India and the resentment and revolts it inspired, it is arguable that its overarching aim: to germinate public resentment and revolts within the Indian forces of the British Indian Army to overthrow the Raj was ultimately successful.

Establishment

The direct origins of Azad Hind can be linked to two conferences of Indian expatriates from across South East Asia, the first of which was held in Tokyo in March of 1942. At this conference, convened by Rash Behari Bose, an Indian expatriate living in Japan, the Indian Independence League was established as the first move towards an independent Indian state politically aligned with the Empire of Japan. Rash also moved to create a sort of liberation army that would assist in driving the British from India - this force would later become the Indian National Army. The second conference, held later that year in Bangkok, invited Subhash Chandra Bose to participate in the leadership of the League. Bose was living in Germany at the time and made the trip to Japan via submarine.

Rash Behari Bose, who was already aging by the time the League was founded, struggled to keep the League organised and failed to secure resources for the establishment of the Indian National Army. He was replaced as president of the Indian Independence League by Subhash Chandra Bose; there is some controversy as to whether he stepped down of his own volition or by pressure from the Japanese who needed a more energetic and focused presence leading the Indian nationalists.

Bose arrived in Tokyo on June 13, 1943, and declared his intent to make an assault against the eastern provinces of India in an attempt to oust the British from control of the subcontinent. Bose arrived in Singapore on July 2, and in October 1943 formally announced the establishment of the Provisional Government of Free India. In defining the tasks of this new political establishment, Subhash declared: "It will be the task of the Provisional Government to launch and conduct the struggle that will bring about the expulsion of the British and their allies from the soil of India." Bose, taking formal command of the demoralised and undermanned Indian National Army from Rash Bose, turned it into a professional army with the help of the Japanese. He recruited Indian civilians living in Japanese-occupied territories of South East Asia, and incorporated vast numbers of Indian PoWs from British forces in Singapore, Malaya and Hong Kong to man the brigades of the INA.

The Cabinet

The Provisional Government of Free India consisted of a Cabinet headed by Netaji Subhash Chandra Bose as the *Head of the State, The Prime Minister and the Minister for War and Foreign Affairs.*

Captain Doctor Lakshmi Swaminathan (later married as Lakshmi Sehgal) was the *Minister in Charge of Women's Organisation.* She held this position over and above her command of the *Rani Jhansi Regiment,* a brigade of women soldiers fighting for the Indian National Army. For a regular Asian army, this women's regiment was quite visionary; it was the first of its kind established on the continent. Dr. Lakshmi was one of the most popular and prosperous gynaecologists in Singapore before she gave up her fabulous practice to lead the troops of the Rani of Jhansi Regiment.

Other public administration ministers of the Provisional Government of Free India included:

- Mr. S. A. Ayer — the Minister of Broadcasting and Publicity.
- Lt. Col. A. C. Chatterji — the Minister of Finance.

The Indian National Army was represented by Armed Forces ministers, including:

- Lt. Col. Aziz Ahmed.
- Lt. Col. N. S. Bhagat.

- Lt. Col. J. K. Bhonsle.
- Lt. Colonel Guizara Singh.
- Lt. Col. M. Z. Kiani.
- Lt. Col. A. D. Loganathan.
- Lt. Col. Ehsan Qadir.
- Lt. Col. Shah Nawaz Khan.

The Provisional Government was also constituted and administered by a number of Secretaries and Advisors to Subhash Chandra Bose, including:

- A. N. Sahay — Secretary.
- Karim Ghani.
- Debnath Das.
- D. M. Khan.
- A. Yellapa.
- J. Thivy.
- Sirdar Isher Singh.
- A. N. Sarkar — the government's official Legal Advisor.

All of these Secretaries and Advisory officials held Ministerial rank in the Provisional Government. The extent of the Provisional Government's day-to-day management of affairs for Azad Hind is not entirely well-documented, so their specific functions as government officials for the state outside of their positions as support ministers for Subhash Chandra Bose is not entirely certain.

Recognition

Azad Hind was recognised as a legitimate and independent successor state to British rule in India by only a small number of countries, limited almost solely to Axis powers and their affiliate states and puppet regimes. Azad Hind had diplomatic relations with nine countries: Nazi Germany, the Empire of Japan, Fascist Italy, the Independent State of Croatia, Wang Jingwei's Government in Nanjing, Thailand, the State of Burma, Manchukuo and the Philippine Republic. On the declaration of its formation in Singapore, President Eamon de Valera of the Irish Free State sent a note of congratulations to Bose. Vichy France, however, although being an Axis collaborator, never gave formal political recognition to Azad Hind. Recent researches have shown that the Soviet Union too had recognised the Provisional Government of Free India. This government participated as a delegate or observer in the Greater East Asia Co-Prosperity Sphere.

Government Administration and the War

The same night that Bose declared the existence of Azad Hind, the government took action to declare war against the United States and Britain. The government consisted of a Cabinet ministry acting as an advisory board to Subhash Bose, who was given the title "Netaji" (leader) and was no doubt the dominant figure in the Provisional Government. He exercised virtual authoritarian control over the government and the army. With regards to the government's first issuances of war declarations, the "Cabinet had not been unanimous about the inclusion of the USA. Bose had shown impatience and displeasure - there was never any question then or later of his absolute authority: the Cabinet had no responsibility and could only tender advice..."

At the end of October 1943, Bose flew to Tokyo to participate in the Greater East Asia Conference as an observer to Japan's Greater East Asia Co-Prosperity Sphere; it could not function as a delegate because India had technically fallen outside the jurisdiction of Japan's definition of "Greater East Asia", but Bose gave speeches in opposition to Western colonialism and imperialism at the conference. By the end of the conference, Azad Hind had been given a limited form of governmental jurisdiction over the Andaman and Nicobar Islands, which had been captured by the Imperial Japanese Navy early on in the war.

Once under the jurisdiction of Azad Hind, the islands formed the government's first claims to territory. The islands themselves were renamed "Shaheed" and "Swaraj", meaning "martyr" and "self-rule" respectively. Bose placed the islands under the governorship of Lt. Col. A. D. Loganathan, and had limited involvement with the official governorship of the territory, instead involving himself in plans to expand the Indian National Army, ensure adequate men and material, and formulate its course of actions and the administrations and relations of the Indian population in South East Asia and determining Japanese designs in India and his provisional government. In theory the government itself had the power to levy taxes on the local populace, and to make and enforce laws: in practice they were enforced by the police force under Japanese control. Indians were willing to pay these taxes at first, but became less inclined to do so towards the end of the war when the Provisional Government enacted legislation for higher war-time taxes to fund the INA. During his interrogation after the war Loganathan admitted that he had only had full control over the islands' vestigial education department, as the Japanese had retained full control over the police force, and in protest he had refused to accept responsibility for any other areas of Government. He was powerless to prevent the Homfreyganj massacre of the 30th January 1944, where forty-four Indian civilians were shot by the Japanese on suspicion of spying. Many of them were members of the Indian Independence League, whose leader in Port Blair, Dr. Diwan Singh, had already been tortured to death in the Cellular Jail after doing his best to protect the islanders from Japanese atrocities during the first two years of the occupation.

Azad Hind's military forces in the form of the INA saw some successes against the British, and moved with the Japanese army to lay siege to the town of Imphal in eastern India. Plans to march towards Delhi, gaining support and fresh recruits along the way, stalled both with the onset of monsoon season and the failure to capture Imphal. British bombing seriously reduced morale, and the Japanese along with the INA forces began their withdrawal from India.

In addition to these setbacks, the INA was faced with a formidable challenge when the troops were left to defend Rangoon without the assistance of the Japanese in the winter of 1944-45. Loganathan was relocated from the Andaman Islands to act as field commander. With the INA garrison about 6,000 strong, he manned the Burmese capital in the absence of any other police force or troops during the period between the departure of the Japanese and the arrival of the British. He was successful in maintaining law and order to the extent that there was not a single case of dacoity or of loot during the period from April 24 to May 4, 1945.

Indian Areas under the Administration of the Provisional Government

Almost all of the territory of the Provisional Government lay in the Andaman Islands, although the Provisional Government was allowed some authority over Indian enclaves in Japanese-occupied territories. Provisional Government civil authority was never enacted in areas occupied by the INA; instead, Japanese military authority prevailed and responsibility for administration of occupied areas of India was shared between the Japanese and the Indian forces.

The Defeat of the INA and the Collapse of the Provisional Government

Left to defend Rangoon from the British advance without support from the Japanese, the INA was soundly defeated. Bose had fled Burma and returned to Singapore before the fall of Rangoon; the government Azad Hind had established on the Andaman and Nicobar Islands collapsed when the island garrisons of Japanese and Indian troops were defeated by British troops and the islands themselves retaken. Allegedly Bose himself was killed in a plane crash departing from Taiwan attempting to escape to Russia. The Provisional Government of Free India ceased to exist with the deaths of the Axis, the INA, and Netaji Bose in 1945.

The troops who manned the brigades of the Indian National Army were taken as prisoners of war by the British. A number of these prisoners were brought to India and tried by British courts for treason, including a number of high ranking officers such as Colonel Gurbaksh Singh Dhillon. The defence of these individuals from prosecution by the British became a central point of contention between the British Raj and the Indian Independence Movement in the post-war years.

Relations with Japan and View of Azad Hind as Axis Collaborator

Subhash Chandra Bose, while an ally of Japan throughout the war, has become a controversial figure for his stances against imperialism which would run in opposition against what was generally recognised as Japanese imperialism in Asia during World

War II. Bose himself opposed all manner of such colonial practices, but saw Britain as hypocritical in "fighting a war for democracy" but refusing to extend the same respect for democracy and equal rights to their colonial subjects in India. Bose opposed British racial policy and declared working for the abolition of racial discrimination with Burmese, Japanese and other Asians. Criticism of Bose remains, with some accusing him of fascism, citing his strict control over the Provisional Government as evidence of this; some accused him of wanting to establish a totalitarian state in India with the blessings of the Axis powers. It is inaccurate to term Bose solely as a fascist, but it is true that Bose openly admired fascism in the Axis countries and used it as a way to organise the Provisional Government; he believed that parliamentary democracy was unsuitable for India, and that a centrally organised, self-sufficient, semi-socialist India under the firm control of a single party was the best course for Indian government. Some of his ideas would help shape Indian governmental policy in the aftermath of the country's independence from Britain.

The fact that Azad Hind was aligned politically with Japan may have little to do with explicit agreement and support for Japanese policy in Asia, and more with what Bose saw as a pragmatic approach to Indian independence. Disillusioned with Gandhi's philosophies of non-violence, Bose was clearly of the camp that supported exploiting British weakness to gain Indian independence. Throughout the existence of Azad Hind, Bose sought to distance himself from Japanese collaboration and become more self-sufficient, but found this difficult since the existence of Azad Hind as a governmental entity had only come about with the support of the Japanese, on whom the government and army of Azad Hind were entirely dependent. Bose, however, remains a hero in present-day India and is remembered as a man who fought fiercely for Indian independence.

Although Japanese troops saw much of the combat in India against the British, the INA was certainly by itself an effective combat force, having faced British and allied troops and making their mark in the Battle of Imphal. On 18 April 1944 the suicide squads led by Col. Shaukat Malik broke through the British defence and captured Moirang in Manipur. The Azad Hind administration took control of the this independent Indian territory. Following Moirang, the advancing INA breached the Kohima road, posing a threat to the British positions in both Silchar and Kohima. Col. Gulzara Singh's column had penetrated 250 miles into India. The Azad Brigade advanced, by outflanking the Anglo-American positions. However, INA's most serious, and ultimately fatal, limitations were the reliance on Japanese logistics and supplies and the total air-dominance of the allies — which, along with a supply line deluged by torrential rain, frustrated the INA's and the Japanese bid to take Imphal.

With the siege of Imphal failing, the Japanese began to shift priority for resource allocation from South Asia to the Pacific, where they were fighting United States troops advancing from island to island against Japanese holdings there. When it had become clear that Bose's plans to advance to Delhi from the borders of Burma would never materialise due to the defeat of the INA at Imphal and the halt of Japanese armies by British aerial and later naval superiority in the region, Japanese support for Azad Hind declined.

Contributions to the Indian Independence

The true judgement of success or failure of the movement remains open to historians. However, the true extent to which the INA's activities influenced the decision to leave India is mirrored by the views of Clement Attlee, the British Prime Minister at the time of India's Independence. Attlee cites several reasons, the most important of which were the INA activities of Netaji Subhash Chandra Bose, which weakened the very foundation of the British Empire in India, and the Royal Indian Navy Mutiny which made the British realise that the support of the Indian armed forces could no longer be relied upon.

End of the INA

As the Japanese withdrawal from Burma progressed, the other remnants began a long march over land and on foot towards Bangkok, along with Subhash Chandra Bose. The withdrawing forces regularly suffered casualties from allied airplanes strafing them, clashes with Aung San's Burmese resistance, as well as

Chinese guerrillas who harassed the Japanese troops. At the time of Japan's surrender in September 1945, Bose left for Manchuria to attempt to contact the advancing Soviet troops, and was reported to have died in an air crash near Taiwan.

Repatriation to India

Even before the end of the war in South Asia, the INA prisoners who were falling into allied hands were being evaluated by forward intelligence units for potential trials. A small number had fallen into Allied hands in 1943 around the time of the Imphal campaign and subsequent withdrawal, while larger numbers surrendered or were captured during the 14th Army's Burma Campaign. A total of 16,000 of the INA's 43,000 recruits were ever captured, of whom around 11,000 were interrogated. The number of prisoners necessitated this selective policy which envisaged trials of those with the strongest commitment to Bose' ideologies, while those with less strong views and other extenuating circumstance may be dealt with more leniently, with the punishment proportional to their commitment or war crimes. For this purpose, the field intelligence units designated the captured troops as *Blacks* with strongest commitment to Azad Hind, *Greys* with varying commitment but also with enticing circumstances that led them to join the INA, and *Whites,* i.e. those who pressured into joining the INA under the circumstances but with no commitment to Azad Hind, INA, or Bose.

By July 1945, a large numbers had been shipped back to India. At the time of the fall of Japan, the remaining captured troops were transported to India via Rangoon. Large numbers of local Malay and Burmese volunteers including the recruits to the Rani of Jhansi regiment returned to civilian life and were not identified. Those repatriated passed through transit camps in Chittagong and Calcutta to be held at detention camps all over India including Jhingergacha and Nilganj near Calcutta, Kirkee outside Pune, Attock, Multan and at Bahadurgarh near Delhi. Bahadurgarh also held prisoners of the Indische Legion. By November, around 12,000 INA prisoners were held in these camps, from which they were released according to the "colours". By December, around 600 whites were released per week. From amongst the rest, the selection for those to face trial started.

The Red Fort Trial

At the conclusion of the war, the government of British India brought some of the captured INA soldiers to trial on treason charges. The prisoners would potentially face the death penalty, life imprisonment or a fine as punishment if found guilty. It was initially believed by Auchinleck that no less than twenty death penalties were likely to be confirmed. Between November 1945 and May 1946, approximately ten courts-martial were held. The first of these, and the most celebrated one, was the joint court-martial of Colonel Prem Sahgal, Colonel Gurubaksh Singh Dhillon and Major General Shah Nawaz Khan held in a public trial at Red Fort. The then Advocate General of India, Sir Naushirwan P. Engineer was appointed the counsel for the prosecution. Nearly all the defendants in the first trial were charged with *Waging against the King-Emperor* (the charge of treason did not exist in the Indian Army Act, 1911) as well as torture, murder and abetment to murder. The three defendants were defended by the INA Defence Committee formed by the Congress and include legal luminaries of India of the time including Jawaharlal Nehru, Bhulabhai Desai, Kailashnath Katju and others. The trials covered arguments based on Military Law, Constitutional Law, International Law, and Politics and much of the initial defence was based on the argument that they should be treated as prisoners of war as they were not paid mercenaries but *bona fide* soldiers of a legal government, the Provisional Government of Free India, or the Arzi Hukumat-e-Azad Hind, "however misinformed or otherwise they had been in their notion of patriotic duty towards their country" and as such they recognised the free Indian state as their sovereign and not the British sovereign. Those charged later only faced trial for torture and murder or abetment of murder.

These trials attracted much publicity, and public sympathy for the defendants who were perceived as patriots in India. The Indian National Congress and the Muslim League both made the release of the three defendants an important political issue during the agitation for independence of 1945-46. Beyond the concurrent campaigns of non-cooperation and non-violent protest, this spread to include mutinies and wavering support within the British Indian Army. This movement marked the last major campaign in which the forces of the Congress and the Muslim League aligned together; the Congress tricolour and the green flag of the League were flown together at protests. In spite of this aggressive and widespread opposition, the court martial was carried out, and all three defendants were sentenced to deportation for life. This sentence, however, was never carried out, as the immense public pressure of the demonstrations and riots forced Claude Auchinleck, commander-in-chief of the Indian Army, to release all three defendants. Within three months, 11,000 soldiers of the INA were released after cashiering and forfeiture of pay and allowance. On the recommendation of Lord Mountbatten of Burma, and agreed by Nehru, as a precondition for Independence the INA soldiers were not re-inducted into the Indian Army.

Post-1947 Events

Within India, the INA continued to have a strong hold over the public psyche and the sentiments of the armed forces till as late as 1947. Some have said that Shah Nawaz Khan was instrumental in organising INA troops to train Congress volunteers on Nehru's request in late-1946 and early-1947. After 1947, some accounts suggest that the INA-veterans were involved in training civilian resistance forces against the Nizam's Razakars prior to the execution of Operation Polo and annexation of Hyderabad. There are also mentions of some INA veterans leading Pakistani irregulars during the First Kashmir war.

INA-veterans were not allowed to join the Indian Army after India's independence in August 1947. However, a few ex-INA members, notably the most prominent members or those closely associated with Subhash Bose or with the INA trials later have seen prominent public life or held important positions in independent India.

Shah Nawaz Khan served as a Minister of State for Rail in the First Indian Cabinet. Lakshmi Sahgal, Minister for Women's affairs in the Azad Hind govt. is a well known and widely respected public figure in India. In 1971, she joined the Communist Party of India (Marxist) and was later elected the leader of the All India Democratic Women's Association. In 2002, she was also nominated by the Communist bloc's for the post of President of India, when she lost to the candidature of Abdul Kalam. Abid Hasan, Subhash Bose's sole Indian companion in the U-Boat from Germany to South East Asia, joined the Indian Foreign Service in 1948 and served as the Indian Ambassador to a number of countries including Egypt and Denmark. Mohan Singh served for two terms in the Rajya Sabha of the Indian Parliament as a member of the Indian National Congress. Ram Singh Thakur, composer of a number of songs including the INA's regimental march *Kadam Kadam Badaye Ja,* later composed the tune for the Indian National Anthem

Amongst the very few ex-INA members who joined the Indian Armed Forces after 1947 was R. S. Benegal, a member of the Tokyo Boys who was allowed to join the Indian Air Force in 1952 and later rose to be an Air Commodore. Benegal saw action in both the 1965 and 1971 Indo-Pak war, earning a Maha Vir Chakra India's second highest award for valour.

A few members, including Gurubaksh Singh Dhillon and Lakshmi Sahgal were later awarded civilian honours of Padma Vibhushan by the Indian Government in the 1990s. Subhash Bose himself was posthumously awarded Bharat Ratna in 1992 but this was later withdrawn over the controversy over the circumstances of his death.

Outside India, the Malaysian Indian Congress was founded in 1946 by, amongst others, notable members of the INA and of which John Thivy was the founding president. Janaky Athi Nahappan, Second in Command of the Rani of Jhansi Regiment was also a founding member of the MIC, and later was to become a noted welfare activist and a distinguished senator in the Dewan Negara of the Malaysian Parliament. Rasammah Bhupalan, also of the Rani of Jhansi Regiment, later became a noted welfare-activist and a widely respected champion for Women's Rights in Malaysia.

The Impact

The INA's impact on the war and on British India after the war has been analysed in detail. The INA's role in military terms is considered to be relatively insignificant, given its small numerical strength, lack of heavy weapons (it utilised captured British and Dutch arms initially), relative dependence on Japanese logistics and planning as well as its lack of independent planning. Shah Nawaz claims in his personal memoirs that the INA was a very potent and motivated force. Fay however, reinforces the argument that the INA was relatively less significant in military terms. Its special services group played a significant part in halting the First Arakan Offensive while still under Mohan Singh's command. The propaganda threat of the INA, coupled with the lack of concrete intelligence on the unit early after the fall of Singapore made it a potent threat to Allied war plans in South East Asia. It threatened to destroy the Sepoy's loyalty in the British Indian Army and in fact was significant and successful enough during the First Arakan Offensive for the British intelligence to begin the Jiffs campaign as well as engage in campaign to improve morale and preserve the loyalty of the sepoy to consolidate and prepare for defence of Manipur. These measures included imposing newsban on Bose and the INA that was not lifted till four days after the fall of Rangoon two years later.

Later, during the Japanese U-GO offensive towards Manipur in 1944, it played a crucial and successful role in the diversionary attacks in Arakan as well as in the Manipur Basin itself where it fought with Mutaguchi's 15th Army. It qualified itself well in the Battles in Arakan, Manipur, Imphal, and later during the withdrawal through Manipur and Burma. Later, during the Burma Campaign, it did play a notable role in the Battles of Irrawaddy and Meiktilla especially in the latter, supporting the Japanese offensive and tying down British troops. Fay also notes the published accounts of several veterans, including that of William Slim that portrays INA-troops as incapable fighters and untrustworthy, and points out the inconsistencies and conflicts between the different accounts to conclude that intelligence propaganda as well as institutional bias may have played a significant part in the portrayed opinions.

It is however noted that the INA did indeed suffer a number of notable incidences of desertion. Fay notes the significant ones amongst these were not during the offensives into Manipur and the subsequent retreat through Burma, when incidences of desertion did occur but at a far smaller numbers than the fourteenth army told its troops. The significant desertions, Fay notes, occurred around the Battles at Irrawaddy and later around Popa. During the fall of Rangoon, 6,000 INA troops manned the city to maintain order before allied troops entered the city. Nevertheless, Fay argues, the INA was not significant enough to militarily beat the British Indian Army, and was moreover aware of this and formulated its own strategy of avoiding set-piece battles, garnering local and popular support within India and instigating revolt within the British Indian army to overthrow the Raj. Moreover, the Forward Bloc underground within India had been crushed well before the offensives opened in the Burma-Manipur theatre, depriving the army of any organised internal support.

It was however, the INA trials that attracted more attention in India than the war time activities of the unit, and coupled to the decisions to hold the first trial in public, these became a rallying point for the Independence Movement from Autumn 1945, so much so that the release of INA prisoners and suspension of the trials came to be the dominant political campaign in precedence over the campaign for Freedom. Newspaper reports around November 1945 reported executions of INA troops, which deteriorated already volatile situations. Opposition to the trial of the officers for treason became a major public and political campaign, and the very opening of the first trial saw violence and series of riots in a scale later described as sensational. It also saw a campaign that defied communal barriers.

Increasingly violent confrontations broke out between the police and the mass rallies being held all over India, culminating in public riotings in support of the INA men. The Raj also observed with increasing disquiet and unease the spread of pro-INA sympathies within the troops of the British Indian forces. In February 1946, while the trials were still going on, a general strike ratings of the Royal Indian Navy rapidly deteriorated into a mutiny, incorporating ships and shore establishments of the RIN throughout India, from Karachi to Bombay and from Vizag to Calcutta. Amongst the rallying cries of the ratings the central one was the INA trials and slogans invoking Subhash Bose. Significantly, the mutiny received massive militant public support. At some places, NCOs in the British Indian Army started ignoring orders from British superiors. In Madras and Pune, the British garrisons had to face revolts within the ranks of the British Indian Army. Another Army mutiny took place at Jabalpur during the last week of February 1946, soon after the Navy mutiny at Bombay.

British troops suppressed this by force, using bayonets. It lasted about two weeks. After the mutiny, about 45 persons were tried by court martial. 41 were sentenced to varying terms of imprisonment or dismissal. In addition, a large number were discharged on administrative grounds. Fay records Auchinleck as having sent a "Personal and Secret" letter to all senior British officers as having explained the remissions of the sentences in the first trial as

> "...practically all are sure that any attempt to enforce the sentence would have led to chaos in the country at large, and probably to mutiny and dissension in the Army, culminating in its dissolution"

Later historians have pointed out that the INA trials and its after effects brought the decisive shift in British policy. The viceroy's journal describes the autumn and Winter 1945-45 as "The Edge of a Volcano". Intelligence reports at the time noted widespread public interest and sympathy that turned into what has been described as "Patriotic Fury" that was beyond the communal barriers in India at the time. Particularly disturbing for the British, was the overt and public support for the INA by the soldiers of the Indian army. In addition, the use of Indian troops for the restoration of Dutch and French rule in Vietnam and Indonesia also fed growing resentment within the forces. The Raj had every reason to fear a revival of the Quit Indian Movement, especially given the Congress rhetoric preceding the elections and rapidly realised that the Indian army, unlike in 1942, could not be used to suppress such a movement owing largely to nationalistic and political consciousness in the forces which was ascribed to the INA. Some historians cite Auchinleck's own assessment of the situation to suggest this shortened the Raj by at least fifteen to twenty years.

The political effects of the INA trials was enormous and were felt around India as late as 1948, much to the chagrin of the then Indian government. Clement Attlee, the then British Prime Minister, reflecting on the factors that guided the British decision to relinquish the Raj in India, is said to have cited the effects of the INA and Bose's activities on the British Indian Army and the Bombay Mutiny as being the most important.

After the war ended, the story of the INA and the Free India Legion was seen as so inflammatory that, fearing mass revolts and uprisings — not just in India, but across its empire — the British Government forbade the BBC from broadcasting their story.

Relations

The army's relationship to the Japanese was an uncomfortable one. Bose wished to establish his political independence from the regime that sponsored him (he had, in fact, led protests against the Japanese expansion into Manchuria, and supported Chiang Kai-shek during the 1930s), but his complete dependence on them for arms and resources made this difficult. On the Japanese side, members of the high command had been personally impressed by Bose, and were thus willing to grant him some latitude; more importantly, the Japanese were interested in maintaining the support of a man who had been able to mobilise large numbers of Indian expatriates — including, most importantly, 40,000 of the 45,000 Indians captured by the Japanese at Singapore.

The INA's interactions with the British Indian Army occurred over two distinct phases. The first of these was December 1942-March 1943, during the First Arakan offensive at a time that the morale of the sepoy was low and the knowledge about the INA was minimal. The INA's Special Services agents led a successful operation during this time in encouraging the Indian troops to defect to the INA, while those who returned to India beaten in the field took back horrific if unbelievable stories of Japanese troops using their parachutes not only to drop from the skies, but to go back up again. The threat of the INA at this time was significant and successful enough for the British intelligence to begin the Jiffs campaign as well as engage in campaign to improve morale and preserve the loyalty of the sepoy. General newsban on reporting the INA allowed the British Indian Army to consolidate and prepare for defence of Manipur, which it successfully did. By the end of March 1945, the sepoy of the British Indian Army was reinvigorated and perceived the men of the INA little more than savage turncoats and cowards. Bayly and Harper mentions that a number of times, the sepoys in the field units shot captured or wounded INA men, relieving their British officers of the complex task of formulating a formal plan for captured men.

Writing about his experiences in the infantry during the Burma Campaign, the author George MacDonald Fraser stated that INA prisoners had to be guarded by British troops to prevent them from being shot by British Indians. After Singapore was retaken, Mountbatten ordered the INA's war memorial to its fallen soldiers to be blown up.

However, the INA's most significant interaction with the British Indian Army occurred not in the battle field, but after the end of the war. The lifting of the newsban after the fall of Rangoon led to the INA story breaking in India which, within a matter of months if not weeks, had captured the public imagination within India. This nationalistic euphoria swept through the armed forces as well, generally destabilising the Sepoy's loyalty to both the Raj and his regiments. Fay notes that even before Japan surrendered preparations were underway for the trial of selected INA men. The predominant feeling in the Indian officer corps at this time was a resentment was that so *few* were being tried.

This changed dramatically over the following months as the further information on the INA began emerging in the press and its true extent, as well as the stories of its campaigns came to be known. The general feeling within the British Indian army at this time is described by some is that of guilt for having fought for the British and against the INA. The revolts and mutinies within the armed forces in early-1946, during the trial and in a situation of volatile nationalist public mood, are held to be a significant factor in precipitating the end of the Raj.

Although, the British Indian Army remained the largest volunteer force during the World War II and saw action from the theatres of North-Africa to Europe and New Guinea to Manipur, in India today, the stories of the INA form a much more prominent aspect of both appreciation as well as analysis of her role in World War II.

Controversies

A number of different views and controversies surround the history and records of the Indian National Army, borne especially by its integral associations with Imperial Japan, and the course and history of Japanese occupation of South East Asia during the

War. These include views especially among British troops that the recruits were traitors, that they were Axis Collaborators, as well as allegations that INA troops engaged in or were complicit in widespread torture of Allied and Indian prisoners of war. Fay concludes in his 1993 history of the army that the allegations were largely products of the British propaganda campaign and points out that the allegations were not borne out by the charges against the defendants in the Red Fort trials.

Fay also points out that war-time press releases as well as the field counter-intelligence directed at the sepoy portrayed the INA as a small group and attributes to the Jiffs campaign the promalgamation of the view that INA recruits were weak-willed and traitorous Axis collaborators motivated by selfish interests of greed and personal gain. He further notes over the records of Shah Nawaz Khan's trial that officers of the INA had described to their men the possibility of having to fight the Japanese after having fought the British in order to prevent Japan from exploiting India.

Controversy also exists in India with regards to the treatment of the ex-INA soldiers by the post-independence government of India and of historical records of the period leading up to Indian independence in 1947, with some alleging that official histories of the Independence Movement largely omit events surrounding the INA especially the Red Fort trials and the Bombay Mutiny and ignore their significance in terms of rejuvenation of the Independence Movement and guiding the British decision to relinquish the Raj.

Further criticisms have been made in recent years for the general hardships and apathy surrounding the conditions of ex-INA troops including, for example, the circumstances surrounding the death and funeral of Ram Singh Thakur. These have been compounded by a number of conspiracy-theories and news reports in the past on agreements between the Indian political leadership to hand over its leader Subhash Chandra Bose as a War Criminal if he was found to be alive. Later historians have, however, argued that given the political aim and nature of the entire Azad Hind Movement especially the Indian National Army, Nehru's decisions may have been to prevent politicisation of the army and assert civilian authority over the military.

Commemorations

Memorials:

- The INA War Memorial at Singapore to commemorate the *"Unknown Warrior"* of the INA. Started on 8 July 1945 the memorial was situated at the Esplanade Park. It was destroyed on Mountbatten's orders when allied troops reoccupied the city. The words inscribed upon the War Memorial were the motto of the INA: *Ittefaq* (Unity), *Etmad* (Faith) and *Qurbani* (Sacrifice).
- The Former Indian National Army Monument, was established in 1995 by the National Heritage Board of Singapore at the site where the old memorial stood with financial donations from the Indian community in Singapore. The site is now officially one of the Historical sites in Singapore.
- The Indian National Army Memorial at Moirang, Manipur commemorates the place where the flag of Azad Hind was raised by Col. Shaukat Hayat Malik. Moirang was the first Indian territory captured by the INA. The memorial suffered damage in an insurgent attack in 2004 when the Statue of the Springing Tiger on the entrance was blown up.
- *Swatantrata Sainani Smarak* (Memorial to the soldiers of the Independence Army) is an Indian National Army (INA) memorial at the Salimgarh Fort, at Delhi, adjacent to the Red Fort, on the banks of the Yamuna. The site has been neglected for a number of years now and fallen into disrepair. Its exhibits include the Indian National Army uniform worn by Colonel Prem Sahgal, riding boots and coat buttons of Colonel Gurbaksh Singh Dhillon, photographs of Subhash Chandra Bose. In addition, a separate gallery also holds material and photographs from excavations carried out by the Archaeological Survey of India inside the fort in 1995.

Postage and Philately:

- Jai Hind, the INA's battle cry, became Independent India's first commemorative post mark on 15 August 1947.

- The first postage stamp issued by Independent India shows the Indian Flag with the letters Jai Hind in the top right hand corner.

These were a part of the *Jai Hind* series of stamps issued on 15 August 1947.

- Commemorative postage stamps were issued by the Indian government in 1968 and 1993 respectively to commemorate the 25th and the 50th anniversaries of the establishment of Azad Hind at Singapore.

The Indian Postal Department also includes the six unused Azad Hind Stamps in its commemorative book *India's Freedom Struggle through India Postage Stamps.*

Bose's Chair at Red Fort

The following words are inscribed on a brass shield in front of the chair which is symbolic to the sovereignty of the Republic of India, as also to the Psychological upkeep of the Armed Forces of India. The chair rests in a glass case and is a symbol of pride as well as national heritage.

"Netaji Subhash Chandra Bose in order to free India from the shackles of British imperialism organised the Azad Hind Government from outside the country on October 21, 1943. Netaji set up the Provisional Government of Independent India (Azad Hind) and transferred its headquarters at Rangoon on January 7, 1944. On the 5th April, 1944, the "Azad Hind Bank" was inaugurated at Rangoon. It was on this occasion that Netaji used this chair for the first time. Later the chair was kept at the residence of Netaji at 51, University Avenue, Rangoon, where the office of the Azad Hind Government was also housed. Afterwards, at the time of leaving Burma, the Britishers handed over the chair to the family of A. T. Ahuja, the well-known business man of Rangoon. The chair was officially handed over to the Government of India in January 1979. It was brought to Calcutta on the 17th July, 1980. It has now been ceremonially installed at the Red Fort on July 7, 1981."

6

Mystery of Disappearance

In a strange event, the alleged death of Subhash Chandra Bose, the supreme commander of Azad Hind Fauj and Free India Legion in a plane crash in Taiwan on August 18, 1945, has long been the subject of dispute. The third Indian commission that was appointed for enquiring into this confirmed in its report tabled in Parliament in May 2006, that Bose's death was staged to facilitate an escape to the USSR.

Basic Issues

Subhash Chandra Bose, a prominent leader of the Indian Independence Movement against the British Raj in India and a general of the Imperial Japanese army Tsunamasa Shidei were reported to be flying to Tokyo, Japan when the alleged plane crash occurred at Matsuyama aerodrome (now Sungshan Airport) in Taipei, northern Formosa (now the Republic of China, or Taiwan). The news was withheld by Japanese government for five days before it was announced by Japanese news agency Domei. The Allied forces took the Japanese news as a ploy. The then Viceroy of India, Field Marshal Archibald Wavell, is reported to have noted in his diary that "I wonder if the Japanese announcement of Subhash Chandra Bose's death in an air-crash is true. I suspect it very much, it is just what should be given out if he meant to go underground."

The matter was looked into by several allied intelligence teams and soon holes in the Japanese version became apparent.

The findings of the intelligence teams seem to have not confirmed the Japanese announcement. For as late as October 1946, the Government of British India refused to confirm the death of Bose.

After India's independence, the matter was looked into by three official panels formed by the government of India following the public demands. These panels were: Shah Nawaz Committee, Justice G. D. Khosla Commission and Justice Mukherjee Commission of Enquiry. The Shah Nawaz Committee upheld the Taiwan crash version, as did the Justice G. D. Khosla Commission, whereas the Mukherjee Commission negated it.

However, it has also been alleged at various times that the Indian government and political leadership was aware that Bose may have been alive, and according to one theory, in captivity in Soviet Union, but chose to ignore or actively collaborate to suppress this information after Independence.

Shah Nawaz Committee

In April 1956, the Jawaharlal Nehru Government formed a committee headed by Shah Nawaz Khan. Khan had earlier risen to the rank of Lt. Col. in the Second Indian National Army, before he was captured by allied troops after the fall of Azad Hind and was one of the three charged with treason in the Red Fort Trial. He was thus seen as an appropriate person to head the enquiry. Two other members of the enquiry commission were S. N. Mitra and Suresh Chandra Bose, Bose's elder brother. The committee's report that Bose had indeed died in Taipei became disputed due to several reasons. The most important among them was the dissentient report of Suresh Bose. Suresh Bose refused to agree with the findings of his colleagues and accused them and the Government of India of trying to coerce him into agreeing with their views.

In mid-1990s, the released archives of Indian Political Intelligence proved conclusively that Bose was killed in 1945. Since rumours were circulating that he was still alive, Indian Political Intelligence arranged for Military Intelligence in New

Delhi to investigate the matter. Captain Turner of the War Crimes Liaison Section in Taiwan (formerly called Formosa) was put on to the case and he managed to locate the last person to have seen Bose alive. This was Captain (Medical) Taneyoshi Yoshimi, who was under arrest in Stanley Gaol. He gave a statement that resolved the matter: 'I personally cleaned his injuries with oils and dressed them. He was suffering from extensive burns over the whole of his body, though the most serious were those on his head, chest and thighs. During the first four hours he was semi-conscious...he murmured, and muttered in his state of coma, but never regained consciousness. At about 2300 hrs. he died. I injected Formalin into the body and also had the coffin partly filled with lime.' The coffin was then taken away and Bose's body was cremated.

Justice G. D. Khosla Commission

Consequently, in June 1970 the Government of India formed a judicial commission headed by Justice G. D. Khosla, former Chief Justice of Punjab High Court. The decision followed years of lobbying by Indian lawmaker, most notable among them were Professor Samar Guha and Amiya Nath Bose, Subhash Bose's nephew. Unlike Shah Nawaz, G. D. Khosla visited but refused to interact with the ROC Government. Much before the commission's report was made public June 1974, it came under assault of Samar Guha. This report also stated that Bose had died in Taiwan.

Rejection of Shah Nawaz, and Khosla Reports

After Emergency was lifted in India, MP Samar Guha fought a political battle in Indian Parliament, where the matter of Bose's death was debated in 1977-78. On August 28, 1978 Prime Minister Morarji Desai stated that there were "various important contradictions in the testimony of the (mostly Japanese) witnesses" to Bose's death. And that "some further contemporary official documentary records have also become available", making the Government of India think that the conclusions reached by G. D. Khosla and Shah Nawaz Khan were not "decisive".

Mukherjee Commission

The Mukherjee Commission refers to the one-man board of Mr. Justice Manoj Mukherjee, a retired judge of the Supreme

Court of India which was instituted in 1999 to enquire into the controversy surrounding the reported death of Subhash Chandra Bose in 1945.

On 30 April 1998, the High Court of Calcutta gave orders to the then BJP-led Government to "launch a vigorous enquiry as a special case for the purpose of giving an end to the controversy".

Many, however, feel that with a new Congress controlled government now in power, the commission's results may be undermined. Many conspiracies abound, and many contain specific details that are damaging to the Congress Party and Indian Prime Minister Jawaharlal Nehru.

The Mukherjee Commission is also not the first commission created to ascertain the death of Netaji Subhash Chandra Bose. The two previous commissions were the Shah Nawaz Commission (appointed by Jawaharlal Nehru) and The Khosla Commission respectively. The Khosla Commission, created by the government of Indira Gandhi (daughter of Jawaharlal Nehru), reported that all documents relating to Prime Minister Nehru and the reports of Netaji Subhash Chandra Bose were either missing or destroyed.

Objectives of the Commission

The purpose of the commission was the ascertain the following:

- Whether Netaji Subhash Chandra Bose is dead or alive?
- If he is dead whether he died in the plane crash, as alleged?
- Whether the ashes in the Japanese temple are ashes of Netaji?
- Whether he has died in any other manner at any other place and, if so, when and how?
- If he is alive, in respect of his whereabouts.

The commission is also the first to probe into the much publicised Soviet-connection. The basics of which are that Netaji Subhash Chandra Bose did indeed survive the end of the Second World War, and detained in a Siberian camp in the late-1940s. A former Russian General swore under oath to the commission that he had seen a true Soviet-Cabinet paper detailing and discussing a "living" Subhash Chandra Bose, one year after his supposed death.

Findings of Commission

The findings of the commission are following:

- Netaji Subhash Chandra Bose is dead.
- He did not die in the plane crash, as alleged.
- The ashes in the Japanese temple are not of Netaji.
- In the absence of any clinching evidence a positive answer cannot be given.
- Answer already given above.

Rejection of Mukherjee Commission Report by Govt. of India

The Mukherjee Commission report was tabled in the Parliament of India on 17 May 2006. The report said that Netaji did not die in the alleged air crash of 1945 and the ashes at the Renkoji temple are not his ashes. The report also did not comment on Netaji's alleged stay in Russia after 1945 and called for further investigation into the matter. However, the report said that Netaji could be presumed to be dead today.

The Govt of India has rejected the findings of the Commission, saying that it did not agree with the findings.

Controversies

The Death of Netaji remains a mystery. No one cooperated in the investigation and consequently the JMC of enquiry was forced to submit its unfinished work to the home minister Shivraj Patil. The main reason for this is the non-cooperation shown by the home ministry. The dissatisfaction caused resulted in Justice Mukherjee sending the report through his secretary rather than submit it in person.

During the whole tenure of the investigation, only one country, Taiwan has shown any real cooperation. Even the Govt. of India refused to share some important intelligence files under the pretext of them being sensitive. The Govt. of India will be tabling this report along with the ATR to the Parliament. At the moment the home minister has passed on this 500 page report to the CS division of the ministry for scrutiny.

Subrata Bose, who was present in all the international trips made by the JMC has said that apart from Taiwan, no other country has shown any cooperation. On the basis of the information available from Taiwan it is now confirmed that no air-crash took place on 18 August 1945 which could have killed Netaji as previously propagated.

The commission had tried to uncover facts from trips to Japan, Taiwan and Britain. The UPA govt has permitted the commission to visit Russia. Bose said that Russia too did not cooperate in this investigation. Officials in Russia had said that files were present in the former KGB archives but the commission was not even allowed to visit the archives. The hostile posture of the British, Japanese and Indian governments is intriguing and seems to strongly point to an international conspiracy. In any case.it is clear that Netaji Bose was seen in Russia in 1946. Lately American state department has sent information to the commission which corroborate the fact that no aircrash took place in Taiwan. The request for intelligence papers from the Govt. of India elicited the official response that they cannot be opened as they are of a highly sensitive nature that may jeopardise international relations between India and some of its friend nations.

The JMC commission was formed by the former NDA Government to investigate the mystery surrounding Netaji's death at the end of world war II. The only kindness shown by the UPA Govt was to extend the commission's tenure by 6 months — from May 2005 to 14 November 2005. But the commission has now submitted its report to the Govt before the end date.

Also three researchers who helped find the declassified documents in the military archives of Paddolsk, Russia, Purabi Ray, Hari Vasudevan and Shobanlal Dutta Gupta, have also reported threats from unidentified persons upon their lives, if they did not stop their research. Many files and documents by the Union Home Ministry have been deemed a risk to national security and under Sections 123 and 124 of the Evidence Act and Article 74(2) of the Constitution of India, have not been disclosed to the commission.

Justice Mukherjee's Revelations

Justice Manoj Kumar Mukherjee stated in his report that the sanyasi of Faizabad (Bhagwanji) was not Bose as there was no clinching evidence to prove it. However, he inadvertently stated in a documentary shoot that he believed Bhagwanji was none other than Bose. This revelation supports the view that Bose had not died in the plane crash in 1945, and was in fact in India after that.

Justice Mukherjee's Revelation and Mission Netaji's Response

Justice Manoj Kumar Mukherjee who probed into the disappearance of Netaji Subhash Chandra Bose stated in his report that the sanyasi of Faizabad (Bhagwanji) was not Bose as there was no clinching evidence to prove it. However, he inadvertently stated in a documentary shoot that he believed Bhagwanji was none other than Bose. This revelation supports Mission Netaji's stand that Bose had not died in the plane crash in 1945. In light of this revelation, Mission Netaji demanded a thorough enquiry into the mystery.

Bose Mystery in Contemporary India

Mission Netaji is a Delhi based Indian non-profit trust, conducting research on Indian freedom fighter Netaji Subhash Chandra Bose. Mission Netaji mainly looks into the circumstances of disappearance of Netaji. Mission Netaji is of the view that Indian governments over the years have been trying to smother the truth.

According to the Indian government, Netaji Bose died in a plane crash in Taihoku (Now, in Taiwan) on August 18, 1945. His remains are kept at the Renkoji Temple in Japan. But from the documents Mission Netaji could collect, it is clear that Bose had plans to escape to Russia during August 1945 and the plane crash was a cover-up to mislead the British. This possibility was also hinted by Justice M. K. Mukherjee Commission of Enquiry that probed into this case.

Anuj Dhar, one of the founders of Mission Netaji, was instrumental in earning valuable information from the Taiwan government that no plane crash involving Netaji Bose had happened in or around Taihoku airport on or around August 18, 1945. The Mukherjee Commission corroborated this finding. But, the Indian government rejected the findings of the commission. Since then, Mission Netaji has been fighting to bring out the truth, utilising the Right to Information Act.

Mission Netaji approached the Central Information Commission of India, under the Right to Information Act, protesting against the Indian government's indifference in this matter. This has been a legal battle, covering almost all clauses in the RTI Act. Mission Netaji calls this fight by the name 'Right To Information Crusade' (RTI Crusade).

Objectives

The objectives of Mission Netaji are:

- To collect and preserve all relevant intelligence, declassified documents and manuscripts, photographs and films, records and other objects and materials — relating to the mystery surrounding the disappearance of Netaji Subhash Chandra Bose.
- To establish a world wide network of committed individuals, groups and organisations, sharing a common vision.
- To publish materials dealing with the mystery surrounding the sudden disappearance of Netaji Subhash Chandra Bose.
- To provide medical relief to the weaker section of the society.
- To take steps to eradicate illiteracy.
- To encourage and support the efforts aimed at eradicating discrimination based on caste, religion and gender.
- To take appropriate measures for providing aid and assistance to the people affected by natural calamities or devastating accidents.
- To organise and conduct such appropriate schemes, activities and ventures for the welfare of the people in general, and for charitable purposes as decided by the members from time to time.

RTI Crusade

Mission Netaji is of the view that Netaji Subhash Chandra Bose escaped to the Soviet Union towards the end of the second world war. But the Indian government has been holding on to its claim that Netaji died in the air plane crash on August 18, 1945. The Justice Mukherjee Commission of Enquiry that probed into this case said in its report that there was no such plane crash and Netaji didn't die on the said date. The Indian government dumped this report, favouring the findings of two former commissions that probed into this case in the second half of the 1900s, headed by Shah Nawaz Khan and then G. D. Khosla.

Due to these discrepancies in the reports, Mission Netaji decided to launch its information seeking campaign entitled 'RTI Crusade'. The organisation utilises the Right To Information Act to seek evidences from various governmental wings, with pleas submitted to the Central Information Commission of India. This has been an enduring fight between the government and Mission Netaji.

Mission Netaji seeks information from the Prime Minister's Office (PMO), Ministry of External Affairs (MEA), Ministry of Home Affairs (MHA), and the Research and Analysis Wing (R&AW). Mission Netaji, so far, has been successful in creating importance to this issue, which was long forgotten by the public and the administrators alike. The approach from the part of the government has not been encouraging.

Documents Sought by Mission Netaji from Various Departments, with Statuses:

Documents sought from the Prime Minister's Office (PMO)

- Information whether the PMO and R&AW, which reports to the Prime Minister, hold several classified records on Subhash Chandra Bose. If yes, a descriptive list of such records/materials thereof.

Status: PMO has said that the disclosure would harm India's relations with foreign countries. PMO has also sought dismissal of RTI appeal on the destroyed files regarding Bose.

- Release information on Nehru's file enquiring into the death of Subhash Chandra Bose.

Current Status: PMO informed that the file was destroyed as part of a routine housekeeping process. However, it was not informed who ordered the destruction of the file and why.

Documents sought from the Ministry of External Affairs (MEA)

- Certified copies of the complete correspondence the MEA has had with the Governments of the USSR and the Russian Federation over the disappearance of Netaji.

Status: CIC rejects government's stance on Russia correspondence papers. Commission tells government to take up the matter with Russians if it feared that the disclosure would harm relations between the two nations.

- Release correspondence with Russia regarding the investigation done into the disappearance of Subhash Chandra Bose

Current status: MEA informed the Central Information Commission that the Russian government is not in favour of the disclosure of facts.

Documents sought from the Ministry of Home Affairs (MHA)

- Authenticated copies of the all documents exhibited before the Shah Nawaz Committee (1956) and G. D. Khosla Commission (1970-74).

Status: CIC demanded MHA to disclose information on Netaji mystery within three months. This order came on July 5, 2007. CIC later scolded Home Ministry for not parting with the information. The full CIC bench heard MHA-Netaji secret papers case.

- Release documents related to the death of Netaji Subhash Chandra Bose.

Status: Government released 91 documents related to the death of Bose. Records include Intelligence Bureau reports, Ministry of External Affairs' telegrams and prime ministerial correspondence. One note by Prime Minister Jawaharlal Nehru remains classified.

Documents sought from PMO and MEA

- Release the truth regarding M. O. Mathai's note about receiving the remains of Bose in India.

Status: After hearing the views of MEA and Mission Netaji, the Central Information Commission stated that one can only hope that some serious researcher will look into one of the greatest mysteries of modern India and arrive at a definite conclusion.

Documents sought from the Research and Analysis Wing (R&AW)

- Are there any records/materials on and relating to Subhash Chandra Bose in RAW?

Status: Cannot intervene in Netaji-R&AW case, says CIC.

Fischer's Note and Criticism of Italian Ambassador's Views

In January 2009, on the occasion of the 112th birth anniversary of Subhash Bose, Italian ambassador to India, Alessandro Quaroni stated that there was no point in continuing research on whether Bose died in a plane crash or not in August 1945. In a statement issued against this remark, Mission Netaji stated that there was evidence which held that Bose did not die in any plane crash. Mission Netaji cited reference to a note preserved in the Princeton University Library which quotes the former Italian ambassador Pietro Quaroni, father of Alessandro Quaroni, as saying that he did not think the news of Bose's accidental death was true.

The note was written by Mohandas Gandhi's biographer and Pulitzer Award winning American journalist Louis Fischer. Pietro Quaroni had helped Bose escape to Moscow in 1941. Fischer had met Pietro Quaroni in Moscow in November 1946 and quoted him saying it was possible "that Bose is still alive". Quaroni had told Fischer that Bose did not want the British to look for him, so the false rumour of his death was circulated.

Netaji Didn't Die in the Air Crash

After a prolonged wait of more than six decades, at last an Enquiry Commission appointed by the Govt. of India arrived at the conclusion that no air crash ever took place at Taihoku, the venue of the alleged plane crash on 18th August, 1945; and hence no question of Netaji's death in the alleged plane crash. This finding is in spite of the fact that the Govts. of India, the present Govt. as well as it's predecessor, did not provide the requisite cooperation to the Commission.

The Congress led UPA govt. which appeared to be in neck breaking hurry to reject the report of the C omission, till the last day of the functioning of the Commission refused to supply to the Commission some vital documents which could have a decisive bearing on the findings of the Commission. About the present findings of this Commission we can say that these are under the circumstances. Had the govt. made available all the documents in it's possession and had the Govt. helped the Commission in procuring the documents from some countries like Russia, England,

Japan, Taiwan, Vietnam, USA, then much more information would have come out and the Commission might have confirmed more truths.

The Ministry of Home Affairs of India through a notification dated 14.5.1999 appointed a Commission of Enquiry consisting of Mr. Justice M. K. Mukherjee, a retired judge of the Supreme Court of India. According to clause 2 of the notification "The Commission shall enquire into all the facts and circumstances related to the disappearance of Netaji Subhash Chandra Bose in 1945 and subsequent developments connected therewith including:

- Whether Netaji Subhash Chandra Bose is dead or alive;
- If he is dead, whether he died in the plane crash, as alleged;
- Whether the ashes in the Japanese temple are the ashes of Netaji;
- Whether he has died in any other manner at any other place and, if so when and how;
- If he is alive, in respect of his whereabouts."

When one goes through the status reports of the Commission one finds that the Govt. did not sincerely, honestly and timely cooperated the Commission. Still it is great on the part of the Commission that in spite of all the hazards it completed it's work and submitted the report to the Government of India on 8th November, 2005.

Role of Government about Files and Documents

On March 23, 2000, the Commission issued orders to produce file no. 12 (226)/56-PM (investigations into the circumstances leading to the death of Subhash Chandra Bose. The Director of the Prime Minister Office (PMO) replied vide her letter dated May 2,2000 that the above file was not available as it had been destroyed.

Through it's letter dated May 23, 2000 the Commission asked her (Director) to let the Commission know:

- The subject and contents of the file.
- The circumstances under which the above said file had been destroyed.

— Before reply could come from Director, PMO, the Director (Internal Security-1) in the Ministry of Home Affairs A. K. Paitandy, on June 22, 2000 filed the following affidavit before the Commission: "in view of the fact that some of the Departments/organisations have informed that they do not have any papers on Netaji/INA, there seems to be some confusion about filing of affidavits to that effect by them. In view of this fact and in deference to the directions/orders of the Commission, this Ministry is filing this affidavit on behalf of the following and I accordingly further affirm and state that there are reportedly no files/papers concerning Netaji/INA in their (the under mentioned departments') possession (emphasis supplied).

- Cabinet Secretariat.
- Intelligence Bureau.
- Research and Analysis Wing.

— Contrary to what Shri Paitandy said, the Director of PMO in her reply dated July, 2004 to the Commission's letter dated May 23, 2000 stated " file no. 12 (226)/56- PM which contained agenda paper/Cabinet decision regarding "Investigations into the circumstances leading to the death of Sri Chandra Bose" was destroyed in 1972 in course of routine review/weeding of old records since records of Cabinet proceedings are kept permanently in Cabinet Secretariat, from where they may be procured."

When the Commission asked the Secretary, PMO and the Secretary MHA to produce copies of the orders regarding destruction of files/documents concerning Netaji Subhash Chandra Bose as also the copies of the lists of files/documents destroyed, the Director of PMO replied vide letter dated September 21, 2000 that no order regarding destruction of files/documents could be located.

The Deputy Secretary of the Cabinet Secretariat, in a letter dated October 31, 2000 addressed to Shri. A. K. Paitandy of MHA with a copy to the Commission stated that their organisation had no record relating to Netaji because it was formed on September 21, 1968 Here it is important to note that though the PMO is stating that the documents were destroyed in 1972 on the assumption that these are available with the Cabinet Secretariat yet the Cabinet Secretariat is denying the possession in spite of the fact that it had been established in 1968.

Another startling fact is that when the said file was destroyed in 1972, the Khosla Commission was holding the enquiry. Prof. Samar Guha, the then Member of Parliament, in a letter dated January 3,1974 requested the then Prime Minister of India Smt. Indira Gandhi and requested her to investigate into the matter and forward the file, if not destroyed. Smt. Gandhi wrote back to say that the "file contained only copies of certain documents which are still available in other files" and that is why "the file was destroyed." All this makes it very clear that though the file was destroyed in 1972 yet the copies of the documents contained in the files are still there in the Cabinet Secretariat. The government has played a fraud with the nation by suppressing the evidence related to Netaji's disappearance. The Govt. must decalassify the contents of the file and make it public so that the people can know what is there in the file.

Shri Morarji Desai, the then Prime Minister of India, made the following statement on August 28, 1978 in Parliament:

> "There have been two enquiries into the report of the death of Netaji Subhash Chandra Bose in the air crash on 18th August 1945 at Taihoku airfield during his air-journey to Manchuria, one by a Committee presided over by Maj. General Shah Nawaz Khan and the second by a one man Committee of enquiry headed by Shri G. D. Khosla, retired judge of the Punjab High Court. The majority report of the first Committee and Shri Khosla held the report of the death as true. Since then, reasonable doubts have been cast on the correctness of the conclusions reached in the two reports and various important contradictions in the testimony of witnesses have been noticed, some further contemporary official documentary records have also become available. In the light of those doubts

> . and contradictions and those records, Government find it difficult to accept that the earlier conclusions are conclusive."

The Commission asked the Prime Minister Office (PMO), Ministry of External Affairs (MEA):

> The Cabinet Secretariat (CS) and the Ministry of Home Affairs (MHA) to ensure the production of "official documentary records" on the basis of which the Prime Minister had made the above statement in the Parliament, but unfortunately the PMO vide letter dated October 29, 2001 conveyed that no such records could be located in their office. Shri Jarnail Singh, a Joint Secretary in the PMO, through an affidavit dated December 18,2001 conveyed that 'no such records could be found in this office ' and added that their office was not in a position to explain or clarify the circumstances under which such a statement was made. It sounds too jarring and ridiculous to believe that the Prime Minister made a false statement in Parliament. It is the duty of PMO and the Cabinet Secretariat to make available the documentary record on the basis of which P. M. had made the statement. The whole episode reflects that the Govt. has suppressed the documents and evidence which could throw greater light on the issue and has not placed it before the Enquiry Commission. The Govt. of India failed to provide the documentary records to the Commission which were very much required by the Commission for the establishment of the truth. Commission went to England also to study the relevant records there but unfortunately didn't get the positive response. The Commission was not given access to the two files which were marked "closed". In spite of its best efforts, the Commission couldn't get the required information from England, USA and some other countries.

Unfortunately, since independence the Governments of India have not made any serious effort to collect the documents, related to Netaji's mystery, from some foreign countries. Will the UPA govt explain that what efforts have been made by it and it's predecessors at their own to procure any information about Netaji's disappearance from the Governments of the countries like England, Japan, Russia, USA, Taiwan, Vietnam and others? The indifference of the Governments to such a sensitive and historically important matter shows the malafide intentions of the Govt. in this respect. A fraud has been perpetrated on the nation and it needs to be exposed.

DNA Tests of the Ashes at Renkoji Temple

The Commission visited Renkoji temple in Tokyo where the alleged ashes of Netaji are being kept in an urn inside a glass chamber. The Chief Priest was asked to open the urn to ascertain whether there were any bones in the ashes which could be subjected to DNA test. Since no competent mechanic was available, it could not be opened. The Indian Ambassador in Japan was requested to depute two senior officers of the Embassy to inspect the ashes and to report whether there were any bones in the ashes. The two officers went to the temple on October 24, 2002, opened the casket in the presence of the Chief Priest and his wife, and examined the contents. They sent a joint report to the Chairman of the Commission.

The Commission approached Director, Centre for Cellular and Molecular Biology as also to the Director, Centre for DNA Fingerprinting and Diagnostics at Hyderabad for conducting DNA tests on the bones found in the ashes. The Director CCMB conveyed to Commission that the facilities needed for conducting the proposed DNA test was not available in India; hence it could not be carried out in the country.

On learning that the DNA test was not possible within the country, the Commission contacted Prof. Dr. Svante Paabo, Director, Department of Genetics, Max Planck Institute for Evolutionary Anthropology, Liepzig, Germany but he also expressed his inability to conduct the required test. On Dr. Paabo's recommendation, the Commission approached Prof. Sir Alec Jeffreys of the Department of Genetics at the University of Leicester (UK). Prof. Jeffreys also expressed his inability to do the needful. Even the Japanese doctors Prof. Saitou Naruya and Dr. Yamamoto, a forensic DNA expert of Nagoya University reached the conclusion that since all the bones and teeth had received high heat, there was almost no possibility of obtaining DNA from the bone material.

Since the Ancient DNA Facility had become fully functional at CCMB, Hyderabad, the Commission again approached CCMB for re-examination of the bones and opinion. The CCMB opined that if the less charred bones were brought to India from Renkoji temple in a sealed plastic bag at room temperature, then it could be possible to conduct the required tests. Efforts were made in this direction till the last minute before the submission of report but the Chief Priest did not respond to the request of permission for the collection of potentially less charred bone pieces from the casket lying in the Renkoji temple. In this way the DNA test couldn't be performed on the ashes lying in the Renkoji temple.

The Evidences

During the proceedings of the Commission, a lot of evidence came for consideration. 131 witnesses were examined and 730 files and documents were exhibited. Unfortunately the Govt. of India did not produce even a single witness at it's own.

The Commission received 105 books-47 in English, one in Russian and 57, including 14 journals in vernacular-from different deponents and sources. Many tape records, photographs and compact discs were also placed before it.

The Govt. of India claimed privilege under sections 123 and 124 of the Evidence Act and Article 74 (2) of the Constitution of India in the case of three files.

Netaji Subhash Chandra Bose, Dead or Alive

The following five versions relating to Netaji's death were placed before the Commission:

- He was murdered at the Red Fort in New Delhi on August 15, 1945;
- He died at Dehradun, Uttar Pradesh (now Uttaranchal) in 1977;
- He died at Sheopurkalan in the State of Madhya Pradesh on May 21, 1977;
- He died at Ram Bhawan in Faizabad, Uttar Pradesh, on September 16,1985;

- He died in an air crash at Taihoku (now Taipei) in Taiwan (formerly Formosa) on August 18,1945.

The Commission thoroughly investigated into all the five possibilities. Before pondering over the various options, the Commission considered the fact that the average life span of the Indians is 70-75 years, and in exceptional cases about 100 years. There are very rare cases of people having age beyond 100 years. Considering that Netaji was born on 23rd January, 1897, he was to be 108 years at this point of time. Hence, there is no possibility of his being alive now.

The Commission didn't arbitrarily reject any version of death. The various versions were analysed as follows:

- *Death in the Red Fort:* Shri Usha Ranjan Bhattacharjee, a resident of Calcutta claimed that Netaji was deliberately murdered in the Red Fort on August 15,1945 at zero hour. Mr. Bhattacharjee couldn't produce any document in support of his contention. Since this story was given out on assumptions and presumptions, it was rejected outrightly by the Commission.
- *Death at Dehradun:* In 1959, a Sadhu known as Sharadanandji set up his Ashram at a place called Falakata in the district of Cooch Behar which borders Bangladesh, Bhutan and Nepal. This Ashram was known as 'Shoulmari Ashram'. Initially it was very small but after sometime when it grew in size and expanded to an area of over 100 acres and its population grew to around 1500, it gained importance. A rumour spread that the Sadhu was in fact Netaji Subhash Chandra Bose. By 1961 this rumour had spread throughout the country. Many important personalities started visiting this Ashram and this further strengthened the rumour. The sadhu stayed here for 6/7 years and thereafter shifted to Dehradun in 1973 where he died in 1977 in this context the Commission examined 11 witnesses out of which eight held the view that the Sadhu was none else but Netaji whereas three disputed the claim. There was no substantial and undisputed evidence to support the contention that the Sadhu was Netaji. Since the Sadhu was not Netaji, hence there is no question of Netaji having died at Dehradun .

Death in the Plane Crash?

Right from August 23, 1945, when the news of Netaji's alleged death was broadcasted from Japan, the people have been kept engaged by the mystery of Netaji's death in the alleged plane crash at Taihoku air port on 18th August, 1945. Initially a number of enquiries were held at the instance of British, Chinese and Japanese governments. In 1956 a three member Enquiry Committee was appointed under the Chairmanship of General Shah Nawaz Khan and in 1970 a one man Enquiry Commission presided by Justice G. D. Khosla was appointed by the Govt. of India!

Brief Narration of the Facts of the Alleged Accident

In the afternoon of August 15,1945 while Netaji was in Singapore, the Government of Japan officially announced the news of surrender of Japan to the Allied Powers. On hearing this news of surrender by Japan Netaji discussed this matter with his colleagues and Ministers of the Provisional Government of Free India (headed by Netaji) about the course of action to be followed under the circumstances. Though Netaji was willing to surrender to the Allied Powers, yet his colleagues persuaded him to go out of Singapore to some Russian territory, for they felt that no useful purpose would be served by his surrender and being taken as a prisoner. After the decision was taken Netaji along with his colleagues including Col. Habibur Rehman, Col. Pritam Singh and others left for Bangkok on the following day, i.e. August 16, 1945. From there, Netaji along with his colleagues and some officers of the Japanese Army, left for Saigon in the morning of August 17, 1945 in two bomber planes. At Saigon difficulty was experienced in continuing with the two bomber planes in which the journey to Saigon had been performed as the two bombers had to return.

However, Netaji was told that a bomber plane in which some military personnel were to travel to Manchuria would leave Saigon in the afternoon. That plane had come from Manila and was fully loaded with passengers and baggage. Netaji was informed that it would be impossible to accommodate his entire party and he could at best be provided with one seat in the plane. Netaji was unwilling to travel without his colleagues and he sent an appeal to Field Marshal Terauchi, who was in overall Command of military operations in South East Asia, to make necessary arrangements to accommodate his colleagues. His appeal, however, was turned down except that a second seat was offered to him. Netaji hurriedly consulted his colleagues and they prevailed upon his accepting the offer. Left with no alternative, he chose Habibur Rehman to be his co-passenger. Then the plane carrying Netaji, Habibur Rehman and some Japanese officers including Gen. Shidei left Saigon for Tokyo via Manchuria at 5 p.m. and arrived at Tourane at 7.45 p.m. As it was not considered safe to travel beyond Tourane the same day, the party spent their night there.

The next morning (on August 18) the plane left Tourane at 7.00 a.m. and flew to Taihoku (in Formosa) and after a brief halt there for refuelling, the plane took off from Taihoku at 2.30 p.m. Immediately thereafter the plane crashed on the airfield and burst into flames. The Pilot and Gen. Shidei, who were inside the cockpit, met with an instantaneous death.

The remaining crew and passengers including Netaji and Habibur Rehman were able to come out of the wreckage alive but several of them sustained burn injuries. The injured were taken to the Military Hospital a few kilometres away where Netaji and Co-Pilot succumbed to their injuries the same night. The injuries of Habibur Rehman were, however, not serious. Netaji was cremated a day or two later in the crematorium of Taipei and the ashes were collected. Later on the ashes were sent in a box to Tokyo and ultimately enshrined in the local Renkoji Temple and the same still remain there.

The story of Netaji's leaving from Singapore on August 15, 1945 and reaching Saigon on August 17, 1945 via Bangkok has never been challenged before this Commission or earlier Commissions because of the overwhelming evidence in support thereof. Even the departure from Saigon on August 17, 1945 along with Habibur Rehman and some Japanese officers for going to Russia via Manchuria has never been a matter of controversy. Now the evidence regarding the air crash and the subsequent death of Netaji needs to be discussed and analysed.

The following seven witnesses testified before the Commission: Shri. Suman Chattopadhyay, the Executive Director of the Bengali daily 'Ananda Bazar Patrika'; Dr. Col. Laxmi Sehgal, ex member of INA and the Commanding Officer of the Rani Jhansi Regiment; Capt. Barindra Karmakar, ex member of INA; Sh. Pranab Mukherjee, a former Minister of External Affairs and presently the Defence Minister of Govt. of India; Shri K. Natwar Singh, the former Minister of External Affairs; Dr. Tanyoshi Yoshimi, a former doctor in the army hospital at Taipei; and Sh. Husamuddin B. Kapasi, a resident of Bangkok, whose father was a Minister in the Interim Cabinet of Netaji. All these witnesses were examined by the Commission but since none of them had any personal knowledge about the death of Netaji in the plane crash nor did they produce any contemporary document in support thereof; and since their assertions were based on hearsay or belief or result of enquiries including those of Shah Nawaz Committee and Khosla Commission, their statements could not be treated as admissible evidence-much less to be relied upon-to hold that Netaji died in the plane crash. Some of the deponents and their learned Counsels also persuaded the Commission not to believe the evidence of the above witnesses on the following grounds:

There are serious discrepancies and contradictions in the statements made before this Commission, and earlier Commission or Enquiry Committee. These discrepancies and contradictions prove that through their versions they were making out a story which had no basis at all.

Their evidence relating to plane crash is so improbable that no reasonable person can act upon the same, far less draw a conclusive inference there from. It was also submitted that the bomber plane had no seats and for that matter no seat belts and all the passengers had to squat on the floor. If the plane had nosedived from a "fairly high altitude, possibly over 12-14,000 feet', all the passengers and luggage inside the plane would be hurled together near the cockpit and in that event even half of the passengers could not have survived or come out of the plane either unhurt or with some minor injuries as claimed by them. Similarly the story given by some of the witnesses that as Netaji was seated adjacent to the petrol tank, gasoline flashed all over his body resulting in his sustaining third degree burns cannot be believed for the simple reason that Netaji could not be in his original position on the floor of the plane following the nosedive.

All these witnesses could not provide even a scrap of paper-not to speak of any contemporary document, in support of their versions of the plane crash. There has to be some official record to prove the fact of crash. The maintenance of the records becomes all the more important keeping in view the fact that two of the occupants of the plane, who died in the crash, were Netaji, the Head of the Provisional Govt. of Azad Hind which was recognised by the Government of Japan and Shiedei, a General of the Japanese army. The Government of Taiwan and the Taipei City Government admitted before the Commission that in response to the queries of the journalist of English daily Hindustan Times, they had replied that they had no proof of the fact that there was any plane accident on the said date at the said place.

Even Shri Tarakeshwar Pal, the learned Senior Counsel appearing for the Government of India, fairly submitted that there were glaring discrepancies in the evidence adduced regarding the accident as also the date and time of death, news of death, death certificate and cremation of Netaji.

Dr. Yoshimi who was acting as the Chief of the Nanmon Military Hospital, where Netaji and other injured were brought after the plane crash and treated, was examined by Shah Nawaz Committee, Khosla Commission and the present Commission also. Dr. Yoshimi was on duty in the hospital when the news of air crash came. Dr. Yoshimi was told that one of the injured persons was Chandra Bose (as Netaji was so called by the Japanese). Dr. Yoshimi examined Chandra Bose and found that he had suffered severe burns-burns of third degree-and had little chance of survival. As the condition of Chandra Bose was most serious of all, he was treated first and thereafter the other injured persons were attended. Netaji remained conscious for 7/8 hours. At 7.00/7.30 p.m. his condition deteriorated and shortly after 8 p.m. he breathed his last. Dr. Yoshimi informed the Headquarters of the Formosan Army of Netaji's death. The military personnel arrived at the hospital and under the instructions of the commander-in-chief, Dr. Yoshimi injected formalin to prevent decomposition of the dead body. On the night of Netaji's death Dr. Yoshimi prepared and signed a death certificate, writing his name in Japanese (Kata Kana) as "Chandra Bose" and giving the cause of death as " burns of the third degree." The other two doctors Dr. T. Tsuruta and Dr. Yoshimi Ishii also stated that in spite of their best efforts and treatment, Netaji died same night. Besides the above doctors the others who spoke about Netaji's death and treatment included Col. Habibur Rehman, Capt. K. Arai, Tado Sakai, Koji Takamiya, S. Nonogaki, Tara Kono, Takahashi Ihaho, Shibuya Masanari, Makato Nakamura, Makato Yamamoto, K, Sakai, Kazuo Mithui, Interpreter Nakamura and S. Nagamoto. Some of them claimed that they have seen Netaji dying and also being cremated.

Cremation of Netaji's Body

As regards the cremation of Netaji's body, instead of taking the body to Tokyo, it was cremated at Taihoku itself. As regards the date of cremation there are glarig contradictions in the versions of Col. Habibur Rehman. He told Shah Nawaz Committee that Netaji's dead body was cremated on 20th August and gave a detailed description of the cremation ceremony. As regards the injuries, treatment in hospital, death and cremation, the following important contradictions were pointed out by the deponents:

- No records regarding the nature of injuries sustained by Netaji, the treatment given to him, his death and other related matters was available. The death certificate which Dr. Yoshimi claimed to have issued and the copy of the cremation permit was not available.
- No photograph of Netaji to provide evidence of identification of the dead body was taken either at the hospital or at the crematorium.
- Though Netaji was the Head of an independent state which was recognised by nine independent countries including Japan, no military honours befitting the Head of a state appeared to have been given to the deceased at the time of funeral.

Incidently no corroborative contemporaneous official records relating to death or cremation of Netaji were available. The witnesses did not take care to search for the relevant records of Taihoku Airport, the Army Hospital, Taipei Municipal Bureau of Health and Hygiene and Taipei City Crematorium to test the veracity of their assertions.

Shri Harin Shah, the Editor of "Indian Workers", the official journal of Indian National Trade Union Congress, towards the end of August, 1946 paid a visit to Taipei and enquired into the air crash story involving Netaji. He visited the Director of the Bureau at his office and asked for records with regards to Netaji's death and cremation. The Director deputed two clerks for the job and they produced the following three documents:

- the doctor's report on the death of Netaji,
- the police officer's report, and
- the certificate issued by the Bureau permitting cremation.

The death certificate was in the name of the person named 'Okara Ichiro'; the reason of death "by sickness, heart failure;" the time of death "19th August at 4 p.m." This certificate was given as the death certificate of Netaji.

From The Army Hospital To The Bureau of Health and Hygiene

Date of Report: 21st August, 1945

Certificate Of Death:	
Name Of the Person:	Okara Ichiro and Ichiro means eldest son
Sex:	Male
Birth:	Born in the Meiti 22nd year April 9
Occupation	He Was Taiwan Military Army's obedient officer.
Reason of death:	By Sickness
Nature of sickness:	Heart-failure
Time of sickness:	17th August, 1945
Time of death:	19th August 4 p.m.
Place of death:	Army Hospital
The Writer's Certificate;	
Dated:	21st August
The Name of the doctor:	Chhuluta Toyoji Chentze
And the seal	Siskwan (Japanese University)

The clerks on being asked about the false particulars, replied that they were directed by their senior officers that 'the particulars of the person had to be kept confidence. But even a cursory glance at the entries in these documents makes it absolutely clear that they could not-and do not-by any stretch of imagination relate to Netaji.

In 1956 an enquiry was undertaken by the Government of Formosa at the initiative of the Government of India. Following the appointment of Shah Nawaz Committee on April 5, 1956 and it's plan to visit Formosa, the Govt. of India had asked the High Commissioner for United Kingdom in India whether Her Majesty's Counsel in Tamsui (Formosa) could:

- get a copy of cremation certificate; and
- obtain from some or all of those witnesses (detailed by the Govt. of India) signed statements or persuade them to meet the Committee in Hong Kong for which the Government of India was prepared to pay travel and accommodation expenses.

After some correspondence, an enquiry was held by the Department of Health of the Formosan Government and a report was submitted along with a copy of an extract from the cremation register kept by the Welfare Section of the Taipei Municipal Government. It appears that a copy of the said report, duly authenticated by Her Majesty's Consul was handed over to the Ministry of External Affairs, Government of India by the High Commissioner for UK in India on August 10,1956. Incidentally, it may be mentioned that the record of the above enquiry was collected by this Commission from the UK National Archives on it's own initiative and was not received from the Govt. of India. The Government of India has been maintaining a policy of minimum publication of the facts and documents related to this mystery and maximum suppression of these facts and documents.

The Government of India had asked the Govt. of Japan also to obtain and supply the doctor's report on Netaji's death and cremation permit. Pursuant thereto the Ministry of Foreign Affairs of Japan forwarded a copy of an entry under serial number 2641 of the cremation register maintained by the Bureau in the name of one Ichiro Okura with a forwarding letter addressed to the First Secretary, Embassy of India by the Ministry of Foreign Affairs, Government of Japan on July 20, 1956.

It is pertinent to point out here that a bare perusal of the three documents received from Shri Harin Shah, the Government of Formosa and the Government of Japan demonstrate that the particulars furnished therein tally with one another.

Prof. Samar Guha who had all along been disputing the death of Netaji in the plane crash and had actively participated in the enquiry conducted by Khosla Commission, visited Taipei and after all his efforts could find and produce the photocopies of only those two documents, i.e. in the name of Ichiro Okura, which have already been mentioned. Now since it stands established that the contents of none of those documents, i.e. the death certificate, the permit seeking the cremation of the dead body of the person concerned and the relevant entry No 2641 in the cremation register relate to Netaji, this Commission had to search for the documents relating to the death and cremation of Netaji. A mere discovery of documents relating to one Ichiro Okura does not and cannot have any bearing whatsoever on Netaji's death or- cremation. Any attempt to base the finding on the oral evidences of the eye witnesses, is the over simplification of the extremely complex issue and looks like a superficial approach, as had been done by the Shah Nawaz Enquiry Committee and Khosla Commission in the past.

Before arriving at any conclusion about the veracity of the said documents it is essential to ponder over the procedure of issuing cremation permit in Taipei in those days. For the cremation of a dead body a doctor's report of his death had to be first obtained. Armed therewith an application in the prescribed form for a permit for cremation was required to be filled by a family member of the deceased with the Bureau. In that form detailed particulars regarding the date of birth of the patient, nature of illness causing the death, date and time of death, etc. were required to be furnished to obtain permission to cremate the dead body. The body was also required to be brought before the Bureau to enable the authorities there to verify the particulars furnished in the application. After such verification a permit was issued for cremation of a dead body. With the permit so granted, the body was to be taken to the crematorium and after cremation an entry was to be made in the cremation register against be relevant serial number of the permit.

Dr. Yoshimi in a statement before the Shah Nawaz Committee stated very categorically that:

> "On 18th August, I had issued a medical certificate of death in respect of the deceased person writing his name in Japanese (Kata Kana) as 'Chandra Bose' and giving the cause of death as 'burns of the third degree'."

In the cross examination also Dr. Yoshimi confirmed the above statement.

If we go by the statement of Dr. Yoshimi, it is confirmed that he issued a death certificate in the name of 'Chandra Bose' on August 18, 1945 and made an application seeking a permit for his cremation on the same day.

From the evidence of the two doctors and the two employees of the Bureau, the following inferences follow: If Netaji was to be and in fact cremated, his body would have been taken to the Bureau and on the basis of the application filed by DR. Yoshimi a permit for his cremation would have been issued and on his cremation there would have been entries in the cremation register with a specific serial number allotted and Dr. Yoshimi's name in the columns prescribed for writing out the name of the applicant seeking permit for cremation and his rank in the army. Surprisingly, however, in the Enquiry Report submitted by the Department of Health of the Formosan Government it has been stated that in the register of cremation at the Municipal Health Centre there was an entry in the name of Ichiro Okura, who, as already mentioned, was cremated on August 22, 1945.

The absence of death certificate of Netaji filed before the Bureau, the application seeking permission to cremate his dead body, the permit granted for his cremation and an entry in the cremation register in proof of the cremation makes the evidence of the witnesses, who testified to Netaji's death and cremation, vulnerable and raises a strong, reasonable and *bona fide* doubt about the story of his death by air crash.

The Chairman of the Commission vide his letter dated February 01, 2005 requested the Government of Taiwan to send to this Commission certain records including all entries in the cremation register of the old crematorium of Taipei city during the period from August 18 to August 24, 1945. In deference to the said request the Ministry of Foreign Affairs of Taiwan sent copies of some of the documents asked for. In these documents there is no entry in the name of Netaji Subhash Chandra Bose/'Chandra Bose', Pilot Takizawa, Co-Pilot Aoyagi and General Shidhei in the documents of cremation during the period from August 17 to August 27, 1945. The above report, so far as it relates to the entries in the cremation register, clearly discloses that not only there is no entry of cremation of Netaji but also of his co-passengers who, being Japanese, would have, in all probability, been cremated had they died on August 18, 1945 by August 27, 1945. Absence of any entry relating to their cremation defeats the story of the death of Netaji and some of his co-passengers in the plane crash.

Dr. Yoshimi Didn't Tell the Truth

The absence of any record relating to Netaji's death and cremation, in respect of which Dr. Yoshimi claimed to have played a pivotal role, clearly demonstrates that he was not telling the truth. Toshikazu Shimoda of 5-19-6 Inamuragasaki Kamakura-SHI Kanagawa-Ken 248 Japan had addressed a letter to Dr. Purabi Roy on August 26, 1996 enclosing therewith a death certificate of Chandra Bose which he had received from Dr. Yoshimi on August 18,1988. When the attention of Dr. Yoshimi was drawn towards the said certificate, he admitted that it was the photocopy of the certificate issued by him. When asked under what circumstances he issued belated copy of the certificate, he could not give a satisfactory reply. This indicates very clearly that the above said document cannot but be a manufactured one. The above findings are sufficient to hold that the story of Netaji's death in the plane crash has not at all been proved and to answer the related questions in the negative.

Netaji in Russia?

Many deponents believed that Russia was the real destination of the flight of Netaji and he succeeded in reaching Russia. General

Isoda, the Head of Hikari Kikan, had a meeting with Netaji on August 16, 1945 at Bangkok. He confirmed that the destination of Mr. Bose was to go to Russia via Manchuria and Dairen. On 17th August, 1945 he had a discussion with Netaji about the escape plane which he narrated as follows:

> "The purpose of his (Netaji's) flight was to go to the Soviet Union and with the aid of the Soviet Union he was to continue his Independence Movement. That was the aim of his mission. After reaching Dairen, if time allowed he had intended to go to Tokyo to express his gratitude for the Japanese help and also to collect some supplies from Tokyo. I thought no such time would be available to him going to Tokyo. The main purpose of Mr. Bose was to go to the Soviet Union and his desire to go to Tokyo was only secondary."

Col. Pritam Singh of INA, Shri E. Bhaskaran, the Confidential Secretary of Netaji and Mr. Watanabe, his interpreter have also supported this theory of some escape plan to Russia. Dr. Purabi Roy who had been regularly visiting Russian Federation for research work, claimed that there are people and evidence to prove that Netaji was in Russia after the alleged accident. She gave the names of the persons with whom she had interacted and also gave a list of fifteen archives where documents relating to Netaji could be available. The Commission visited Russian federation from September 20 to September 30, 2005 and during this period the Commission visited six archives and examined four witnesses. Nothing concrete came out of this exercise in Russia. Unfortunately the Commission was not allowed access to some of the more important archives where there was greater possibility of information related to Netaji.

The British Approach

The Commission took note of the references from the Transfer of Power Volume VI. On 23rd August, 1945 Sir F. Mudie wrote (Home Member to the Viceroy's Executive Council) to Sir E. Jenkins (Private Secretary to the Viceroy) giving alternative proposals for dealing with Subhash Chandra Bose. If Netaji had died in fact, there was no need to give these proposals. On October 25,1945 in a meeting of India and Burma Committee of British Cabinet presided over by Prime Minister Attlee, the minutes included "It was generally agreed that the only civilian renegade of importance was Subhash Chandra Bose." This also indicates that till that time even the British Cabinet did not treat Netaji as dead.

Col. Habibur Rehman's Role

Col. Habibur Rehman, being the only Indian who accompanied Netaji in flight from Dairen, was the most important evidence and link in the air crash story. There have been contradictions and discrepancies in his statements, leading to confusion and suspicion about the story. If it is accepted that the plane had no seats and no seat belts and everybody was squatting on the floor, then it was inevitable that the moment plane nosedived, everybody in the plane and the whole luggage will roll down to the cock pit. As already explained, under such circumstances some people remaining unhurt or not seriously wounded looks absurd. He also testified that the plane nose-dived from a fairly high altitude "possibly over 12-14000 feet". If this evidence of Col. Habibur Rehman is to be believed then none of the 12/13 passengers could have survived. In this context the explanation sought to be given that as Netaji was sitting by the side of the Petrol Tank, gasoline flashed all over his body resulting in his sustaining third degree burns, cannot also be believed, because Netaji could not have been in his original seat or position, the moment plane nosedived. Habibur Rehman gave the following version before the Shah Nawaz Committee regarding the injuries sustained by him in the plane crash:

> "As for myself, my both hands were very badly burnt. As I came through the fire, right side of my face was burnt and I noticed I had received a cut in the forehead which was bleeding and also the right side of my right knee was also bleeding profusely as it had hit some hard substance. The head cut was caused by hitting the floor as the plane crashed. My clothes did not catch fire. My hands were burnt very badly in the attempt to take off Netaji's clothes. Both my hands, up to the wrist, show marks of deep burning even after a lapse of more than ten years."

He claimed that he was treated for his injuries at Nanmon Hospital (the army hospital) and Hokuto Hospital for a number of days. However, no documentary evidence was available at either of the places. He gave different versions to different people at different times, raising suspicion about the truthfulness of his statements. Besides this if he was the real witness of Netaji's death in the crash, it was expected of him to immediately report about it to his colleagues in Bangkok, Singapore, Saigon and Tokyo but he opted to maintain suspicious silence. This conduct shows that he was playing a vital role with the Japanese army authorities in formulation and execution of Netaji's escape plan.

From the evidence which appeared before the Commission, the Commission concluded:

- There is no satisfactory evidence of the plane crash; on the contrary, the story given out in that respect is rather improbable;
- In absence of any contemporaneous record in the hospital, the Bureau and/or the crematorium, the oral account of the witnesses of Netaji's death and cremation cannot be relied upon to arrive at a definitive finding on the basis thereof; and
- A secret plan was contrived to ensure Netaji's safe passage to which Japanese military authority and Habibur Rehman were parties.

From the statements of Col. Habibur Rehman, Dr. Yoshimi, Dr. Tsuruta, Gen. Isoda, the clerks of Health Bureau and others it is apparently very clear that there was no plane crash or death or cremation of Netaji; there was an escape plan for Netaji and many facts, statements and documents were fabricated to support it; and many procedural rules were overlooked to conceal the real identity of Ichiro Okura. If the Japanese authorities wanted to create documentary evidence to make people in general, and the Allied Powers in particular, believe that Netaji had died in a plane crash, the best course open to them would have been, if the story in respect of the plane crash was true, to avail of the documents relating to the death and cremation of the few co-passengers of the ill fated plane and to pass off the same as those of Netaji, to maintain secrecy. In that case, the date of death, the cause of death and nature of injuries would have been common with those of Netaji, thereby making the story of his death more probable and acceptable. This tell tale circumstance not only supports the successful implementation of the escape plan but also negates the story of the air crash.

The Conclusions

In view of the evidences, arguments, witnesses placed before the Commission, the Commission arrived at the following conclusions:

- Netaji Subhash Chandra Bose is dead;
- He did not die in the plane crash, as alleged;
- The ashes in the Japanese temple are not of Netaji;
- In absence of any clinching evidence a positive answer cannot be given; and
- Answer already given in (a) above.

As regards the ancillary query the Commission is of the view-consequent upon it's above findings-that in undertaking the scrutiny of publications touching upon the questions of death or otherwise of Netaji, the Central Government can proceed on the basis that he is dead but did not die in the plane crash, as alleged."

Findings of Commission and Voice of People

The Commission, after extensive, intensive and prolonged efforts, arrived at the conclusions which amounted to not only the rejection of the findings of Shah Nawaz Enquiry Committee and the Khosla Commission but also acceptance of the views of the various deponents and the beliefs which the people of the country have been nursing since the day of the broadcasting of the news of the air crash involving Netaji. The people across the country welcomed the findings of the Commission but the Congress led UPA Govt. shocked the nation by rejecting the report and that too without giving any reason or explanation for it. There is no justification in govt. rejecting the report in such an arbitrary and unjust manner.

7

Great Nation Builder

Basic Concepts of Bose's Political Philosophy

Idea of History

Subhash interpreted Indian history and asserted that it has to be recorded not in decades or in centuries but in the thousands. India has passed through various vicissitudes of fortune. Neither the individual nor the nation can have an uninterrupted career or progress and prosperity. The same is true for India which has always been characterised by a very high level of culture and civilization. Bose summarises his readings of Indian history as follows:

- A period of rise has been followed by a period of decline to be followed again by a upheaval.
- The decline is the result chiefly of physical and intellectual fatigue.
- Progress and fresh consolidation has been brought about by an influx of new ideas and sometimes an infusion of fresh blood.
- Every new epoch has been heralded by people possessing greater intellectual power and superior military skill.

- Throughout Indian history all foreign elements have always been gradually absorbed by Indian society. The British are the first and the only exception to this.
- In spite of change in the central government, the people have all along been accustomed to a large measure of real liberty.

To regain lost glory Subhash wanted regeneration of energy in India.

Political Views

Subhash Chandra Bose, believed that the Vedanta and the Bhagavad Gita were the sources of inspiration for the struggle against the British. Swami Vivekananda's teachings on universalism, his nationalist thoughts and his emphasis on social service and reform had all inspired Subhash Chandra Bose from his very young days. The fresh interpretation of the India's ancient scriptures had appealed immensely to him. Many scholars believe that Hindu spirituality formed the essential part of his political and social thought through his adult life, although there was no sense of bigotry or orthodoxy in it. Subhash who called himself a socialist, believed that socialism in India owed its origins to Swami Vivekananda. As historian Leonard Gordan explains "Inner religious explorations continued to be a part of his adult life. This set him apart from the slowly growing number of atheistic socialists and communists who dotted the Indian landscape."

Bose's correspondence (prior to 1939) reflects his deep disapproval of the racist practices of, and annulment of democratic institutions in Nazi Germany. However, he expressed admiration for the authoritarian methods (though not the racial ideologies) which he saw in Italy and Germany during the 1930s, and thought they could be used in building an independent India.

Bose had clearly expressed his belief that democracy was the best option for India. The pro-Bose thinkers believe that his authoritarian control of the Azad Hind was based on political pragmatism and a post-colonial recovery doctrine rather than any anti-democratic belief. However, during the war (and possibly as early as the 1930s) Bose seems to have decided that no democratic system could be adequate to overcome India's poverty and social inequalities, and he wrote that an authoritarian state, similar to that of Soviet Russia (which he had also seen and admired) would be needed for the process of national rebuilding. Accordingly some suggest that Bose's alliance with the Axis during the war was based on more than just pragmatism, and that Bose was a militant nationalist, though not a Nazi nor a Fascist, for he supported empowerment of women, secularism and other democratic ideas; alternatively, others consider he might have been using populist methods of mobilisation common to many post-colonial leaders. Bose never liked the Nazis but when he failed to contact the Russians for help in Afghanistan he approached the Germans and Italians for help. His comment was that if he had to shake hands with the devil for India's independence he would do that.

On August 23, 2007, Japanese Prime Minister Shinzo Abe visited Subhash Chandra Bose memorial hall in Kolkata. Abe said to Bose's family "Japanese are deeply moved by Bose's strong will to have led the Indian Independence Movement from British rule." "Netaji is a much respected name in Japan."

Social Philosophy of Subhash Chandra Bose

Deep spiritual feeling and inherent love for God of a boy of the age of fifteen or sixteen predetermined the direction of his future life. Since his boyhood, Subhash was an introvert and preferred loneliness. He himself admitted that in some respects he had a touch of abnormality in his mental make-up and was also precocious.

The result was that at an age when he should have been busy in the football field, he was brooding over the problems which should rather have been left to a more mature age.

Hence, it was not unnatural for the young Subhash to leave home and wander in the Himalayas.

This spiritual feeling was intensified with the passage of time. In a letter to Haricharan Bagchi from Mandalay Jail in 1926, Netaji advised the former to meditate every day, twice if possible, and to read regularly the letters and the speeches of Vivekananda. He further observed that one should not try other books before reading Swamiji's letters and speeches. In the same letter, Netaji wrote, 'The purpose of worship is to develop strength within one's self. You must contemplate some form of Power every day, seek strength from Her, offering all the five senses and all evil at Her feet.'

S. A. Ayer, the Minister of Propaganda of the Provisional Government of Azad Hind, wrote that many a night, after dinner, while in Singapore, Netaji used to send his car to the Ramakrishna Mission to bring the Swamiji in-charge of Singapore Mission or his fellow-worker, Brahmachari Kailasam, and spend about two hours or so in spiritual communion before retiring into his study sometime after midnight. Or, late at night, he used to drive incognito to the Ramakrishna Mission, there change into a priestly silk dhoti, shut himself up in the prayer-room, rosary in hand, and spend a couple of hours in meditation. This helped him face and solve complicated problems. Ayer further wrote that whenever Netaji was not actually doing some work or talking to somebody, he would withdraw within himself in a trice and would be in communion with God. His faith in the Supreme Being was an inexhaustible reservoir of courage and optimism.

To quote Ayer: 'It was his intense spiritual faith that give him poise, tranquillity, quiet strength, infectious self-confidence, tolerance, charitability, natural humility and, most important of all, a touching and overpowering spirit of humanity.' 'Sanyasi (ascetic) was writ large on his forehead even when the Supreme Commander's cap rested majestically on his head at an alluring angle over his right brow' he added.

This deep spiritual conviction determined the future life-direction of Subhash Chandra, without understanding of which it will not be possible to comprehend the social philosophy of Netaji. Only at the age of fourteen, in a letter to his mother from Cuttack, Subhash Chandra was asking his mother what sort of career for her children would please her most?-whether she would be the happiest if her children in later life became the judges, magistrates, barristers or high-placed officials and came to be admired for wealth and fortune by the men of the world, or if they could earn the respect of the learned and the virtuous for having grown up to be 'real men' even though they might be poor. The intensity of realisation of a boy of fourteen years astonishes us. At the same age in a letter to one of his classmates, Subhash Chandra wrote: 'My life is not for my own enjoyment. My life is of course not devoid of happiness but is not for enjoyment-my life is a mission-a duty.'

We know that Subhash Chandra secured fourth position in the Indian Civil Service (ICS) Examination. At that time the selection of the Deputy Magistrate in the provincial service created stir in the society, not to speak of the ICS. Subhash Chandra joined the Indian Civil Service as a probationary, but soon resigned. During that period he had been undergoing mental conflict which was reflected in one of his letters of 22 September, 1920, written from England to his elder brother Sarat Chandra Bose. He wrote: 'A nice fat income with a good pension in after life, I shall surely get. Perhaps, I may become a Commissioner if I stoop to make myself servile enough. Given talents with a servile spirit, one may even aspire to be the Chief Secretary to a provincial Government. But after all is service to be the be-all and end all of my life?'

After almost six months, on 16 February, 1921, in another letter from Cambridge to his elder brother, he said: 'I have written to father and to mother to permit me to take the vow of poverty and service. They may be frightened at the thought that path might lead to suffering in the future. Personally I am not afraid of suffering-in fact, I would rather welcome it than shrink from it.'

In one more letter on 6 April 1921, written from Oxford Subhash Chandra informed his elder brother that he was fully conscious of the 'sacrifice' what he was determined to make. It meant poverty, suffering, hard work and possibly other hardships to which he did not expressly refer. But the sacrifice had got to be made-consciously and deliberately.

Is it possible to make such a great sacrifice 'consciously and deliberately' for a person lacking deep spiritual realisation? While imprisoned in Insein Central Jail in 1927, the health of Subhash Chandra broke down. The British Government suggested his treatment in a foreign country, preferably in Switzerland but tagged, two conditions: (1) he would not be allowed to go home and meet his family members and friends before he sailed abroad. The ship by which Subhash Chandra would travel must not touch any port in India; (2) Subhash Chandra would have to stay abroad till the expiry of the Bengal Criminal Law Amendment Act, i.e. till January 1930, and he would not be allowed to interact with anybody while in abroad.

Subhash Chandra, however, rejected these conditions as humiliating. While expressing his reaction to the first condition, Netaji, in a letter to his elder brother Sarat Chandra Bose on 4 April 1927, observed from Insein Central Jail: 'It is not easy for a Westerner to appreciate the deep attachment which Oriental people have for their kith and kin It would be typical only of a Western mind to presume that because I have not married-therefore I have no family (taking the word in its large sense) and no attachment for anyone.'

Regarding the second condition, the stand of Netaji was that it was not certain whether he would at all be allowed to return to India, as there was no guarantee that the Bengal Criminal Law Amendment Act would not be given another lease of life after January 1930.

The well-wishers of Netaji were insisting on him to accept these humiliating conditions if not for anything else, but solely for the sake of his better treatment abroad. At this Netaji, in a letter dated 6 May 1927, wrote to Sarat Chandra Bose from Insein Jail: 'I am not a shopkeeper and I do not bargain. The slippery paths of diplomacy I abhor as unsuited to my constitution. I have taken my stand on a principle and there the matter rests. I do not attach so much importance to my bodily life that I should strive to save it by a process of higgling. My conception of values is somewhat different from that of the market place and I do not think that success or failure in life should be determined by physical or material criteria. Our fight is not a physical one and it is not for a material object either.'

This incident again illustrates that one cannot develop such a determined and detached outlook on life without having a deep-rooted spiritual conviction. Social service: The second component of Netaji's social philosophy is his spirit of social service which is the product of his deep spiritual realisation. Since boyhood he was actively associated with social work. During his school-days at Cuttack, accompanied by some friends, he used to go to the primary village schools situated in the outskirts of the town and did some teaching. In 1913, when he came to Calcutta, he gradually realised that 'social service was an integral part of Yoga and it meant not merely relief to the halt, the maimed and the blind, but national reconstruction on modern lines.'

Towards the end of 1913 or the beginning of 1914, he joined an organisation whose purpose was to give aid to the poor. This organisation used to collect money and foodstuff every Sunday by begging from door to door. The begging used to be done by the student-volunteers and he was one of them.

After he had returned to Cuttack to spend his vacation with his parents, he, along with his friends, went to an interior village to nurse the cholera patients. In those days, cholera was a fatal disease and they took hardly any precautions against infection. This 'nursing expedition' continued for one week and this week's experience, in the words of Subhash Chandra, 'opened a new world before my eyes and unfolded a picture of real India, the India of the villages-where poverty stalks over the land, men die like flies, and illiteracy is the prevailing order.'

In 1915, there took place flood and famine in Bankura, Kumilla, Noakhali, etc. A flood and famine relief committee was set up at Presidency College which was chaired by the Principal, H. R. James. Subhash Chandra was one of the secretaries of the committee.

In a letter, dated 29 July 1915, to his friend Hemanta Kumar Sarkar, Subhash Chandra wrote: 'They have made me the Secretary of the College Famine Fund. I must work for it to a certain extent. There is no one else available .... Experience of famine is something that you cannot have all the time. My emotions want me to go-in fact I am eager to go ..."

After Subhash Chandra had returned to Cuttack as a 'rusticated student' in March 1916, he found enough time to devote himself to social service with 'passionate zeal'. At that time Cuttack and the surrounding areas were afflicted with cholera and small pox. Along with his old friends he used to go to different parts of the town and did voluntary nursing. This group of young men also worked in the cholera ward of the local Civil Hospital, for there were no trained nurses there. Further, they carried the dead bodies to the cremation ground and performed the funeral rites.

Subsequently, when Subhash Chandra joined active politics and emerged as one of the top leaders of the Indian National Congress, he set up a 'Sevasram' in South Calcutta. Till now this organisation is functioning. Even from jail he kept detailed information about its activities. In a letter from Mandalay Jail in 1926, he wrote that he had not taken up Sevasram work as a whim. He could give up Congress work. But it was impossible for him to give up Sevasram work. 'Where else shall I get such a wonderful opportunity of serving 'Daridra Narayana' asked Netaji. According to him, the first step towards equipping oneself for public service is to sacrifice all worldly interests and then devote oneself whole-heartedly to the national cause.

In a letter from Cambridge to Sarat Chandra Bose in February 1921, Subhash Chandra gave vent to his feeling on this subject. With a heavy heart he wrote to his fellow-traveller Bhupendra Nath Bandyopadhyay: 'Today many workers in Bengal have developed a strong business and traders' mentality. They have started saying: "give me power-else I shall not work". I should like to ask-since when has service to the poor been converted into a business or a contract? I always knew that the ideal of service was:

> "Give away, never turn to ask in return, Should there
> be the wealth treasured in thy heart".

There is nothing surprising in that the Bengali who has already forgotten about Deshbandhu's sacrifice, should have forgotten Swami Vivekananda's 'Bir-Bani', preached so many years ago."

Netaji linked social service with spiritual feeling. In his autobiography, Netaji wrote: '...for spiritual development social service was necessary. The idea came probably from Vivekananda' for... he had preached the ideal of the service of humanity which included the service of one's country.'

Political action The political activism of Netaji is the result of his same spiritual conviction. Politics is a vital component of society. In Political Science we draw a line of distinction between the state and the society. There is a consensus among political scientists that the society is wider in concept than the state and that, in order of time, society is prior to the state. Nevertheless, the state is the most significant and society is an integral part of the state. Hence, any discussion of social philosophy shall include political philosophy. However, we do not intend to deal in detail with the political philosophy or thinking of Netaji. We like to mention only that Subhash Chandra was not a political philosopher, but was a selfless political actionist. He was never a systematic political thinker, nor he ever staked his claim to be so. He did not have the time to indulge in theorisation about the political concepts. But he possessed a highly intellectual bent of mind and had enough foresight to plan well ahead of his time. From his diverse activities one can have a glimpse of his political thinking.

Attitude to alien rule As noted earlier, Subhash Chandra was the product of resurgent extremist nationalism of Bengal which was based on the cardinal principle that no sacrifice was too great for the cause of liberation of the motherland. He devoted himself to the Non-cooperation Movement body, heart and mind. But the sudden withdrawal of the movement in February 1922 by Gandhiji broke his heart. Subhash Chandra wrote in 'The Indian Struggle': 'To sound the order of retreat just when public enthusiasm was reaching the boiling-point was nothing short of a national calamity.'

After Gandhi-Irwin Pact and the postponement of the Civil Disobedience Movement in 1931, Netaji became sceptical about India's success under Gandhiji's leadership. At the Karachi Session of the Congress in March 1931, he opposed the Gandhi-Irwin Pact.

Netaji Said: 'No real change in history has ever been achieved by discussions. The only alternative is war.'

In a joint statement, Subhash Chandra and Vithalbhai Patel observed: 'Mr. Gandhi as a political leader has failed', and called for 'a radical reorganisation of the Congress on a new principle with a new method, for which a new leader is essential.

After becoming the Congress President for the second time in 1939, Netaji wanted to give a notice to the British Government to leave the country within six months.

At the personal level both Subhash Chandra and Gandhiji had admiration for each other. Both were the two formidable sons of India who had a common goal to liberate India from the British rule and make a new India free from exploitation and oppression. The candidature of Subhash Chandra for the Congress

Presidentship at the Haripura Session of the Congress in 1938 was sponsored by Gandhiji. In a conversation with Louis Fischer, an American journalist, Gandhiji described Netaji as a 'patriot of patriots.'

Gandhiji visited the INA detention camps more than once and in an address said: 'Netaji was like a son to me. I came to know him as a lieutenant full of promise under the late Deshbandhu Das ...'

In his turn, Netaji, in an address from the Azad Hind Radio on 6 July 1944, described Gandhiji as the 'Father of our nation.'

In a broadcast on the occasion of Gandhiji's 75th birthday on 2 October 1943, Netaji said: 'The service which Mahatma Gandhi has rendered to India and to the cause of India's freedom is so unique and unparalleled that his name will be written in letters of gold in our national history for all time.

Subhash Chandra and Gandhiji differed in their political technique. The former was convinced that the British rulers were so unscrupulous and inhuman that Gandhiji's non-violent means would not yield any result. According to him, it is futile to expect a change of heart in the British rulers merely through our own suffering and by trying to love them. There is no alternative to uncompromising struggle against British imperialism. In the Radio Broadcast address to Gandhiji over the Azad Hind Radio on 6 July 1944, Netaji said: 'The British Government will never surrender to persuasion or moral pressure or non-violent resistance.'

Hence, the adoption of any means to drive out the British rulers from the Indian soil will be justified, and in this respect, Bose and Gandhiji differed. Incidentally, it may be noted that the concept of 'Satyagraha' was not simply a political strategy to Gandhiji, but was a philosophy of life. Besides, the unique contribution of Gandhiji was to involve all sections of the Indian masses in the Liberation Movement, and that was not at all possible before Gandhiji who, in fact, fulfilled the dream of Swami Vivekananda in this respect. In Swamiji's view, the mission of any national organisation should be for the destitute, the poor, the illiterate peasantry and the labouring classes.

In May or June 1897 at Almora, in his conversation with Ashwini Kumar Datta, a prominent leader of the Indian National Congress,

Vivekananda impressed upon him the urgency of involving the masses in the activities of the Congress.

It was Gandhiji who, for the first time, succeeded in involving the 'masses', in the true sense of the term, in the mainstream of the Congress and thereby of the Indian National Movement.

Netaji's political modus operandi is described as militarism which is the natural corollary of his social philosophy. Netaji put emphasis upon the urgent need of a national army, strong and well-organised, to fight for the liberation of the country and also the maintenance of its freedom. Examples of Washington and Garibaldi, who achieved independence with the help of their national army, were in his mind. Netaji felt that unless the might of British imperialism was wrecked from outside, it would be difficult to ask them to surrender. To him, there is no harm in taking the help of outside powers on the basis of reciprocal relationship. Citing example from history, he argued that Garibaldi had taken the help of Austria's enemies. For the downfall of Czarist regime in Russia, Lenin had taken the help of 'reactionaries' even.

Concept of Samyabad

According to Netaji, after independence, nationalism should be based on socialism. Establishment of socialism or 'samyabad' (he himself coined the term) was his important political goal. He was the first political personality within the Indian National Congress to define the objectives of Indian freedom in terms of socialist objectives. In his presidential address at the Haripura Session of the Congress in 1938, Netaji said: 'I have no doubt in my mind that our chief national problems relating to the eradication of poverty, illiteracy and disease and to scientific production and distribution can be effectively tackled only along socialistic lines.'

Although a separate subject of comprehensive discussion, the cardinal principles of Netaji's socialism included the adoption of economic planning as a technique to achieve the goal of socialism (Indeed, the history of our freedom struggle will remember with profound regard Netaji as the father of Indian National Planning), assigning limited role to the private sector and greater role to the public sector in the initial years after independence, special emphasis on improving the lot of the peasants (agrarian reform on the basis of reform of land-system, including abolition of landlordism, abolition of agricultural indebtedness, formation of co operative institutions, etc.), ensuring the linguistic and cultural autonomy for all sections of the Indian community, assimilation of all the knowledge that the outside world could give and which would be of benefit to the material prosperity of India without, however, sacrificing the original character of the Indian society and culture. Among other things, Netaji put emphasis upon the development of heavy industries and planned industrial development (In this respect Netaji sharply differed from Gandhiji and came closer to Nehru) and categorically stated that there should be no discrimination on gender ground. He also advocated Municipal Socialism, i.e. to utilise the municipality for the service of the community as a whole.

Netaji rejected the concepts of materialistic interpretation of history and class-struggle, the two basic postulates of Marxism-Leninism. He said: 'Class-conflict is something that is quite unnecessary in India.'

Likewise, Vivekananda observed: 'You must take care not to set up class-strife between the poor peasants, the labouring people and the wealthy classes.'

Having deep-rooted spiritual feeling and conviction, Netaji disliked the anti-religious and atheistic stance of Marxism-Leninism. Besides, Netaji observed: 'Communism today has no sympathy with Nationalism in any form and the Indian Movement is Nationalist Movement, a movement for the national liberation of Indian people.'

In brief, Netaji's idea of socialism did not conform to socialism of the Marxian model or any conventional form. He said: 'Indian Socialism did not derive its birth from the books of Karl Marx. It has its origin in the thought and culture of India.'

Strong government For the implementation of socialist principles, Netaji advocated a strong government with a single party rule committed to the principles of nationalism and socialism as well as military discipline, for a temporary period. In his own words, 'there must be a strong central government by a strong party bound together by military discipline.' There is, however, disagreement of views among the political thinkers whether Netaji had a feeling of contempt or abhorrence for the British system of parliamentary democracy.

To sum up, Netaji's political activity and thinking, though scattered, are the reflection of his social philosophy, and deep spiritual conviction is a basic determinant of his social philosophy.

Militant Nationalism and Patriotism

Subhash angered that a spirit of militant nationalism is essential to rejuvenate Indians to achieving freedom. Subhash believed in the non-violent path and mobilisation of the people for the cause of freedom; that is why he supported the non-cooperation and Civil Disobedience Movement but its withdrawal at a crucial moment on the pretext of violence and opportunist compromise was severely criticised by him. He wrote, "If our policy had been one of uncompromising militancy, the Bardoli surrender of 1922 never would have taken place — nor would the Delhi Pact of March; 1931 when the situation was opportune." He felt that, 'Freedom intoxicated' missionaries who are 'morally prepared' to undergo the maximum sacrifice and suffering. These are necessary to attain success in the mission.

Bose's Views on Nation Building

For Bose a nation is not there merely to satisfy narrow selfish ends. Addressing the students of the Central Provinces at Amravati and Berar, he said, "I have already said that we shall have to change some of our existing ideas of values with regard to good and evil." He advocated the need of a complete overhauling and recasting of the present stereotyped ^node of existence, which in turn would lead to genuine national solidarity and would give India a position of glory.

For him life, only when inspired above the ordinary by some greater and nobler ideals, has value or significance. Bose asserted that a nation need not exist, or alternately it has no right to exist or live if it has no ambition. However, he also warned that a nation should not strive for progress just to satisfy narrow selfish ends, but should march onwards so that it effectively contributes towards the evolution of the human society.

For nation building Bose asserted the need of 'Swadeshi'.

Swadeshi and Nationalism

Nationalism is not only a political movement but ethical as well, according to Bose. Its ethical aspect is reflected in the adoption of Swadeshi which was a common cause to be practised religiously. Because when one buys an indigenous product, even though of the worst quality and on higher price he helps the nation. Swadeshi is better than the protection of the native industry. Thus, Swadeshi combines sacrifice for the nation and ensures improvement in the indigenous industry.

Bose's Concept of Freedom

Overthrowing the foreign yoke nevertheless was the immediate task towards the ideal of achievement of freedom, which Bose made clear in his address to the students at Lahore in October 1929. He said that the ideal we have to hold up is an ideal which will galvanise our whole life. That ideal is freedom. But freedom is a word which has varied connotations. For Bose freedom is an all-round freedom, i.e. freedom for the individual as well as for the society; freedom for the rich as well as for the poor; freedom for men as well as women; freedom for all individuals and for all classes. This freedom implies not only emancipation from political bondage but also equal distribution of wealth, abolition of caste barriers and social inequalities and destruction of communalism, and religious intolerance. Thus, for Bose, freedom has many facets as there are different aspects of it. He held socialism necessary for really achieving Freedom.

Bose's Conception of Socialism

Subhash Chandra Bose was a believer in socialism. He asserted that he wanted a 'Socialist Republic of India'. However, his concept of socialism was different from that of the others and he called it Indian socialism. Addressing *Bharatiya Naujawan Sabha* in 1931, he said, "If we undertake a comparative analysis of different social and political ideals that have inspired human endeavour and activity throughout the ages, we shall arrive at certain common principles that should form the basis of our collective life. These are justice, equality, freedom, discipline and love." In order to be just and impartial, he advocated treating all men as equal. He asserted that bondage of any kind, economic or political, robs men of their freedom and gives rise to inequalities of various kind. Therefore, in order to ensure equality it is necessary to get rid of bondage of every kind.

However, he also warned that freedom did not mean indiscipline or license or absence of law. It rather means the substitution of law and discipline, which is very necessary for the struggle for freedom the basis of life. Besides these fundamental principles, Bose asserted that love is the highest principle. Without a feeling of love for humanity neither one could be just to all, or treat men as equal, nor feel called upon to sacrifice, and without that the right sort of socialism could not emerge. Thus, for Bose the cardinal principles of socialism are justice, equality, freedom, discipline and love. He advised his countrymen and women not to ignore the history and traditions of the country while adopting the social and political institutions of the other countries. He asserted that there were all kinds of active nation building programmes and socio-political ideologies in the Western world, such as Socialism, State Socialism, Guild Socialism, Syndicalism, Philosophical, Anarchism, Bolshevism, Fascism, Parliamentary Democracy, Aristocracy, Absolute Monarchy, Dictatorship, etc. He accepted some wisdom in each of them.

However, he warned that in a progressive world like ours it would not be proper to accept any one of them as the last word for an ideal or the final solution of all the social and political problems. Because he reasoned that the results of the transplantation of an entire idea or institution in one country from another may not necessarily be agreeable or fruitful. A national institution is the natural result of the history of the people concerned — their thoughts and ideals and the activities of their day to day life. This should be borne in mind. According to Bose social and political institutions cannot be built by ignoring history and the traditions of the people of the country, besides their present condition or prevailing atmosphere of life.

For the above reason, he could not agree with the communists in India also. He felt that the Bolshevik Socialism of Soviet Union did not suit India. There should be assimilation of only those socialistic principles which could suit on Indian requirements. He explained that the Bolshevik theory had been passing through an experimental stage and the communists were departing from Lenin and other Bolsheviks. This departure had been caused by the peculiar conditions and circumstances prevailing in Russia, which compelled a modification of the original theory. He also warned against the unsuitability of Marxian ideas and said that Marxian ideas were coming from the West like 'boisterous breakers' and some people in India we unnecessarily excited and stirred up with these. Most of them, Bose said, who believed that adoption of Marxism in its pure and complete form would make India a land of joy and plenty and pointed their fingers towards Russia, in fact were wrong because the Bolshevism adopted and practised in Russia was not the same as classical Marxian socialism.

The other reason for rejection of communism was the methodology and tactics communists generally employed to achieve their ends. These methods and tactics, he thought, did not suit India and that is why communism could not make much headway in this country.

Indian socialism would therefore be different, he asserted. He said that at that stage it was difficult to chalk out the details of a socialist state (of his dreams). He could only give an outline, the main features and principles of the socialist state. He said, "We want political freedom whereby it meant the Constitution of an independent Indian state, free from the control of British imperialism. It should be quite clear to everybody that independence means severance from the British Empire, and on this point there should be no vagueness or mental reservation. Secondly we want complete economic emancipation. Bose elaborated his view of economic emancipation and held that every human being must have the right to work, and the right to a living wage. There shall be no drones in the society and no unearned income. There must be equal opportunities for all, and there should be a fair, just and equitable distribution of wealth. For this purpose, it may be necessary for the state to take over the control of the means of production and distribution of wealth.

Besides economic equality Bose also felt that the third essential feature of real socialism is complete social equality. Social equality means that there shall be no caste or depressed classes. Every man will have the same rights, the same status in society. Bose was not only a believer of eradication of caste hierarchy, but also a supporter of women's equality in social status or in law. Woman will be an equal partner of man was Bose's firm faith.

Nevertheless, the ideal of socialism could not be achieved without social change. Bose had a specific view about social change.

Social Change

Bose was of the view that social reforms and the movement for national freedom in India were inextricably related. Aş President of the Hooghly District Students Conference in July 1929, he said that those who imagine they can make their country politically free leaving its social order untouched and those who think social change is possible without political freedom belt are wrong. He explains that the former were wrong because once the desire for freedom was aroused in the people, it could not be postponed on the ground that society had not changed. Similarly, the latter were wrong because a society as 'tattered' as ours and where social repression and economic inequality were dominant, people could not be inspired for political independence.

Thus, a kind of social revolution had been envisaged by Bose. He asserted that there was no fundamental difference between evolution and revolution. Revolution is nothing but evolution taking place within a comparatively short span of time, whereas evolution is only another name for revolution spreading over a longer period of time.

Technique of National and Social Revolution — Guerrilla Warfare

In a broadcast over Azad Hind Radio Subhash Bose chalked out his methodology of national struggle. He said that the campaign that was going on in India was non-violent guerrilla warfare. He asserted that the object of this guerrilla warfare would be twofold, one to destroy war production in India and the other to paralyse the British administration and all people of India should participate in the struggle. He chalked out a detail programme for the people. He suggested that payment of the taxes be stopped which directly or indirectly brought revenue to the government. The workers in all industries should either launch a stay in strike or try to hamper production by conducting a go-slow campaign inside the factories. They should also carry out sabotage to impede production. The students should organise secret guerrilla bands for carrying on sabotage in different parts of the country. They should also invent new ways of annoying the British authorities, for example, burning stamps, etc. in post offices, destroying British monuments, etc. The women, especially girl students should do underground work of all kinds, especially as secret messengers or provide shelter for the men who fight. The government officials who are prepared to help the campaign should not resign their posts but those in government offices and in war industries should give all available information to fighters outside and should try to hamper production by working inefficiently. The servants who are working in the houses of Britishers, should be organised for the purpose of giving trouble to the masters, for example, by demanding higher salaries, cooking and serving bad food and drink, etc. The Indians should give up all business with foreign banks, firms, insurance companies, etc. For the general public he suggested the following activities:

- Boycott of British goods, industry, burning of British stalls and government stores;
- Total boycott of Britishers in India, and those Indians who are pro-British;
- Hold demonstrations in spite of official prohibition;
- Publishing of secret bulletins and setting up of a secret radio station;
- Marching to the houses of British government officials and demanding their departure from India;
- Organising of processions for entering and occupying government offices, secretarial buildings, law courts, etc. with a view to hampering administration;
- Arranging to punish police officers and prison officials who oppress and persecute people;
- Begin erecting barricades in the streets where there is a likelihood of attack from the police and military;

- Setting fire to government offices and factories which a re working for war purposes;
- Interrupting postal, telegraph, telephone and communication as frequently as possible;
- Interrupting railways, bus and tram services, whenever there is a possibility of hampering the transport of soldiers or of war material;
- Destroying police stations, railway stations and jails in isolated places.

Bose and Fascism

Bose has been called a believer in Fascism. This assumption arose from the fact that he wanted to associate India's freedom struggle with Second World War politics and sought the help of Fascist Italy and Nazi Germany. He also showed his admiration for Mussolini. Besides in a chapter 'A Glimpse of the Future' in his book 'The Indian Struggle' he wrote "In spite of the anti-thesis between communism and fascism, there are certain traits common to both. Both communism and fascism believe in the supremacy of the state over the individual. Both denounce parliamentary democracy. Both believe in Party rule. Both believe in the dictatorship of the party and in the ruthless suppression of all dissenting minorities. Both believe in a planned industrial reorganisation of the country. These common traits will form the basis of the new synthesis. The synthesis is called 'Samyavada." Bose asserted that it will be India's task to work out this synthesis. Besides the advocacy of this synthesis, in 1941 in Kabul, Bose had said that dissensions in the country would disappear only when an iron dictator rules in India for twenty years. He asserted that at least after the end of British rule in India there must be a dictatorship. And it is for India's good that she should be ruled by a dictator to begin with. None but a dictator can wipe out such dissensions. He believed India needed a Kamal Pasha to cure its many ailments.

Nevertheless, Bose had advocated dictatorship as a panacea for India's problems. However, he could not be branded as a fascist. He never sanctioned the extreme tenets of fascism which sanctioned imperialistic expansion and believed in racialism. He was a votary of the rights of the exploited masses. Thus, although he took armed help from the fascist powers of Europe and Asia, and organised national army for India's liberation, yet he did not preach the ideology of fascism. The Forward Bloc, the party he belonged to summarised its dominant guiding principles on January 1, 1941.

- Complete national independence and uncompromising anti-imperialist struggle for attaining it.
- A thoroughly modern socialist state.
- Scientific large-scale production for the economic regeneration of the country.
- Social ownership and control of both production and distribution.
- Freedom for the individual in the matter of religious worship.
- Equal rights for every individual.
- Linguistic and cultural autonomy for all sections of the Indian community.
- Application of the principle of equality and social justice in building up a New Order in Free India.

The Summary

Bose's political philosophy has a close link with his political life. Bose stood for militant nationalism for achieving India's freedom. According to him freedom and equality are interrelated. So freedom could be achieved only with socialism. There are four bases of socialism, national freedom, economic equality, social equality and equality of sexes, according to him. Bose felt that India should have its own indigenous socialism, and she should not imitate others' way of life. For national freedom, Bose sought the help of the fascists. However, he himself did not believe in fascism. National freedom and national construction were the core of his political ideology.

8

Great Revolutionary

During freedom struggle Gandhi was the most powerful force within the Congress, and, it's probably fair to say, in nationalist politics. By this I mean not only that Gandhi was able to make the big decisions, or at least influence those decisions, but also that Gandhian methods had become the primary tactics of the Nationalist Movement. These tactics involved an emphasis on non-violence, and a vacillation between non-cooperation and active participation. In other wards, the Gandhi and the Congress would go for years quietly coexisting with British rule, then launch a non-cooperation campaign, gain some concessions from the British, and then go back to another period of relative quiet. For the most part, there were few challenges to this approach outside the Congress. The terrorists carried on in certain areas of the country, especially Bengal, but they were, at the most, a nuisance. By the time of WW II, it had long become evident that elite terrorism was not going to inspire a popular revolution. After Gandhi came along and demonstrated how a popular movement might be generated, the terrorists became even less relevant.

The challenge to the predominance of Gandhi and Gandhian tactics in Indian nationalism came from within the Congress. It came from a man named Subhash Chandra Bose, who, at the height of his political influence, was one of the two or three most powerful leaders in the Congress. Gandhi certainly saw Bose as a rival and a dangerous upstart, and did his best to destroy him politically.

Whereas Gandhi sought compromises with the British, Bose sought absolute victories. Gandhi was willing to wait a long time for independence, Bose wanted immediate action, if not immediate results. Gandhi was anti-materialistic and hostile to modern technology, Bose saw technology and mass production as essential to survival and dignity. Gandhi wanted a decentralised society and disliked the modern state; Bose wanted a strong central government and saw the modern state as the only solution to India's problems. And finally, Bose did not share Gandhi's dedication to non-violence.

Mahatma Gandhi and Subhash Chandra Bose

Mahatma Gandhi and Subhash Chandra Bose were two legendary personalities, gigantic in their political moral and ethical stature. Both of them were two worthy sons of Mother India. In 1915, soon after his return from South Africa Gandhiji became the unquestioned leader of India's Freedom Movement and Indian National Congress. He transformed 'an unarmed, politically subjugated, dumb and illiterate mass of humanity into a fearless, non-violent, politically awakened, resurgent militia. Verily out of dust, he made Indians into men'. Subhash Chandra Bose, 'the stormy petrel of Indian Renaissance' younger to Gandhi by 28 years who had resigned his brilliant career in the much coveted heaven-born Indian Civil Service with the resolute aim and determination to devote himself entirely to the fight for India's freedom.

The saga of relationship between Subhash and Gandhi starts with Subhash meeting Gandhi on the very day (on 16th July, 1921) of his landing at Bombay. Their first meeting set the contours of the relationship over the coming quarter of a century between these two foremost leaders of India's freedom struggle.

To Subhash Bose, Gandhi always remained 'India's greatest man'. His appreciation of the unique contribution of Gandhi was unequivocal. He recognised and admitted Gandhi as the undisputable, unrivalled leader of the masses. Subhash had all praise for Gandhi' unflinching patriotism, firmness in character, love for truth, etc. In fact, Bose bowed before Gandhi's 'single hearted devotion, his relentless will, and his indefatigable labour'. To Gandhi, Bose was like a son whose 'self sacrifice and suffering, drive, integrity and commitment to the national cause and the capacity to bind all Indians into one people were unsurpassed.'

Both Gandhi and Bose were totally honest men. They were internationalists and humanists. They were secular in approach and anti-racial in outlook. In whatever situations they were and whatever they were doing, their minds were always diverted towards the liberation of their motherland. The whole life of both the leaders was an epic struggle for India's independence. In fact, the life long "Tapasya" of both, ended with the ultimate sacrifice of their very lives.

In spite of all these, there were glaring differences between Gandhi and Subhash and in political life both were posed against each other. Young Netaji was a firebrand nationalist who believed in the tradition of Tilak and Aurobindo. Gandhiji, on the contrary, was a reluctant nationalist who belonged to the tradition of his mentor Gokhale and Tagore. Bose's strong revolutionary urge for the emancipation of his motherland made him critical of many of Gandhiji's techniques.

In 1920, at the age of 23, Subhash joined the Non-cooperation Movement which was going on with all its fury in Bengal under the leadership of Deshabandhu Chittaranjan Das. He took prominent part in the agitation against the Prince of Wales's visit. In protest against the decision of Gandhi in calling off the Non-cooperation Movement as a sequence to the Chauri Chaura incident in 1922, Bose felt highly dejected. In 1927, Subhash was elected as one of the General Secretaries of the Indian National Congress. A British Parliamentary Commission, known as Simon Commission was appointed, to fix up the exact status of India's Constitutional development. Indian leaders had long been thinking in terms of early Dominion Status. For Subhash, the demand of Dominion Status appeared to be too short of his dream of full freedom. To the utter astonishment of everybody he roared before the Commission. 'India shall be free, the only question is when'? For this bold statement he incurred the displeasure of the Mahatma who rebuked Bose in the sharpest language such of which was never before heard in the public from Gandhiji.

The year 1927 brought Subhash closer to Jawaharlal Nehru at the annual session of the Indian National Congress, which was held at Madras. They formed the Independence of Indian League and under their joint effort, resolution for 'Complete Independence' was passed. In the next year due to the opposition of Gandhi the resolution to reiterate the demand for Complete Independence could not be approved. Thus, Bose's proposal was defeated. In 1929 to separate Nehru from Subhash, Gandhiji nominated Jawahar as the President of Indian National Congress. The Mahatma was happy as he thought that Bose would be ineffective without support from Jawaharlal. But Subhash a different stuff altogether, despite opposition both from Nehru and Gandhi declared 1929 to be the year of preparation for a massive Civil Disobedience Movement.

In the subsequent events that immediately followed the same sort of ambivalence in the relationship between these two leaders are clearly discernible. Subhash praised Gandhiji for Dandi March and Salt Satyagraha (1930). He wrote nostalgically 'The march of Dandi — an event of historical importance which will rank on the same level with Napoleon's march to Paris'. He particularly admired Gandhiji success in involving women into the Freedom Movement. At the same time Subhash severely criticised Gandhiji's participation in the Second Round Table Conference in London. Bose was much perturbed by the way Gandhiji played his cards at the Round Table Conference. Gandhiji should have spoken, he felt, at the Round Table Conference, with a firm voice. In his treatise 'The Indian Struggle' which was published in November 1934 Subhash wrote:

> 'If the Mahatma had spoken in the language of dictator Stalin, Duce Mussolini or Fuhrer Hitler, John Bull would have understood and bowed his head in respect'.

In 1937, Gandhiji felt that Bose was a force to be reckoned with and hence he should no longer be neglected. He was further convinced that Subhash alone could be an instrument in the split of the Congress. Hence, he decided to elect Subhash as the president of the Indian National Congress even when Subhash was not a member of that party. In the 51st session of the Congress held at Haripura in 1938, Subhash was unanimously elected as the

President. Unfortunately both for the Congress and the country, the alliance between Bose and Gandhi remained precarious. Subhash not only condemned Gandhi's favourite Charakha but gave a call to modernise India. He called upon the people to get united for an armed struggle against the Britishers.

At the presidential election in January 1939, Subhash was vigorously opposed both by Gandhi and Nehru. Nevertheless, he has achieved a decisive victory over his opponent Dr. Pattabhi Sittaramayya, Gandhi's nominee by 1580 to 1375 votes. Gandhiji openly declared that Sitaramayya's defeat was his defeat. He said that Subhash's references to his colleagues were unjustified and unworthy. He remarked that since Subhash had criticised his colleagues as 'rightists', it would be most appropriate on his part to choose a homogeneous Cabinet and enforce his action. At the Tripuri Congress, Bose as the president made a clear proposal that the Indian National Congress should immediately send an ultimatum to the British Government demanding independence within six months. It was opposed by the Gandhian wing and Nehru.

In the midst of the hostile situation Subhash resigned the Presidentship of the Congress on 29th April, 1939, and immediately proceeded to form a radical party bringing the entire left wing under one banner. In this connection, it would be most appropriate to mention that Bose's innate devotion and respect for Gandhiji remained as firm even though his path was diverging. He clearly stated 'it will always be my aim and object to try and win his confidence for the simple reason that it will be tragic for me if I succeed in winning the confidence of other people but fail to win the confidence of India's greatest man'.

Subhash had his 'last long and hearty talk with the Mahatma on 20th June, 1940.' He had pressed Gandhi to launch the struggle taking advantage of the critical position of the British in the Second World War. He told that it was the most opportune time and it was impossible to think of any other situation in which India could start the struggle. Mahatma replied, 'why do you think that we cannot get better opportunities later on? I am sure we will have many such opportunities. Whether England wins or loses the war, she will be weakened by it; she will have no strength to shoulder the responsibilities of administering the country, and with slight effort on our part she will have no alternative but recognise India's independence'.

The whole nation was aroused when Subhash Bose made his spectacular escape on 17th January, 1941 (it was the day fixed for his trial for sedition) while under house detention at Calcutta and finally reached Germany in order to lead struggle for freedom from outside. Gandhi, on his part, could never endorse Subhash Bose joining with the Axis powers. Even outside India, Bose remained unshaken in his deep allegiance to Gandhiji. His praise and devotion for Gandhi were again obvious in his broadcast on Gandhiji's birthday on 2nd October, 1943. 'The service which Mahatma Gandhi has rendered to India is so unique and unparalleled that his name will be written in letters of gold in our national history for all time'.

Even Gandhiji, while differing from the extreme methods of Subhash Bose, had utmost admiration for his unique effort for India's freedom. On one occasion Gandhiji wrote to Subhash, 'regarding your love for the country and determination to achieve freedom, you are second to none. Your sincerity is transparent. Your spirit of self-sacrifice and suffering can not be surpassed by anybody'. On another occasion in a conversation with an American journalist, on the eve of launching the Quit India Movement, Gandhiji defended Bose as 'a patriot of patriots'. Netaji's last broadcast on 6th July, 1944 addressed to Gandhiji through Azad Hind Radio, was like a brilliant report in which he described how 'the high esteem in which you are held by patriotic Indians outside India and by foreign friends of India's freedom, was increased a hundred fold when you bravely sponsored the Quit India Movement in August 1942'. Concluding his speech he fervently sought the blessings of Gandhi, 'Father of our Nation, in this holy war of India's liberation we ask you for your blessings and good wishes.'

During 1945 and 1946, Gandhiji came to know a lot about the exploits of Subhash and his Indian National Army. While addressing the INA prisoners he paid unreserved tributes in hailing Bose as 'Netaji'. He also paid unqualified tribute to the INA. 'The greatest among its achievements was to gather together, under one banner, men from all religions and races of India, and to infuse in them the spirit of solidarity and oneness, to the utter exclusion of all communal and parochial sentiments. It is an example which we should all emulate.'

It is thus clear from the above that both Gandhiji and Subhash discussed all the problems that confronted them, honestly realised their differences. Their relationship was based on truthfulness, transparency, sacrifice and suffering. No wonder, they had the deepest concern for each other till the end.

Netaji vs Foreign Powers

Utterly convinced that passive protestations and civil disobedience to the English rulers of India alone cannot guarantee freedom, his overwhelming passion for India's independence drove Netaji out of India — in search of, and to secure, international diplomatic support and military cooperation.

Bose firmly believed that India needed allies in its struggle for freedom even if that meant forging a tie with an 'intolarable' regime as the Nazis of Germany. He said to Kitty Kurti:

> It is dreadful, but it must be done. It is our only way out. India must gain her independence, cost what it may.

With the help of a selected few confidants of his revolutionary organisation Bose left Calcutta on 17th January 1941 for Kabul — where previously arrangements were made with German and Italian embassies — for his eventual transfer to Europe. He took grave security risks and braved the rugged mountainous route from Peshawar to Kabul on bare foot in the companionship of only one other person Vagatram.

Equipped with an assumed identity and passport from the Italian Legation in Kabul in the name of Signor Orlando Mazzitto, with diplomatic immunity as an official wireless operator, and in the company of Dr. Voelger Bose left Kabul on 18th March for Samarqand. On 20th March they boarded a train from Tarmeez bound for Moscow.

Disappointed with Russian response to his proposal for help, Bose eventually leaned towards Germany. He despised Nazism — but he was ready to make friends with the devil himself — if that was any assistance to his cause.

His earlier stay in Germany and close contact with Hitler and his top deputies in the mid-thirties and credentials from the Italian and German diplomatic offices in Kabul were supposed to have helped him a great deal when he flew from Moscow to Berlin. Alas! it was not easy!

German foreign office was very well informed about Bose through its pre-war Consul General in Calcutta and from its representative in Kabul. The Foreign Office had all the information about his great past and knew from their reports that as an active fighter against British imperialism Bose could be trusted with any help that the Government thought to extend to him.

But at the time the leading lights of German politics must have been so busy that they had no time to consider in detail the case of a man, even of Bose's political status, who had appeared suddenly on the scene, with his uncommon demands.

Another reason has also been advanced for some of Hitler's reticence to welcome Bose's proposal. The superiority of Nordic races was a mania with Hitler and accordingly, he had a soft corner in his heart for England. His order on victorious German forces to allow British troops to retreat unharmed from the battlefields of Dunkirk has been cited as evidence to support this hypothesis.

It was therefore not very easy to change this pro-British attitude of Hitler into a friendly gesture towards India which was in direct opposition to England.

Bose's burning desire to forge a tie with all enemies of the British imperialists, his endless patience and his untiring perseverance eventually won the day. After his fruitful contact and negotiations with Adam von Trott Zu Solz (head of the German Eastern Affairs, later made head of Special India Division) and his deputy Alexander Werth:

> ... it was ultimately decided that Netaji should be given every help to choose his men out of PoW (Prisoner of War) camps and the German Wehrmacht should give him all the help necessary on the lines suggested.

In this regard Werth observed:

> Very soon we felt the strength of his will power, the honesty of his intentions and the inexorability of his personal dedication to India's cause, ... we could not help being influenced by his ideas and wishes.

One of the demands, Bose was able to extract from the German authorities, was the release of all Indian prisoners from War camps and jails in countries under German occupation. Also, with great difficulty and considerable research, Bose was able to make a reasonable list of Indians living at the time in Europe. Soon he (in the name of his assumed identity of Orlando Mazzitto) invited them ali to a tea party — to be held at none other than the former British diplomatic mission. It is here that everyone eventually worked out who this host Signor Orlando Mazzitto really was. Here they started the Free India Centre, Azad Hind Radio centre in October 1941 and finally here was born the Indian Legion (Azad Hind Fauj) later known as the Indian National Army (INA) comprising enthusiastic Indian students, political activists and Indian PoW's imprisoned by General Rommel, primarily from the battle grounds of Africa.

Converting the PoW's, who fought under the British generals and thoroughly indoctrinated by their masters, was a rather difficult task for Bose and others. All of a sudden, this largely uneducated band of soldiers, had to come to grips with the idea as soldiers of free India. Dr. Girija Mukherjee, who himself was a patriot journalist, wrote about this subject:

> I saw how the whole audience was coming under his spell [as] they were lightening. ...when he finished they had acquired new life, new animation, new excitement...

Bose kept working with furious pace and determination to strengthen the Azad Hind Fauj, Azad Hind Radio — his only medium of contact with India his beloved motherland, and ever so relentlessly in the diplomatic front to secure a tripartite declaration of support from Germany, Japan and Italy.

He saw Mussolini. He frequented between the German foreign office and Japanese mission. He saw Hitler on 26th May 1942 to plead the urgency of his case. At the time Hitler was a little hesitant as his forces were advancing towards Leningrad and did not, understandably, want to take on additional burden right then. The German Chancellor suggested that the time was not right then and wanted to know exactly what kind of 'political concept' Bose had in mind. Netaji was extremely annoyed at this last comment and replied through the interpreter, Von Trott — chief of the Special India Office:

> Tell his excellency that I have been in politics all my life and that I don't need advice from any side.

A remark about Hitler very few would be brave enough to make in the Spring of 1942 — when he was at the Zennith of his success and glory! But we are describing here a man of steel — he had no fear!

Meanwhile, following the attack of Pearl Harbour on 7th of December 1941 Japanese forces made significant naval and army inroads in the East and South East. They virtually controlled everything from Sea of Japan to Bay of Bengal. Cities after cities fell under the Japanese forces by May 1942. Hong Kong, Singapore, Manila, Penang and Rangoon. The Japanese Government, persuaded by another fearless Bengali revolutionary, Rash Behari Bose, who was in exile in Tokyo for a considerable length of time and married a Japanese girl, Tosshiko Soma, declared its whole-hearted support for Indian revolutionaries in their fight against the British Raj. Prime Minister General Tojo announced:

> It is a golden opportunity for India having, as it does, several thousand years of history and splendid cultural tradition, to rid herself of the ruthless despotism of Britain and participate in the construction of the Great East Asia Co-prosperity Sphere.
>
> Japan expects that India will attain her proper status as India for the Indians...

Mussolini, who sent separate communication to Hitler on the subject, advised Bose to form a government in exile. But Germany considered the proposition a little premature. The above announcement from Japan, however, gave Netaji immense encouragement. Now convinced that he could play a much more active role on the soil of Asia — rather than agonising for ever staying in Berlin. Time was running out. He must be where the centre of action was. So, he decided to transfer to the East and asked for Axis help. The security risk of Bose's transfer was phenomenal. He needed special assistance to safely come to the East. In this matter Rash Behari, who was the Chairman of the Bangkok Conference (of Indians in East Asia), having chaired the Tokyo Conference a few months earlier, was a catalyst. Under his guidance the Bangkok Conference resolved that:

> This Conference requests Subhash Chandra Bose to be kind enough to come to East Asia and appeals to the Imperial Government of Japan to use its good offices to obtain the necessary permission and conveniences from the Government of Germany to enable Subhash Chandra Bose to reach East Asia safely.

After fall of Malay, Japanese Major Fujiara transferred 30,000 Indian PoW's under the control of the fallen British Army Captain Mohan Singh of the Punjab Regiment in Malay under a deal cut by Preetam Singh and Debnath Das both close revolutionary colleagues of the fiery Rash Behari Bose. The Indian Independence League (under the leadership of Rash Behari Bose) took control of this military wing — the INA counterpart in the East — under the command of Captain Singh — to fight side by side with the Japanese forces to forge their way through Burma and march to India, on to Delhi.

Meanwhile the Cripps mission failed, Congress became increasingly more impatient with Britain and was not prepared to wait until the end of the War for India's independence. Even Gandhiji started to look a little moved by Bose's activities in Europe. Joyprakash Narain openly supported Bose's armed revolution saying:

> My own interpretation of the Congress position (not Gandhiji's) is quite clear and definite. Congress is prepared to fight aggression violently if the country become independent. Well, we have declared ourselves independent, and also named Britain as an aggressive power; we are, therefore, justified within the terms of Bombay resolution itself to fight Britain

> with arms. If this does not accord with Gandhiji's principles that is not my fault.

Quit India became the slogan. Do or die became the motto. The August movement crystalised. All political leaders of India were despatched to jail by the British Raj. The authorities disbanded the provincial Congress committee of Bengal — the most militant in India on 10th of August 1942. Even Gandhiji himself conceded, at C. R. Das's residence that 'had India sword, I would have asked her to draw it'. This was the kind of electric energy Bose radiated from a long distance. Thousands of Indians in the British Army started defecting and wanted to sacrifice their lives for the cause of India. Because it was the wish of their leader. That's what Bose wanted. Fight till your last breath, fight for India! The English author Coupland writes:

> "The Revolutionaries of extreme left, specially in Bengal, were still ready to take their orders from Mr. Subhash Chandra Bose, even if they came by Radio from Berlin".

The desperate killing machine of the so-called civilized English rulers of Churchill started indiscriminate firing on the aroused mob on the streets of Calcutta and other parts of the country. On 11th August, 13 died in Bombay, casualties in Calcutta rose to 6 at the end of 12th with 3 in Bombay, 7 in Bangalore on 13th, 14 in Bombay and 4 in Madras on 14th, 6 in Ramnad, 5 in Godavari and 1 in Nilgiri districts, 40 in Delhi in 7 days, 218 in Vagalpore, 38 in Dwarbhanga, 5 at Katihar, 67 in Sultanganj, 8 in Bidpur, 8 in Sahabad, 9 in Laheria, 6 in Dhaka, 4 in Munsiganj, 3 in Taltala ... the list goes on for ever. Churchill wasn't going to be the first minister of the monarch to dismember the British Empire. If Bose was alive in free India, he surely would have demanded a trial of Prime Minister Churchil and all the King's men in India for brutal genocide and crime against humanity perpetrated by them.

The Japanese Government was a little unsure as to whether it was a good idea to bring Subhash Bose to the East in view of the impending perilous risks. Further, they already had another Bose (Rash Behari) who was already doing a commendable job of uniting the East Asian Indians against Britain. As to Rash

Behari's request for speedy transfer of Subhash Chandra Bose to the East Lieutenant General Seizo Arisu of Japanese Ground Self Defence is quoted as saying:

> Myself and my colleagues had no objection to comply with it, but we were much worried as to the seniority positions between the two Boses after arrival of Mr. Chandra bose. So asked his frank opinion in the matter. in reply he assured me that we should have no worry on this point and that he would subordinate himself to Mr. Chandra Bose... This impressed me very much and I felt great respect towards him since I saw very plainly that he felt no hesitation to work under the other Bose for the success of the Indian Freedom Movement. Further, I could clearly understand how much he was devoted to the independence of India.

On the other hand, Subhash facing the same question from Mr. Higuti — Japanese Military Attache at Berlin embassy replied that he did not know Rash Behari personally. But as he was fighting for India from Tokyo, he would be quite happy to fight as a soldier under Rash Behari Bose. This clearly shows the depth of devotion to their motherland of these two revolutionary Bengali greats. It's a pitty that in half a century since India's independence, she had done very little to uphold their ideals to the new generation of Indians.

Mussolini rejected Netaji's request to fly in an Italian long-distance plane as too risky, even though a trial flight was successful from Rome to Singapore without any incidents. Alexander Werth wrote:

> After long and complicated discussions with the Italian and the Japanese Embassies in Berlin and Rome, the following was agreed upon between the Special India Division and the German military authorities: Netaji accompanied by only one friend should be taken by a German submarine by way of the British Channel, Bay of Biscay, West Africa, South Africa to the south of Madagascar where he should be transferred to a Japanese submarine which would take him to the nearest Japanese base in East Asia.

All these arrangements were successfully carried out through joint efforts of Netaji and the Special India Division and thanks to the initiative of General Oshima, Ambassador of Japan in Berlin, his military attache Mr. Yamamoto and other members of the Japanese Embassies in Berlin and Rome, as well as competent German military authorities.

Eventually, on the night of 7th Feb. 1943 Boses deputy Nambiar, German State Secretary Keppler and Alexander Werth from the Special India Division took Bose and his companion Abid Hassan to Kiel port where a submarine was awaiting the arrival of the INA's Supreme Commander.

At dead of night on the 26th April, 1943 the two submarines could see each other at the pre-appointed location off Madagascar coast. They did not make initial contact with each other until the following day. But as the weather was pretty rough it was decided to travel further northeast in search of calmer sea. On 28th, despite inclement weather, Bose and Hassan were transferred from the German sub to the Japanese sub with the help of a rubber boat. On 6th May they landed at Saban, not Penang as originally intended. Yamamoto, the Japanese Military Attache at Berlin Embassy who arrived here earlier to receive the INA Chief, welcomed Bose. Because of the unplanned delay in arrival of the plane which was supposed to fly him to Tokyo, he was stranded at Saban for 5 days and reached Tokyo on the 16th. Ready

Thus, the stage was for Bose to emerge as the leader of the Independence Movement in East Asia.

Initially, Prime Minister Tojo refused to even see Bose claiming pressure of work. It was not unknown to him that Mr. Bose came all the way from Germany responding to offer of his government's help. Why then this sudden change of heart! Whilst nobody will ever discover the real truth, it is often speculated that the misgivings created by INA General Mohan Singh's unilateral decision to liquidate INA unit in Malay, thus trying to disfranchise Rash Behari from continuing Japanese Imperial assistance, may have annoyed Tojo no end. On the other hand, he could well have been genuinely under a tremendous pressure of work. Yamamoto was disillusioned with Tojo's behaviour and resigned in disgust. Other leaders convinced General Tojo to eventually see Subhash on 10th of June.

Hugh Toye wrote about Bose:

> For most, the personality of the man was overwhelming, there was great genius of enthusiasm, of inspiration. Men found that when they were with him only the cause mattered, they saw only through his eyes, through the thoughts he gave them, could deny him nothing.

General Tojo was not an exception. The Japanese Prime Minister was charmed as Bose stood before him and spoke of his iron will and determination to snare India's independence off the British hands. He saw fire in this man's belly, hunger for freedom in his eyes and nothing in his words but great devotion to his motherland. The rest is history. The history that the English rulers never wanted to tell the world, the history which even the Congress party wanted to hide, and it was a history which Gandhiji tried to forget. Subhash met General Tojo on 14th June again. The latter agreed to each and every proposal that Bose made to him one by one. He announced in the Diet forthwith:

> We are determined to extend every possible assistance for the cause of India's independence. It is our belief that the day is not far off when India will enjoy freedom and prosperity after winning independence.

At a press conference on 19th June, Bose declared that 'we would, however, get freedom only by shedding our own blood. We will be able to preserve our freedom only if we get it through our own sacrifice and toil'. On 20th June Nisi Nippon Shimbun openly published his arrival in Tokyo. Before he left Japan, Bose proposed his plan to establish a Provisional Government of Free India to the Japanese authorities who had little time to consider it properly before his departure for Singapore. When he arrived at Singapore on 2nd July he received a tumultous welcome there from soldiers and civilians alike.

His personal enthusiasm, his vitality, his authority and his world view won him the real allegiance of Indians in East Asia.

At a reception held on 4th July in his honour Rash Behari transferred the mantel of the Indian Independence League to

Subhash. On 25th of August he was formally appointed the commander-in-chief of the INA.

When Bose took command of the INA the army was in a bad shape with low morale and lacked discipline. This he changed in a very short period of time. On 21 October 1943 Bose announced his Provisional Government of Free India.

On 23rd October Japan announced its official recognition of the Bose Provisional Government:

> The Provisional Government of India, having been established with Mr. Subhash Chandra Bose as its head, the Nippon Government in its firm belief that it is a great step towards the realisation of an independent India for which the Indian people have long aspired, has recognised it as the Provisional Government of Free India and hereby declares its intention to extend every possible cooperation and support in the Provisional Government's efforts to attain its object.

Soon came General Tojo's personal message congratulating His Excellency President and Prime Minister of Azad Hind Government. Recognition came from Dr. Ba Maw's Provisional Government of Burma on 24th, from the German Government on 29th, from Italy on 9th November. Recognition was extended by Thailand, Nanking, the Philippines and a number of other nations.

The preparation for assault on the British Raj went along at a lightning pace. The head quarters of the INA was moved from Singapore to Rangoon on 7th January 1944. On the same day, in accordance with previous understanding with Bose, Japanese General Sugiyama, the Chief of General Staff, issued an Army Instruction paving the way for his forces, when conditions are favourable, to attack, occupy and consolidate the Imphal Area in NE India in order to secure GOC in Burma. The INA Chief Bose agreed with Japanese generals in regards to the following code of conduct by respective armies:

- The two armies would work on a common strategy.
- Officers and men of the INA would be under their own military law and not under that of Japan.

- Liberated territories were to be handed over to the INA.
- A definite independent sector would be allotted to the INA.
- The only flag to fly over the Indian soil would be National Tricolour.
- No indiscriminate bombing was to be carried out in Calcutta.
- Any Japanese or Indian soldiers found looting and raping was to be shot at once.

The first success of INA was recorded in Arakan's Mayu Valley when Major L. S. Mishra's unit quickly cut off the 7th Indian Division on 4th of February 1944. The foreign minister of Japan Sigimitsu congratulated Bose and his INA:

> Your Excellency! Allow me to tender to your Excellency my heart-felt congratulations upon the splendid achievements of your gallant troops who have demonstrated their prowess in fighting shoulder to shoulder with Nippon forces.

The success stories continued in the Arakan and Kaladan sectors. Seatabin, Taung Bazar, Lanacot and Fort White were occupied in early-March. The INA Gandhi Brigade, Subhash Brigade and Azad Brigade marched ahead towards the promised land — Free India.

Kohima fell to INA's Subhash Brigade on 8th April under the command of Col. Thakur Singh (2IC). Moirang fell to INA on 14th April, Col. S. Malik raised the Tricolour flag. The wonderful work done by Major Gen. Kiani's troops, and by Subhash Brigade under Shah Nawaz Khan's command allowed INA to surround the British troops in Imphal for around three months.

The battle of Imphal turned out to be a protracted battle — for which INA's timing was too late in summer. Soon monsoon, not the British army, was to become their biggest adversary.

'With continuous pounding of the only connecting link between the INA Headquarters and the Advance forces' by British B29 bombers and nothing to combat them with it was getting tougher by the day. Wrose still, INA did not have any aerial cover of their own — as most Japanese planes left the area to fight the Americans elsewhere. This inevitably meant that it was almost impossible to ensure continuity of supplies. Further, with the onset of monsoon, extensive rainfall caused widespread flooding.

INA morale, however, was dampened neither by flood, nor for lack of supplies. They 'lived on grass and leaves for long', they could have gone on longer. Their leaders call was 'We must keep marching on'. Even the defection of Gandhi Brigade's Commandant B. J. S. Garewal and Major Prabhudayal to British army with maps and papers pinpointing exact locations of INA positions could not destroy the fighting spirit of the INA troops. Outbreak of malaria and dysentery in the face of a total lack medical facilities and supplies dealt, however, a severe blow and took a heavy toll.

On Bose's instruction the troops eventually retreated. The extent of loss during retreat was significant.

Bose and his INA troops did not give up there. The task of rebuilding and strengthening INA continued in Burma. They fought many other battles in Burma against the advancing Allied forces. On 7th May 1945 Germany formally surrendered to the Allied forces. Fuhrer Adolf Hitler had fallen, The Fuhrer was dead.

Following the fall of Okinawa, despite Japan's proposal of surrender, nuclear attack on 6th of August in Hiroshima, followed by a similar explosion in Nagasaki on 9th, left a terrible mark on the history of an unprecedented account of loss of life and destruction. On 10th August USSR declared war on Japan. And the inevitable followed — Japan surrendered. Bose in his ever-calm voice said to his people:

> Japan's surrender [is] not India's surrender... The INA would not admit defeat.

Netaji wanted to stay in Singapore. But impending arrival of the Allied forces was only a matter of time. On advice and under extreme pressure from his Cabinet members, he decided to leave Singapore. On 17th of August 1945, Bose met up with Field Marshal Terauchi in Saigon. With him were a number of top INA officials and Japanese General Isoda and Hachaiya. Netaji, Habibur Rehman who was to accompany Netaji, General Isoda, Hachaiya and Field Marshal Terauchi had a meeting which took place behind closed doors. The rest of the INA officials were not privy to the content or subject matter of that meeting. Whatever was decided was secret and remained so to this day. Netaji and Habibur flew with General Isado and Hachaiya. They reached Taihoku airport the following afternoon, after an overnight stopover at Turan.

After a short break at the airport and following maintenance checkup of the aircraft and a light refreshment the plane took off from the runway. Mechanical troubles caused the aircraft, hardly elevated 300 ft, to collapse and it crashed down to the ground. Bose was badly injured and was taken to the Nanmoon Hospital where he died later that night.

At least that was the official announcement.

The British never believed that story, neither did the 400 million Indians. To this day and as long as India exists, to hundreds of millions of Indians and oppressed people of the world, the leader of Free India — the Supreme Commander of the Indian National Army Netaji Subhash Chandra Bose shall live for ever!

The Prince among the Patriots

Bose came from a upper-class Bengali family. His father was a well-known lawyer in Cuttack. He was the ninth child in a big, busy family; but his parents were aloof, and Bose grew up as a loner. He was a voracious reader, and he was especially attracted to the writings of the 19th century Hindu social reformer, Swami Vivekananda. From Vivekananda he picked up a desire to take India, especially Hindu India, back to an idealised past in which Indians had been strong, moral and free. As he grew older, and became interested in socialism, he lost this interest in mythical golden ages and his overtly Hindu outlook. But he kept his determination to do something about what he saw as social injustice towards low-caste groups, the poor, and women.

He was a brilliant student, and became active in student politics at Calcutta's Presidency College. In those wartime years, the university offered military training to students who were interested (sort of like the ROTC today), and Bose eagerly signed up. Bose did not join because he saw it as his duty to the Empire. He joined because he believed military training was an important part of a nationalist's education. He fervently believed that India, and especially Hindus, had become politically subjugated because of their military weakness. If the nation was to be free and worthy of respect, Bose felt, its citizens must know how to fight.

Also at Presidency College, he had one of his first direct encounters with the British. He became involved in an assault by students on a British professor, and was kicked out of school. This incident has since become one of the major myths of Indian nationalism, with Bose presented as the hero and Edward Oaten, the professor, presented as a racist villain. The truth is probably not so clear-cut. What is more likely is that Oaten was tactless, and Bose was hot-headed. A sense of humour was not one of Bose's strong points; he tended to be touchy and took everything very seriously.

He eventually graduated from Scottish Church college in Calcutta (after his father pulled a few strings to get him admitted), and was then packed off to England by his family to prepare for the ICS (Indian Civil Service) exams. He arrived in England in 1919, when he was 23 years old.

It's interesting to compare Bose's English experience with Gandhi's. Bose was probably a bit less socially isolated than Gandhi had been when he had first arrived; there were more Indians around for him to spend time with. As with Gandhi, the time Bose spent in England made a deep impression on his thinking. Like Gandhi, Bose became something of a dandy in England, always wearing expensive, perfectly pressed clothes. Like Gandhi, Bose was terrified of sex, and put all his guards up when he was around English women. And like Gandhi, Bose became more conscious of his Indian identity when he was in England.

But there were some very significant differences, as well. Gandhi did not become a nationalist while he was in England. That came later. Gandhi's nationalism developed slowly over the decades, and if we had to look for pivotal movements we would have to find them in South Africa and later in Jallianwalla Bagh. Bose arrived in England as a budding nationalist, and as somebody who was very conscious, and very resentful, of the racial basis of British rule in India. In England, he wrote one of his friends: Nothing makes me happier than to be served by the whites and to watch them clean my shoes. In England, Bose's nationalism became more clearly defined, and more militant, than it had been before.

At the same time, Bose liked England. He enjoyed the openness of English society, the freedom of expression, the debates in Parliament and at the university, the fact that students weren't shadowed by the police. It made him acutely aware of how different life was in colonial India. Also, there was a lot that Bose admired about the British in England. He found them efficient and energetic, he appreciated their sense of a national interest, and what he saw as their can-do attitude. These qualities — efficiency, energy, discipline, a sense of punctuality — are all central to modern industrial society, and they became central to Bose's vision of what India should be like.

He did very well in the ICS exams, and then faced a dilemma that had, by the 1920s, become common for Indian nationalists. Should he join the IAS, and participate in the administration of India, or should he keep his distance from the colonial government? Would participation constitute collaboration? Eventually Bose decided to stay away from the IAS.

Quite apart from his qualms about the Indian Civil Service, there was another major factor that influenced his decision. Bose was one of those people who desperately needed a father-figure in his life. Ever since he had been a child, he had attached himself to his teachers and to various swamis, hoping to find somebody who could be a combination of spiritual advisor, political mentor, and intellectual guide. For Bose, who was already leaning towards a career in nationalist politics, one possible choice might have been Gandhi, who served those functions for Nehru. But Bose never developed this intimacy with Gandhi. He admired Gandhi, but the philosophical differences were too great.

As he resigned from the Indian Civil Service, Bose finally found his father-figure. This was C. R. Das, who was another one of those nationalist lawyer-politicians active in the Congress. In some ways, Das was a curious choice of mentor for a hot-headed extremist like Bose. Das was the ultimate machine politician. He believed in building an administrative organisation within the framework of the colonial government, and then running that organisation as independently as possible. He did not look for revolution; rather like Gandhi, he believed in a gradual process of piecemeal concessions. Like Gandhi, he had responded to the Rowlatt Acts by throwing himself into the Non-cooperation Movement. He had abandoned his legal practice and his western suits, and adopting khadi and frugality, although he was never quite as frugal as Gandhi.

Bose was drawn to C. R. Das primarily because he admired the latter's personal sacrifices. The fact that both men were Bengalis was also a factor. And perhaps, at a psychological level, Das — with his social, cultural and professional background — was sufficiently like Bose's own father.

So Bose wrote to C. R. Das, offering his services, and rather boldly outlining his own ideas of how to build a nationalist organisation. Congress, he wrote, should have a permanent house. It should come up with a set of policies for all of India, including the princely states, It should have policies for improving the conditions of low-caste groups, It should have its own research and intelligence wing, and a well-organised public relations machine.

These ideas are important for several reasons, For one thing, they tell us a lot about how Bose was thinking about the present and the future. Already, in 1921, he wanted the Congress to function as a parallel government, This is something that very few people inside the Congress, including Gandhi, had given much thought to, or were comfortable contemplating, For another, these ideas highlight the emphasis Bose would place on efficient organisation. They reflect his conviction that society's problems could be solved not through moral persuasion — which was the Gandhian line — but through pressure exerted by powerful organisations, such as a parallel government, or an independent nation-state.

Das was impressed by Bose's ideas, and invited Bose to work with him in Calcutta. So he went, and in 1921 he plunged immediately into hectic political activity mat fully utilised his talents as an organiser. Seeing a need to develop alternatives to the colonial educational system, Bose threw himself into creating a nationalist college. He set himself up as the principal, found professors who were willing to lecture, invented courses, developed course schedules, and even planned on taking some courses himself. All this was typical of the man: he wanted to be the leader, he wanted to plan and to organise, and at the same time he wanted to learn.

When he was not working on the nationalist college, Bose was organising strikes and demonstrations in Calcutta as part of the Non-cooperation Movement. The British threw him in jail, along with C. R. Das and thousands of other activists, but this was pretty much what the Non-cooperation Movement aimed to achieve. He was released after six months, and was immediately back at work, doing what he did best: organising large-scale operations. There had serious flooding in parts of Bengal. Bose, working with Congress volunteers, set up relief operations that were bigger and more effective than anything the Congress had done along those lines until then. Since the colonial government didn't do much to help the flood victims, Bose's reputation as an effective political leader grew larger.

At around this time, Bose began to have his first open disagreements with Gandhi. Actually, it was Das who had the disagreement with Gandhi, and initially Bose was involved only as Das' right-hand man, Das wanted the Congress to contest elections to local councils under the Montagu-Chelmsford Act of 1919, and to become actively involved in local government. Gandhi felt this would undermine non-cooperation, and refused. But Das had support within the Congress on this issue, particularly from the two Nehrus. They got together and formed the Swaraj Party. This was not really a separate party, but a group that remained within the overall Congress organisation. Faced with this tension within the Congress, Gandhi compromised and allowed the Swaraj Party to participate in the elections.

In the 1924 elections to the Calcutta Municipal Corporation — i.e., the city government of Calcutta — the Swaraj Party won a two-thirds majority. Bose became the Chief Executive Officer. In other words, at the age of 27, he was one of the most powerful men in the second-largest city of the British Empire. He loved the job: it allowed him to use his talent for developing and running big operations, to be innovative, and to be the boss. He took charge of all kinds of details, from designing city employees' uniforms, to creating new municipal programmes for education and public health.

In the meantime, the colonial secret service kept a close watch on him, and tried to come up with evidence that would bring him down. The colonial government had first noticed Bose during Oaten episode, and now he was seen as a particularly dangerous nationalist politician, who was becoming too powerful too fast. Eventually, in the fall of 1924, Bose was arrested on vague charges of conspiring with terrorists to kill the police commissioner of Calcutta. The charges were almost certainly false. Bose probably sympathised with the terrorists, and may have helped them find jobs, etc. but it's totally implausible that he would have jeopardised his career at that stage by trying to kill his own police chief.

In any event, the British wanted to get him out of the country, and he was sent off to jail in Burma. His health broke down in prison, and he was eventually released in 1927. He came back to India and found that a lot had changed in his political fortunes. For one thing, C. R. Das had died, and the leadership of the Swaraj Party had been taken over by Gandhi loyalists. This left Bose without a secure foothold in the political establishment. He remained active in the Congress, but his moment at the centre of power had passed. He went back to being the permanent outsider. In sonic ways, this freed him up, especially when it came to being able to criticise Gandhi. Now he had less to lose.

He spoke out strongly on two issues. Firstly, he criticised Gandhi's hostility to modern technology and mass He declared: "We have to live in the present and to adapt ourselves to modern conditions. The days of the bullock cart are gone forever." And, for those of you who have been following the recent controversy over the Indian nuclear programme, he added: "Free India must arm herself for any eventuality as long as the whole world does not accept wholeheartedly the policy of disarmament."

His second point of disagreement with Gandhi was over the pace and the objectives of the Nationalist Movement. Gandhi tended to give the British a lot of time to respond to Congress demands, and there were long gaps between the periods of active agitation. Bose wanted immediate agitation, and could not understand why Gandhi always waited for the right moment. A true revolutionary, he felt, created the moment, rather than wait for it to arrive.

Also, Gandhi and his allies within the Congress were not, in 1928, ready to come out and demand complete independence. They preferred to define the nationalist goal as dominion status, i.e., as autonomy within the British Empire. Bose found this unacceptable, and he did not hesitate to say so.

Nevertheless, he was still working closely with the Congress. During the Congress' convention in Calcutta in 1928, Bose organised the ceremonies. In the process, he allowed his imagination to run wild: he put Congress volunteers in military-style uniforms, named himself General Officer Commanding, and held a military-style honour guard for Nehru senior. Once again, this was his childish delight in uniforms and smart salutes coming to the forefront. Most people didn't know whether to laugh or to cry. Gandhi, most likely, was not amused.

In 1929, Bose was elected president of the Bengal branch of the Congress, defeating Gandhi's candidate. Not long after that, he was jailed for protesting the government's treatment of revolutionaries and political prisoners. In 1930 Gandhi finally gave the call for complete independence, and launched a new campaign of civil disobedience. Bose watched the campaign from prison. While in prison, he was elected mayor of Calcutta. When he was released in the fall of 1930, he immediately went back to being the organiser of massive nationalist demonstrations. After a confrontation with the police in which he was violently assaulted, he was sent back to jail. For the time being, his career as an active politician in India came to an end.

Bose's health failed again in prison, and he went to Europe to recover. He spent most of the 1930s in Europe, shadowed by the British secret service. Nevertheless, he travelled extensively in Switzerland, Germany, Austria, Italy, Ireland and eastern Europe. He developed extensive contacts with the European left as well as with the right, both of which had reasons to be anti-Britain, and to welcome Bose as a man who was fighting the British in India. He met Mussolini, discussed his revolutionary plans with him, and Mussolini was suitably impressed.

This period in Europe had a profound effect on Bose's politics. For one thing, his exposure to the left sharpened his faith in revolutionary socialism, and his determination to lead a socialist revolution in India. For another, his exposure to the right gave him an admiration for the techniques of organisation and administration that the Nazis were trying out in Germany, and that Mussolini's fascists had been trying out in Italy.

We now have to deal with the question of Bose's political ideology at this point, especially the question of whether or not he was a fascist. Well, in a word: yes, Bose was now a fascist. He had no problems with openly admiring fascism. At the same time, he was not a Nazi, in the sense that he was not a racist, and he had no interest in theories of national purity and cultural supremacy. Bose did not seek a Hindu India, or some pure version of Indian culture. He had long outgrown his old politics of Hindu nostalgia. He welcomed Muslim participation in Indian nationalism, and he did not hesitate when it came to forming alliances with Muslim politicians.

For Bose, fascism was a technique of political organisation, and a diagram for relations between government and society. Bose was not a democrat. He may have been one in the 1920s, but by the late-1930s he was quite certain that parliamentary democracy was not suitable for India. In his mind, India needed firm control by a single party, which would direct every aspect of social, political, economic and even personal life.

He believed that India's problems — such as caste discrimination, class injustice, the need for economic modernisation, etc. — were so deep-rooted that they could only be weeded out through massive state intervention. For this, Bose believed, the machinery of the state had to be in the hands of a single, powerful, reforming party organisation, such as the Nazi Party in Germany or the Communist Party in the Soviet Union. At this point, he still believed that this party would be the Congress.

Bose finally returned to India in January of 1937. He was now much more radical than he had been when he had left. He was quick to reject the Government of India Act of 1935, which had allowed for greater Indian participation in the provincial governments. For Bose, the law was too little too late. He was unhappy that the Congress had agreed to participate in the government under the Act, but this did not keep him away from Congress politics. The years in Europe had not diminished his popularity in India, and he had no trouble getting elected as the president of the Congress. He remained president for only a year, before Gandhi schemed to bring him down.

But for that one year, Bose was king, and he enjoyed himself thoroughly. As in the past, he threw himself into building Congress up as a practical parallel government. In keeping with his faith in modern technology, he set up a committee of prominent scientists to develop a viable industrial policy. He raised funds, and he campaigned tirelessly all over India. He emphasised his socialist ideals, and along with Nehru, became the recognised leader of the Congress left.

But Bose and Nehru did not become political allies. There are several reasons. There were the philosophical differences: Nehru was a democrat, Bose was authoritarian. Also Nehru, at heart, was something of an Anglophile, in the sense that he had a soft spot for India's connection with England. Bose had no such sentimental attachment. Then there were differences in temperament that played out in the way they each approached socialism and policy-making. Nehru was a visionary without much interest in the details of implementing his visions. But details mattered to Bose. And finally, there was the Gandhi factor.

In spite of his philosophical differences with Gandhi, Nehru was Gandhi's protege, and everybody knew it. Nehru would disagree with Gandhi on specific issues, but when push came to shove and a decision had to be made, he would give in and let Gandhi have his way. This was partly Out of a genuine respect for Gandhi's leadership, and partly because Nehru understood very well that his own political fortunes were linked to Gandhi's. As long as Nehru was Gandhi's boy, his own future within the Congress organisation was insured. This reluctance to go up against Gandhi meant that when Gandhi turned on Bose, Nehru made no real effort to defend his fellow-socialist.

When Bose had been elected Congress president, Gandhi had accepted it. The break came in the fall of 1938, when war in Europe became a distinct possibility. Bose and the left saw the possibility of war as a tremendous political opportunity, and wanted to use this opportunity to pressure the colonial government for immediate concessions. Gandhi and the Congress right, on the other hand, wanted to issue a much weaker resolution, hoping that the British would simply do the right thing if war broke out. Bose and the left refused to give in, and Gandhi was furious. Even though Bose was the Congress president at this time, Gandhi had long enjoyed the status of the unofficial super-president of the Congress, and he did not like Bose's disobedience.

Bose was up for re-election in January of 1939, and Gandhi decided to block him. Quite apart from his personal animosity, there were real issues involved. Bose wanted the Congress to walk away from implementing the Government of India Act of 1935. He also wanted to give the colonial government an ultimatum demanding immediate independence, and to begin all-out civil disobedience if the government refused. Gandhi and the Congress right felt otherwise. In any event, Bose won his re-election, narrowly defeating P. Sitaramayya, who was Gandhi's chosen candidate.

Gandhi now worked actively to bring Bose down. The Congress constitution provided only two ways for getting rid of the president: he could be voted Out of office, or he could resign. Since Gandhi was unwilling to wait for the next election, he decided to force Bose to resign. Even though Bose was the Congress president, Gandhi's supporters controlled the party's Working Committee. Without their cooperation, the president could not operate effectively; it was a system of checks and balances similar to what we have in the US government.

Gandhi's supporters now resigned, and Bose found himself unable to form a new Working Committee against Gandhi's opposition. He tried hard to work out a compromise with Gandhi. He even offered to let Gandhi nominate the entire Working Committee, if Gandhi would only accept Bose's plan to launch an agitation for immediate independence. Gandhi politely refused, and Bose had no option except to resign, four months into his second term as president.

One of the interesting things about this whole episode is that Bose blamed Nehru more than he blamed Gandhi. He never completely cut his ties with Gandhi, and continued to try to rebuild his bridges. But he never forgave Nehru for not helping him during this crisis.

On September 3 of 1939, war finally broke out in Europe. And not just in Europe, because the Viceroy Lord Linlithgow declared war on India's behalf, without consulting a single Indian. This was a major embarrassment for the Congress, which was now faced with two choices. It could either get some significant concessions from the colonial government. Or it could resign from the ministries it controlled under the Government of India Act. So the Congress went to the government, and asked for a clear statement of its military objectives.

The government stonewalled, saying that it was too early in the war to talk about military objectives. It also refused to talk about Indian independence, saying that any such discussion would have to wait until after the war. Since there was no clearly defined military objective, it meant that the government would decide when the war was over, and when Indian independence could be discussed. Congress now resigned from its ministries. It's been suggested that the British deliberately manoeuvred Congress into resigning, to have a free hand in running the government during the war. Whatever the case may be, the Congress now found itself out of office, and with nothing but moral outrage to show for it. Still Gandhi refused to launch an agitation.

Bose, meanwhile, had been busy organising his own party, called the Forward Bloc. This was initially within the structure of the Congress. But by 1940 it had become an independent political party, mainly because the Congress had refused to tolerate its allegiance to Bose instead of to Gandhi, and had kicked its officers out of office. Things were happening very fast for Bose, as usual. In July of 1940, he was arrested and sent to prison again for planning to lead a march demanding the removal of a memorial to the victims of the Black Hole of Calcutta. He went on a hunger-strike, and in December he was released.

Then began his great adventure. Even before his last arrest, Bose had begun to think about getting himself Out of India. He felt that there was little that he could achieve in India under the circumstances. His career in the Congress had stalled, and besides, the Congress was unwilling to do what he wanted it to do. The war, he felt, was too important an opportunity to waste. So he came up with a plan. He would escape from India, get to the Soviet Union, and then go on to Germany. When he got to Germany, he would persuade the Germans to help him in his fight against the British in India.

Bose now contacted a communist organisation in Punjab. He asked if they might be able to smuggle him across the border into Afghanistan, and through Afghanistan into the USSR. They told him it was possible. In the winter of 1940-41 his journey began. Disguised as a Muslim life-insurance agent, Bose escaped from his family home in Calcutta in the middle of the night. He boarded a train at a remote rural station, and travelled to Peshawar on the border between Punjab and Afghanistan. From there, in a new disguise as a deaf-mute Pathan, and accompanied by his communist contact, he trekked across the desert to Kabul. His plan to travel across the border directly into the Soviet Union had been discarded as impractical. His current plan was to contact the Soviet embassy in Kabul.

Kabul in the 1940s was basically a truck-stop village with embassies. Bose, still posing as a deaf-mute, stayed at truck-drivers' hotel for weeks, trying to contact the Russians. He had no luck, the Russians suspected that he was a British agent trying to infiltrate the Soviet Union. Next Bose contacted the Germans. They heard him out, and were intrigued by his ideas, but dragged their feet. Eventually it was the Italians who rescued him. The Italian diplomat in Kabul was fascinated by Bose's plans. He gave Bose an Italian passport and the name Orlando Mazzotta, and persuaded the Germans and the Soviets to help him. Finally, in March of 1941, Bose travelled to the Soviet border in a diplomatic car, took a train to Moscow, and then flew to Berlin.

Bose remained in Germany for the next two years. He offered the Germans a deal. If they helped him, he said, he could trigger a revolution in India. Having to deal with a revolutionary situation in India would distract British forces from the war against Germany. In the process, Britain would lose the war with Germany, and lose India simultaneously. This was the big picture. To bring all this about, Bose put forward several ideas. Some of these he accomplished; in others areas he was frustrated. Let's look at his political objectives first.

Bose wanted facilities for broadcasting radio messages into India. This the Germans readily provided, and he made regular speeches directed at the Indian public. In his broadcasts, Bose urged people to use the war as an opportunity to break free. Germany would win the war, and the British should not be allowed to hang on in India. The first broadcasts created a sensation in India, largely because Bose's disappearance had generated a lot of public interest. But it didn't go much further than that. This was because in spite of Bose's presence in Berlin, to most Indians the war with Germany was still far away, and people couldn't really visualise the German army sweeping through the Caucasus to liberate India. Also, by this time, Gandhi and the Congress had finally launched the Quit India movement, and a violent revolutionary situation already existed in India.

Bose's other major accomplishment in Germany was organising the Indian Legion. In the course of the fighting in north Africa, the Germans had taken thousands of Indian PoWs. Bose went to the PoW camps, and asked the Indian soldiers to join him to fight against the British. This idea was not entirely new. An expatriate Indian named Mohammed Iqbal Shedai had already made a start organising Indian PoWs captured by the Italians. For a while, Bose and Shedai ran parallel efforts with the PoWs. Then the Indian soldiers in Shedai's camp mutinied, This discredited Shedai, and left Bose as the only Indian organising an army to fight on the side of the Axis.

Ultimately, the Indian Legion that Bose organised in Germany numbered about 3000 soldiers. It was not easy putting this force together. Initially, when Bose visited the PoW camps to talk to the soldiers, he got a hostile reception. The British Indian Army may have been an army without a nationalist ideology, but it would be a mistake to think of it as a purely mercenary force. The colonial army had its own ideology, which was a combination of loyalty to the British throne, loyalty to the commanding officer, loyalty to the regiment, and a tradition of service in which the same family or same village sent many generations of soldiers into the Army.

But Bose persisted. He had the men separated from their officers, and talked to them one on one. Eventually, he got through. He promised them proper treatment from the Germans, appropriate rank, pay and benefits, and he promised them victory. The British, he told them, were certain to lose the war; they were like a dead snake that people continue to fear. If only they shook off this fear, Bose said, victory and freedom would be theirs.

Bose had planned that when the German swing through the southern USSR and the Middle East reached India, the Indian Legion would spearhead the attack on India. He anticipated that this would have two results. One was that when the soldiers of the colonial Indian Army faced the Indian Legion, they would refuse to continue to fight for the British and desert *en masse* to Bose's side. The other was that an invasion of India by Indian Legion would galvanise the Indian population into rising up against the British, and make Bose's task easier.

As things turned out, however, the Indian Legion came to a rather sad end. First, the Russians stopped the German advance at the battle of Stalingrad. This, combined with the defeat at El Alamein, meant that the Germans would be unlikely to get anywhere near India. Second, after Bose left Germany in 1943, the Legion was left without an effective leader to look Out for them. They were absorbed into the German army and deployed in France. Now they knew they weren't going to be fighting for India's freedom, and their morale and discipline disintegrated. Many deserted, some joined the French resistance, and the rest disappeared in the chaos of the German retreat.

Bose's biggest frustration in Germany had to do with diplomatic recognition. He wanted Germany to officially recognise India as independent, and him as the leader of a government in exile. This the Germans refused to give him. The reasons lay partly in apathy, partly in the Master Race mentality, and partly in the peculiarities of Hitler's vision of the post-war world.

Hitler was not entirely comfortable with the idea of helping Indians — whom he saw as racially inferior — to defeat the British. The British were Aryans, after all. In his own way, Hitler admired the English, and through much of the war he continued to hope that he could come to some kind of an understanding with Britain: essentially, that Germany would get a free hand in Europe, and England would get to keep most of its empire. He was perfectly willing to use Bose to make trouble for the British, but he had no long-term interest in India's future, one way or another. Bose knew this, of course. He wanted to use the Germans for his own purposes. But eventually, as things turned out, neither was able to do very much for the other side.

But by the middle of 1942, Bose was already looking beyond Germany, to Japan. The string of Japanese victories after Pearl Harbour had achieved two things. One was that Singapore, which was a major British military stronghold, had fallen to the Japanese. This placed tens of thousands of Indian soldiers in Japanese hands. What Bose had tried to do with the Indian Legion in Germany, he could try in South East Asia on a much larger scale. The other thing that encouraged Bose was the fact that Japanese forces had come all the way to the Indian border with Burma. In other words, if he could organise an army in Japanese-occupied territory, and attack on India would be a relatively practical idea.

So, in February of 1943, the Germans did Bose one last favour: they helped him get to Japan. He travelled in a German submarine to the coast of Mozambique, where he transferred to a Japanese submarine. This submarine took him to South East Asia.

The former British colonies of South East Asia — Burma, Malaya, and Singapore - had large Indian populations, and Bose was welcomed as a conquering hero. In a sense, they had been waiting for him; in spite of all efforts to keep his plans secret, rumours had been circulating that he would come. The Japanese welcomed him also, and were far more enthusiastic about working with him than the Germans had been.

I'll give you an example of the difference in attitude: when Bose was on the German sub, he ate bread that tasted like it had been dipped in diesel. On the Japanese sub, the crew had brought along Indian spices especially for him, and cooked him Indian curries until he protested about the frequent meals. After he reached Asia, Bose travelled widely in the Japanese-help territories: to Burma, Malaya, Singapore, the Philippines, Vietnam, occupied China, and of course Japan. Unlike his uneasy relationship with Hitler, he quickly developed an excellent relationship with Tojo.

The Japanese gave Bose two things which he had wanted very badly: diplomatic recognition as the premier of free India, and a real army. Let's talk about his political status first. He didn't have a territory, but he had a people: the Indian population of South East Asia was placed under his jurisdiction. Bose got all the privileges and trappings of a head of state: the motorcade, the official aircraft, the honour guards, the works, He enjoyed it. In part, this was sheer megalomania: his old love of playing the great leader was resurfacing with a vengeance. In part, however, Bose recognised that it was necessary for him to play this role if was to deal effectively with the Japanese. He did not have any illusions about how the Japanese treated subject peoples. He knew that if he, and the Indians of South East Asia, were to be taken seriously as allies, he had to insist upon his own status as an important political leader.

Bose did in fact run a real government in South East Asia. We are referring not to his status as leader of the government-in-exile of India, but to his status as leader of the local Indians. The regime Bose put together in Singapore, with the help of people who came forward to work with him, had the power to make and enforce laws, to collect taxes, and to recruit soldiers for the army. This people who paid the taxes and obeyed the laws did so willingly at first. Towards the end of the war, this cooperation became strained. As the Japanese collapsed and Tokyo's funding for Bose's army dried up, Bose pressed the local Indians for higher war taxes, and punished people who tried to hold back. This cost him some of his local popularity.

The army, to some extent, already existed when Bose arrived in Asia. After the fall of Singapore, an Indian officer named Mohan Singh had created the Indian National Army, or the INA as it came to be known, from Indian PoWs. This force was much larger than the Indian Legion in Germany. As such, it was a viable military and political resource. Mohan Singh himself had rather an unhappy career with the INA. Soldiers had joined the INA on the understanding that they would fight only on the Indian front. When the Japanese tried to send the INA to fight in other parts of South East Asia, several units mutinied. These units were disbanded, and Mohan Singh ended up in a Japanese prison.

This was, in a way, a parallel of what had happened in Europe with Shedai's army. When Bose came to Asia, he quickly assumed command of what was left of Mohan Singh's old INA. At this time, this force had only 13,000 soldiers. But Bose had big plans. He wanted to expand the INA in two phases, first to 50,000 soldiers, and then to a force of 3 million. The men would come from the colonial Indian Army as well as from the South East Asian Indian community.

The Japanese were shocked at such an ambitious plan, and told Bose that they would be able to arm a much smaller force, of about 30,000. Eventually, the INA reached a peak strength of around 50,000. It was an interesting social experiment in more ways than one. The colonial Indian Army had organised its units around ethnicity and religion, so that the British could play off one group of Indians against another if necessary. In contrast, the INA had fully integrated units. It also had a regiment of female troops: this was the Rani of Jhansi Brigade, named after the Queen who had died fighting the British in the Rebellion of 1857.

For Bose, the big numbers were necessary for their political effect. It didn't matter if most of the 3 million weren't equipped with adequate weapons. He saw the INA as a psychological force as well as a military asset. He knew that if people in India became aware that a nationalist army of 3 million was waiting just across the border, ready to invade, it would have a tremendous effect on the way Indians related to the British. It would inspire pride and confidence, it would take away the fear of British power, and it would make it impossible for the British to maintain control.

In fact, Bose's whole strategy for using the INA depended upon this psychological factor. He wanted the force to spearhead a Japanese invasion, expecting that this would totally demoralise and dissolve the colonial Indian army, drawing its soldiers into the INA. He expected also that the general public would respond with overwhelming support.

It turned out that he was half right. The INA lost the war, but won the peace. In the summer of 1944, the Japanese were finally ready to begin their invasion of India. They attacked from Burma in a two-pronged approach, hoping to capture the town of Imphal. This would then become the base for the rest of the invasion. But, at this critical point in Bose's plan, everything that could go wrong went wrong, The monsoon came early, and the Japanese assault became bogged down in the rain and the mud.

Also, by this point, the war in the Pacific was going very badly for the Japanese. Therefore, the Japanese had allocated most of their air power to the Pacific theatre, leaving their forces in the Burma-India theatre without any air cover. This gave the British a crucial advantage.

Then there were other factors. Food rations became exhausted. Allied air strikes cut the supply lines. Japanese and INA units found themselves eating grass and jungle flowers to stay alive. Japanese commanders on the ground made some serious tactical errors. Normally, when things are going well, a few mistakes don't have to be fatal. But by 1944 the Japanese had overreached their capabilities. The attack on Imphal failed, and the counterattack was devastatingly effective.

The INA became caught up in this disaster, and never recovered. The INA's coordination with Japanese units was poor to begin with. Once things began to go badly for the Japanese, INA units became stranded. Some units fought well and there were plenty of individual heroics to go around, but it made no difference to the overall failure.

The biggest failure was the INA's inability to break up the morale of the colonial Indian Army, which did most of the fighting at Imphal, and which played a major role in the Allied counterattack. Bose had expected that when the INA met the British Indian Army, colonial troops would immediately desert to the nationalist side. This did not happen. Bose had seriously underestimated the ideological strength of the colonial military. In fact, what often happened was the reverse. Starving and out of ammunition in the jungle, shocked by the failure of the Japanese offensive, many INA troops were eager to return to their old units and their old comrades in the colonial army. There were over 700 desertions, and eventually Bose had to give orders that deserters would be shot on suspicion.

After the Imphal defeat, the Japanese retreated steadily through Burma and into Malaya, pursued by British and colonial Indian troops. The INA retreated with them. This retreat, ironically, brought Out Bose's best quaiities as a leader. On the long trek from Burma to Bangkok, followed closely by British tanks and under frequent attack from the air, he marched for days on end, refusing the offer of a car while his men had to walk. Throughout the march, he made sure that INA troops had proper food and medical care. In the chaos of the retreat, Bose was their best protection, and everybody knew it. Without him, the Japanese would have been only too eager to abandon the INA.

Bose returned to Singapore and tried for a while to rebuild the INA. This was the period when he demanded ten per cent of the value of peoples assets to pay for military expenses, and made himself unpopular with the wealthier Indians in Malaya. But for Japan, the war was almost over. After the nuclear bombing of Hiroshima and Nagasaki, there was nothing left for Bose in working with Tokyo.

He now made a political gamble. The Soviets had been an ally of the British during the war, and an enemy of his allies, the Germans and the Japanese. But Bose correctly foresaw that the Soviet alliance with the west would not last. He decided to travel to Manchuria, which had just been overrun by the USSR. He planned to continue his fight against the British, but from Russia this time.

On 16th August, a day after the Japanese surrendered, Bose boarded a Japanese bomber in Saigon, on his way to Darien, in China. On the 18th of August, after a refuelling stop in Taipei, the bomber crashed. Bose was still alive, but badly burned. He died in a Japanese military hospital in Taipei, soon afterwards.

The story didn't end there, During the war, the British had carefully suppressed all news about the INA. This news now finally broke in India. Bose immediately became a hero of mythical proportions. People refused to believe he was dead; in fact, people refused to believe it for decades.

Also, Bose's predictions about the psychological value of his army were finally vindicated. The British played into his hands by making a series of miscalculations about how to deal with 25,000 captured INA soldiers. Misreading the public mood, the British decided to stage a series of highly publicised trials of INA officers in New Delhi. Incredibly, they believed that since the INA had taken up arms against Indians in the colonial army, the Indian public would want them to be severely punished.

Exactly the opposite happened. When three INA officers — Shah Nawaz Khan, G. S. Dhillon and Prem Kumar Sahgal — were put on trial for treason and murder in the Red Fort, the public quickly grasped the symbolism of the affair. The three officers included a Hindu, a Muslim and a Sikh. In other words, all three of India's major religious communities were seen as being on trial for having come together to fight for their country. The fact that the trials were being held at the Red Fort, where the last independent Indian regime had been based, was seen as an added insult.

Even before the trials began, celebrations honouring the INA were held all over India. When the trials did begin, anti-British crowds besieged the Red Fort, and more than a hundred people were killed or injured by police firing. In Calcutta, Hindus and Muslims, flying the flags of the Congress as well as the Muslim League, attacked British and American military bases. Scores of military vehicles were damaged or destroyed. Over 200 military personnel were injured, and 32 Indians were killed. The violence soon spread across much of northern India, all the way to Bombay and Karachi.

Congress leaders like Gandhi and Nehru, who had been uncomfortable with Bose while he was alive, now eagerly jumped on the INA bandwagon. Nehru put on his old lawyer's robes and participated in the defence of the officers on trial. Gandhi made speeches praising Bose.

Confronted by this public hostility, the British found themselves unable to punish the INA prisoners as severely as they would have liked. Most got commuted sentences, or short prison terms. Nevertheless, the British persisted with the trials, and the violence continued to grow. Early in 1946, martial law had to be declared in Calcutta.

At around the same time, Indian troops in the colonial navy and air force mutinied, citing sympathy for the INA as well as unhappiness about their conditions of service. Within days, 78 warships had pulled down the Union Jack. Fierce battles erupted in the streets of Karachi and Bombay, in which tanks and machine-guns were used. In Bombay, the mutineers were supported by the working class. 600,000 textile workers went on strike, and joined the sailors in street battles against British forces.

The rebels eventually failed, in part because they didn't have the firepower that the British were able to call in, and in part because the Congress panicked and told them to stop fighting. The mutineers had looked to the Congress and the Muslim League to lead them. By the spring of 1946, however, the Congress and the League were too deeply implicated in the government of the country to see any good in this kind of unrest. Leaders like Nehru and Jinnah knew that independence was now at the most only a couple of years away. As such, they did not want to encourage something as messy, as volatile and as dangerous as an armed rebellion. They had no experience and no stomach for leading this kind of movement, and they quietly supported the British efforts to crush the rebels.

But Bose's predictions about what would happen when the INA entered India had, to a considerable degree, come true, He had predicted a public uprising and sympathy from colonial troops, and now he was proved right. This is what I meant when I said that the INA lost the war but won the peace. But if Bose was right, where did he go wrong?

Well, as we have argued, that Bose misread the nature of the colonial army. On the battlefield, when everything was at stake, the colonial army retained its loyalties. It was only after the war that sections of it mutinied.

It can also be argued that Bose misread the political situation in India in the 1940s. Being away in Germany and South East Asia had isolated him from the political realities of wartime India, and he had missed some crucial changes in the way the wind was blowing. By 1942, the British were willing to discuss independence for India when the war ended. By 1945, there was no doubt that negotiations would soon begin. Yet Bose continued to fight a military battle, instead of rejoining the political process.

Was this unnecessary, and a mistake? Not if you were in Bose's shoes. He had taken up arms against the British, and his relations with the Congress had collapsed. He had reason to believe that if he returned to India while it was controlled by the British or the Congress, he would be treated as a war criminal.

Also, although India was clearly on its way to independence by the mid-40s, this was not the kind of independence that Bose had wanted. For Bose, the revolution at home was as important as throwing out the British, and for this he needed to be completely in charge. He did not believe that the replacement of British rule by a conservative parliamentary democracy would not bring about fundamental changes in the structure of Indian society.

This brings us some of the most basic questions about Bose, the nationalist and the politician. What are we to make of the fact that he wanted to invite the Germans and the Japanese to invade India? And how do we reconcile his heroic status with the fact that he aligned himself with Nazi Germany, and that he openly advocated dictatorship as the best form of government for India?

Perhaps the biggest weakness in Bose's plan was his belief that even after bringing the Japanese into India, he could maintain effective control of the country. At a diplomatic level, he had grounds for believing he could pull this off. He refused to take India into the Japanese Co-Prosperity Sphere, which was the euphemism the Japanese used for their new empire in Asia, The Japanese accepted Bose's decision on this. Still, if the invasion of India had succeeded, it is difficult to see how he could have remained fully independent of Japanese control.

Bose felt that since the people of India would be with him, he would be able to resist Japanese demands. He knew that India was a long way from Japan, and that the Japanese were already at the limits of their capabilities. He also pointed out that the American revolutionaries had accepted assistance from France, and this didn't make the US a French colony. He may have had a point. But this analogy has its limits. Given the fact the INA was completely dependent on Japan for arms and ammunition, and that it would take time to develop an industrial infrastructure in India, Japan would probably have had a lot of leverage.

There is no getting away from the fact that Bose deliberately ignored the moral evil that Nazi Germany represented. He had lived in Germany for much of the 1930s and the early-40s. He must have known something of what was going on. He had the courage to speak out against some of the racist aspects of the Nazi ideology, and even speak his mind to Hitler himself. But he was not sufficiently disturbed by Nazism to reject Hitler's help.

Similarly, his alliance with Japan ignored the atrocities that the Japanese had perpetrated against people in the countries they had occupied.

Unlike Gandhi and Nehru, Bose believed that the end justified the means. He wanted freedom for India, and to some extent, he didn't care who he had to approach for assistance. But this explanation is too kind to Bose. At some basic level, Bose had an ideological affinity for fascism, and he was a little too comfortable with using the state to crush dissent and ideological diversity.

Indians who refused to believe that Bose was dead, and who continued to believe for decades that he was alive somewhere in the Soviet Union, hoped he would just surface again some day like a messiah, and solve all of India's problems. Yet these people misunderstand Bose, and what he stood for. Had the INA and Bose succeeded on the battlefield, a free India would have been a totalitarian society.

Bose was passionate in his patriotism, and genuinely well-intentioned. He was genuine in his desire to help the disadvantaged segments of Indian society. But good intentions are not enough. Some of the greatest tyrants of the 20th century had good intentions: Lenin, Mao, Pol Pot. (You'll notice that these are all tyrants of the left. Tyrants of the right like Hitler, Franco, or the Shah of Iran, don't get credit for good intentions).

Bose didn't seem to realise that the methods you choose do matter in the final analysis. Totalitarian institutions inevitably corrupt even the best-intentioned people. Even if it hadn't corrupted Bose himself, even if he had remained a so-called benevolent dictator, there would have been no guarantees that his successor would have been benevolent. Ultimately, dying at the end of the war was the best thing Bose could have done for India.

There is much confusion and controversy surrounding the death of Bose. He is said to have died in the crash of his Japanese plane in (then Japanese-occupied) Taiwan on the way to Tokyo on 18th August 1945. Some of his followers refused to believe this and a few hopelessly hopefuls still think that Bose is alive today, even if though he would be massively over 100 years old now.

In 1999 the Indian government appointed a one-man Commission of enquiry under Mr. Justice Manoj Mukherjee to look into the controversy surrounding the disappearance of Subhash Chandra Bose. Mr. Mukherjee was a retired judge of the Supreme Court of India and reported his incomplete findings in 2005 as follows:

- Subhash Chandra Bose is dead.
- He did not die in a plane crash.
- The ashes in the Japanese temple are not those of Bose.
- In the absence of any solid evidence no positive answer can be given.
- Bose must be assumed to be dead.
- Further investigation into the matter is recommended.

Mukherjee's report was tabled in the Parliament of India on May 17, 2006. The Government of India did not agree with Mukherjee's findings and rejected his report.

Manoj Mukherjee's task was doomed from the start. He received little cooperation and was especially stonewalled by the crucial home ministry. In the end he had to submit his unfinished work to the then home minister Shivraj Patil. Mukherjee expressed his protest against the way he had been treated by sending in his the report through his secretary rather than submit it in person.

The Greatest Revolutionary and Socialist Leader

Since the very beginning of his political life, Netaji Subhash Chandra Bose as the President of Bharat Navjawan Sabha, All India Trade Union Congress, Indian National Congress, the All India Forward Bloc and the Head of the Provisional Azad Hind Government had always advocated uncompromising struggle against the British Imperialism and had clearly preached that the salvation of India, as of the world depended on full blooded Socialism Scientific Socialism, but he also clearly held that India would evolve her own methods to achieve Socialism. Due to his taking help from Germany, Italy and Japan to lead the Indian National Army to liberate India from the clutches of British Imperialism during the Second World War, some interested parties and individuals held wrong notions and created impression that Netaji was not a full-fledged socialist but a national socialist.

Though Lenin during the First World War took all help from Germany which was at war with UK and Russia, to reach St. Petersburg (now Leningrad) safely to conduct the Great October Revolution, no body doubted his sincerity and called him as agent of Germany.

Now it is a well known fact that just after the All India Anti-compromise Conference at Rangrah (Bihar) in March 1940 in which it was decided to start a national struggle against British Imperialism, Netaji consulted some of us on the question of seeking active help from USSR and late Lala Shankarlal the then President of Delhi Pradesh Congress Committee and the then General Secretary of the All India Forward Bloc was sent to Japan on a false Passport to finalise this agreement with the Soviet Ambassador in Japan. In the meanwhile, Netaji was arrested in Calcutta in connection with the removal of the Holl-well Movement.

Lala Shankarlal came back to Calcutta from Japan incognito after finalising the agreement with the Soviet Ambassador in Japan and through Late Mr. Sarat Chandra Bose the elder brother of Netaji, the message of agreement was communicated to Netaji in Calcutta jail.

To come out from the jail and finalise plans to go to USSR via Kabul. Netaji started a fast into death. He was released and how he escaped from India to Kabul via Peshawar and again from Kabul to Moscow and Berlin. It is now well known. Due to non-aggression pact with UK, Stalin and Molotov advised Netaji to take help from Germany and Italy. And Netaji did take help from Germany, Italy and Japan because; these three countries were also fighting UK in Second World War.

The writer had to give out this background and reasons as why Netaji had to go to Berlin and Rome because later on the Soviet Press and the Communist Party of India had depicted Netaji as fascist and used vulgar and abusive terms against him. Even after the defeat of the INA in the battlefield, Netaji decided to go USSR via Manchuria to continue the struggle against British Imperialism. While going to Manchuria, the fateful an accident took in which he died.

It may be remembered here that after the formation of the Azad Hind Government on the 21st of October, 1943, Netaji and his Provisional Azad Hind Government declared war against USA and UK but not against USSR and China though they were the allies of UK in the Second World War. This foreign policy of Azad Hind Government proves that Netaji was not against any socialist country.

Presiding over the Third Indian Political Conference held in London on June 10. 1933, Netaji said; "During the nineteenth Century, Germany made the most remarkable gift through Marxian philosophy and during twentieth Century Russia had enriched the culture and civilization of the world through her achievement in proletarian revolution and proletarian culture. The next remarkable contribution to the culture and the civilization of the world. India would be called upon to make." Further he said "we know for example that in Soviet Russia, a new scheme of national (or political) economy has been evolved in keeping with facts and conditions of the land. The same thing will happen to India. In solving our economic problems, Pigeon and Marshall will not be of much help."

As the Editor of "the Forward Bloc" the organ of the All India Forward Bloc, writing on the role of the Forward Bloc said Netaji "that the Forward Bloc would prepare the ground to grow into a Marxist Party". This declaration of Netaji as the President of the All India Forward Bloc in the official organ of the Party proves that he was a genuine scientific Socialist and was neither a national socialist nor a Fabian Socialist.

On the 15th of March, 1935, writing a letter to the United Press of India from Vienna, Netaji said "further if I am not mistaken, the Congress Socialist Party seems to be under the influence of Fabian Socialism which was the fashion in England 50 years ago".

The writing in his famous book 'The Indian Struggle' about the post-independence struggle period Netaji said "The Party that is going to fight for freedom is the party that is entitled to draw up the Constitution of India and rule over the country. If we are to have a socialist economy, socialism cannot be established by the Western Democracy. Socialist reconstruction can be done only by Dictatorship but that Dictatorship should not be of individuals or of the cliques but of general masses" Citing the constituent Assembly of Kerensky's government, Netaji said that "if Lenin would have joined it, the Bolshevik Government of Lenin would have never come into existence".

Presiding over the fifty first session of the Indian National Congress on Feb. 9, 1938 at Haripura (Gujarat) Netaji said "I am afraid there is lack of clarity in the minds of many congressman as to the Congress in the history of the national struggle. I know that there are friends who think that after freedom is own the Congress Party, having achieved its objectives should wither away. Such a conception is entirely erroneous. The Party that wins freedom should be also the party that will put into effect the entire programme of post-war reconstructions. Only those who have won can handle it properly.

If it were to forcibly liquidate itself, chaos would follow. We have no doubt in our mind that our chief national problems relating to the eradication of poverty. Illiteracy and disease and to the scientific production and distribution can be effectively tackled along socialistic lines. The very first things which our future national government will have to do would be to set up a Planning Commission for drawing up a comprehensive plan for construction. Last but not the least, the State, on the advice of Planning Commission, will have to adopt a comprehensive scheme for gradually socialising our entire agriculture and industrial system in the sphere of both production and distribution. Extra capital will have to be procured for this whether through internal or external loans or through inflations".

Just after the Haripura Congress Session, Netaji as President of the All India Congress Committee set up a Planning Commission and appointed Pandit Jawaharlal Nehru as the President, Shri V. V. Giri (the present President of the Indian Republic) as Convenor and Shri H. V. Kamath as the Secretary of the Planning Committee.

Presiding over the All India Forward Bloc Conference at Nagpur in June. 1940 he declared "the All India Forward Bloc as a full-fledged socialist Party within the Indian National Congress and he gave a clarion call to All power to the Indian people" and observed "We shall also bear in mind that the Forward Bloc will have a role to play in the post-struggle phase of our history. It will have to build up a new India and happy India on the basis of eternal principles of liberty, democracy and socialism"

These writings and observations of Netaji Subhash Chandra Bose given here clearly prove that Netaji was not only the greatest revolutionary leader of India but he was also a genuine scientific socialist leader of the country.

Netaji and INA

Netaji is a great and illustrious son of India whose memory has an abiding place in the mind of every Indian. It was Netaji and his Indian National Army who paved the way to India's freedom and struck the last nail in the coffin of British Imperialism.

The more we look to that great son of Bharat for guidance the more pure, patriotic and energetic we shall grow in the service of the motherland.

The Goddess of Independence needs blood at its alter. Therefore, Netaji said "GIVE ME BLOOD I WILL GET YOU FREEDOM" Jallianwala martyrs were the first to give their contribution. Blood donations made by Revolutionaries like Bhagat Singh, B. K. Dutt, Udham Singh and many others will also remain immortal in the annals of India's freedom struggle. Netaji's Indian National Army gave the *puran ahuti.*

Those who say that India got Independence without shedding a drop of blood really lessen the importance of those groups the Jallianwala Bagh innocent victims, the Revolutionaries and the heroes of the INA

The Last Straw that Broke the Back of the British Empire

It is difficult to realise in these days of power politics and of the merry game of plucking the golden spoils of office by fair and foul means that around six decades ago we were an enslaved people. The British were our masters completely and entirely. Their might had the sway over land and on sea all the world over. So powerful was the Royal Navy that it was said. "Britannia rules the waves" and she did. One of the pet questions in Geography used to show and prove why the Sun never set on the British Empire. In schools children were made to admire the British ways and sing songs of their glory. We used to pray for a happy, glorious and victorious life of the British Sovereign "Long to reign over us." And yet the tallest amongst us were behind bars of the British Jails. The British Government was entrenched behind the Army, the Police and the Administrative Services. Surprisingly there was no dearth of people who really recognised the British Raj as a dispensation of the Providence. Others took it with that resignation which is one of our national characteristics. Late in the nineteenth century it required people as great as Swami Vivekananda and the like to awaken our national conscience and restore our spirit.

The story of the Indian Freedom Fight is indeed fascinating. It covers more than a century of continuous struggle unparallel in heroism and self-sacrifice as well as in forms of weapons, strategy, tactics and areas. It was at times spiritual, at times terroristic, at times peaceful, at times violent, at times non-violent, at times within the country or in a part of it, yet at times without and at times in many forms, at a time and all over the subcontinent as well as in other continents. The last straw however to break the British back was in the form of the Indian National Army of Netaji Subhash Chandra Bose. Carrying the Tricolour Flag with the emblem of the Leaping Tiger on it and with the slogan, "Chalo Delhi" (on to Delhi) on the lips, from the battlefields of Asia and of Europe, it burst out on the Indian scene like an avalanche overwhelming all and everyone causing a revolutionary and emotional upheaval turning and churning the very depths of the national soul, sparing not even the Indian Armed Forces of the British the very means of keeping India enslaved. They recovered their national conscience. The soul of India became free. The people could no longer tolerate the foreign Rule. The climax came with the Naval uprising in Bombay. The days of Military and Police Raj were over. It could hold no more.

The story of the INA is a legend in itself. Its historical evidence shows that never, never in the long history of man and war did a people in exile raise an army so big in order to liberate their country from a foreign rule.

In this historic struggle, the part played by the Indians overseas can never be appreciated enough. It was entirely due to these Indians that the Provisional Government of Free India could attain the status of a duly organised, recognised and a belligerent

Government enjoying the allegiance of two million people. These Indians were the State with Indian Independence League as the Executive of that State and the INA as its Army of Liberation.

The Provisional Government of Free India was proclaimed on 21st October 1943 having all the requisites of a Government. It had a Cabinet headed by Netaji as the Head of the State, The Prime Minister and the Minister for War and Foreign Affairs. Shri Rash Behari Bose-the very incarnation of service and sacrifice-having vacated the Presidentship of the Indian Independence League and all its offices to make room for the younger Leader Netaji Subhash to come and to take over so as to lead according to his genius stepped aside.

Netaji requested him to be the Supreme Advisor. The Senior Leader accepted the post with grace which has been conspicuously absent during the past-Independence era. His tall inspiring personality was full of courage, spirit of sacrifice, wit, humour and the never failing sense of duty. This great man in spite of his ill health accepted to do the most difficult job, the Governorship of Andamans and Nicobar Islands which having been annexed to the Provisional Government had been renamed "Shaheed" and "Sawaraj" respectively. Though ill health and non-cooperation by the Japanese Forces of Occupation made his job more and more difficult, yet he stood it out.

Again he had to act as the G.O.C. Burma Command after Netaji's departure from Rangoon. With the INA Contingent about 6,000 strong he manned the Burmese Capital in the absence of any other Police force or troops during the period between the departure of the Japanese and the arrival of the British. And he was successful in maintaining law and order to the extent that there was not a single case of decoity or of loot during that period 24th April to 4th May 1945. Throughout the difficult stages of the INA, whether it was its formation or the crisis in it, or the move to the battlefields or the withdrawal, this old man held the fort like a Knight from the medieval ages. He was affectionately called "Uncle" by all those who were fortunate enough to approach him. In return the old man would call us all "Uncle" irrespective of the age. While in captivity in the Red Fort he was suffering very badly from an ulcer in the stomach, yet he seldom let us know the agony he was passing through.

Logistics of the INA in action are awe-inspiring. It had to operate under ever-increasing difficulties and against fearful odds. Wireless Communication was a rare luxury. We normally had to use runners or at times a dispatch rider on a motorcycle to carry messages to and fro. Often our only means of transport was the good old bullock cart. It was more difficult to find a cover from fire for the oxen than for the men. When they got killed or ran away because of the battle noise, our backs carried the pack and that would be only belongings or rations in the world. Once we hired a cart with a stubborn pair of bullocks. They were too difficult to be controlled. General Shah Nawaz Khan personally tried to drive the cart. The pair ran away with the cart and the Divisional Commander (Maj. General Shah Nâwaz Khan) on it. The owner of the cart had jumped off but the Commander would not give in. The situation became worse as an enemy aircraft appeared overhead. In spite of his own predicament Shah Nawaz shouted to us to take cover while he was having the dangerous ride up and down a dry riverbank. It was after a good half an hour that we could retrieve him and that too luckily intact. The athlete in him saved us our Commander.

Undoubtedly, Netaji's personality was greatest strength which could sustain his fellow-men in spite of their deficiencies in numbers, weapons and resources. On August 1944 after Imphal had been lost to INA. As he was reviewing the war situation, somebody asked him that as war appeared to have been lost and to their allies and there was a little hope of taking over the offensive again, what exactly was left to fight or what were they fighting for. Netaji's reply was quick, "To pay the price of India's liberty". He further elaborated his point and everybody surprised at his frankness and clarity of vision. Little has happened ever since, on the political stages of India, Asia and Europe, which he could not foresee and foretell. He had a very good memory, seven months later in a letter from Rangoon dated 21st March 1945 he repeated the same concept thus:

> "Whatever happens to us individually in the course of this heroic struggle, there is no power on earth that can keep India enslaved any longer. Whether we live and work or whether we die fighting, we must, under

> all circumstances have complete confidence that the cause for which we are striving is bound to triumph. It is the finger of God that is pointing the way towards India's freedom. We have only to do our duty and to pay the price of India's liberty. Our hearts are with you and with all who are with you in the present struggle which is paving the way to our national salvation. Please convey my warmest greetings to all the officers and men under you and accept same yourself. — *JAI-HIND. Subhash Chandra Bose."*

The INA apart from serving India as it did, has undoubtedly been also the forerunner of a Freedom Movement all over the Asian and African countries. Shri Bhula Bhai Desai had appropriately said during the opening of his Defence Address in the First INA Trial in the Red Fort of Delhi that, "What is on trial before the court now is the right to wage war with immunity on part of a subject race for their liberation." Is it not so that the age of a liberation of subject races started thence onward, destroying all forms of Empires and Imperialism!

It is indeed unfortunate that in spite of fighting for a free and united India, the powers to be cut up our divine Motherland into pieces. But having accepted the fact, today it behaves us that in the name of God, in the name of Netaji Subhash, in the name of our Dead Heroes and in the name of bygone and future Generations, we try our best to keep our people and country united. Netaji used to recite to himself a quatrain of Kipling, replacing in it India for England. This noble exhortation while an aspiration of Netaji's soul is the vital need of India today.

Battle of Imphal and Adherence to Fundamentals by Netaji

History bears indelible imprints of acts of faith and trust that remain ever bright, fruitful and dynamic; the climate wherein mistrust and lack of conviction infiltrates and pollutes remains dim and unproductive. The chapters that are created under this unhealthy climate dim insignificant in the history of march of people whereas those that are born of faith in Man and God remain forever phenomental in history. So this act of faith once more helped Netaji Subhash Chandra Bose in raising his moral and political stature in not submitting to Japanese pressure and arrogance vis-a-vis the setting up of an Indo-Japanese War Cooperation Council to function in liberated areas and in deciding fundamentals to India's favour.

The call of Netaji for total mobilisation in East and South East Asia found a tremendous echo into the minds of the three million Indians because they found in him a pillar of Indian manhood, courage and conviction and an image of honesty and sacrifice. Now, when the Liberation Forces were to establish and consolidate bases in Liberated Areas, the only compelling thought that naturally Netaji's mind was that such bases must bear an unblemished record of healthy nationalism, robust patriotism, modest yet determined conduct and last but not the least an uncompromising mood for total sacrifice of men and women of India through armed revolution, reflecting the real image of the Provisional Government of Azad Hind.

It was a tremendous trial of Netaji's patriotic fervour, statesmanship, intimate sense of history on India's struggles for Freedom, Himalayan patience, keen strategic sense and logical move, and unassailable tact in his pragmatic approach to all problems that were not only delicate in nature but also extremely difficult to solve. Anything derogatory to the dignity, integrity and sovereignty. Of Free India was against the very being of Netaji. But, war is war. To win the war becomes the war aim and everything however noble, is of secondary value. Philosophy and sentiments do not bother those who handle military machine especially at a time when both sides strong and powerful, stand, face to face to onslaught each other. Military expediency then reigns supreme to decide the clear and compelling purpose of military strategist.

The situation becomes more intricate when a dependent country throws herself in military alliance with the powerful enemy of her enemy lodged deeply and strongly in its soil, for the political emancipation of her people. And most intricate the political strategy becomes when the country to be liberated is a great country with a great past having to her credit a glorious history in struggles for freedom in her own way within and that too under the leadership of the greatest man of the age, that is, India.

It is therefore, not the consideration of military triumph alone that was the moot point in discussion with the Japanese Military Command but as every detail involved in total Mobilisation of men, money and materials was scrupulously attended to buy Netaji due to his innate faith in Indians by way of exhorting his compatriots to shoulder the sacred task.

Netaji was equally emphatic and keen on the question of independence and integrity in role INA's Advance Force and in governance of Liberated Areas. All discussions therefore with the Japanese civil or military, were held in that context. Temporary military gains were not necessarily all important values to Netaji until and unless Netaji was convinced that such gains would appear commensurate with the ideals of Independence Movement in India itself. How it will act and react psychologically in the minds of the Indian people in general and to what extent such gains would have impact on morals on the political stream of thoughts in minds of men and women in motherland in general was Netaji's concern. What was the image of India, then.

Following the 'Quit India' resolution led by Mahatma Gandhi India entered the final phase of her struggle. Its impact on the use of India's manpower and resources by Britain was not so impressive and effective, viewed from practical point of view in so far as Britain's war machine in India was concerned. But it was symbolic of India's stand.

All national leaders were incarcerated and hundreds of thousands were within prison walls. Revolutionaries were more active and inflicted great damage on enemy's war efforts. But all in all, cumulative effect of national struggles could not call a halt to Britain's stream-roller in exploiting India's men, money and materials, for her imperialistic end. Britain could also succeed in increasing a sense of hatred and horror against Japanese imperialism and Nazi fascism with all their brutalities and nakedness that appeared only before the mind's eye of intelligentsia and common people.

The Congress leaders did, no doubt, stand by Mahatmaji's call but in heart most of them did not like the total collapse of Britain. In fact, they do not think of India, independent of Britain. That the cruelties and hypocrisy of British imperialism far surpassed those inherent in fascism and Japanese imperialism were conveniently forgotten to meet Britain's war needs and to divert people's mind.

The Muslim League helped Britain. The Communist Party of India called the war as the people's war and extended all help and cooperation to Britain not only in her war efforts but also in her organised machination to crush the revolutionary upsurge inherent in the 'Quit India Resolution' and in the call for upsurge by the revolutionaries all over India. The Muslim League, Hindu Mahasabha and the Communist Party of India got all help and assistance in crushing the Inherence Movement.

The industrialists, businessmen and traders and job seekers found in war great opportunities to enrich themselves. Educated men and women were reconciled with lucrative jobs. Mahatma Gandhi's call for 'DO or Die' and the revolutionaries march to martyrdom were eloquently manifested by limited people only-a band of patriots-albeit significant but not overwhelming while compared with the total population and the cause involved. A sad contrast, indeed, when one witnessed the total response from the total people to the total mobilisation call by Netaji in East and South East Asia, for the emancipation of motherland.

The Bengal famine — a man-made famine that was created to serve Britain's imperialist's need, took a toll during the period of 1943-44 of four million lives. With all the revolutionary tradition and spiritual and moral values that Bengal was proud of, not a single shot was fired against the criminals-nor a drop of tear was shed outside Bengal in the rest part of India. People died in front of sweetmeat shops, restaurants and hotels but the common man moved in and out, quite unconcerned and unmoved, as if the 'Quit India Resolution' and the urge of revolutionaries concerned only the followers of the Mahatma and members of revolutionary parties. The people were not to blame-sandwiched as they were between two forces of indecision. The leaders and workers of the Congress took the 'Quit India Resolution', as symbolic and a moral injunction binding on them in India's patriotic stand vis-a-vis Britain's war efforts. In absence of a concerted programme for total struggle country wide for independence by striking the enemy — its roots and branches, the people's mind was at bay, bereft of a clear conscience. Again they lacked in that robust conviction that India's strength and power if generated and directed point blank against the only enemy could match in defeating Britain that was strong and powerful and deeply consolidated in our soil, it would equally match in defeating all machinations of Japan or for that matter any other power, if and where faced, once India was free. Indecision seized the mind of the people during the most crucial period when India was in peril. Her resurgent soul should have remained unconquered and asserted to restore her glory.

Netaji Subhash Chandra Bose proved his mettle as patriot, a statesman and diplomat, during the crucial days of India's destiny. The question of military operation in liberating the advance areas of Manipur State. Assam and Bengal, was most important from the viewpoint of the Azad Hind Government and the Japanese military authority.

The formation of an Indo-Japanese war cooperation council to conduct war operations on the soil of India was therefore considered a logical step. General Isoda. Chief of the Hikari Kikan. Proposed that a Japanese General be the chairman of the council. Netaji refused to consider the proposal. Japan continued on the insistence for a Japanese chairman of Netaji, equally refused to consider the proposal and insisted on an Indian chairman; in taking this stand he was as uncompromising as he was in his conviction to fight British imperialism. He would not compromise with anything that appeared to him as derogatory to the sovereignty of Free India. He would not concede to anything that would harm India's honour and self-respect of Indian patriots at home.

Any student of history will be amazed at the stand taken by Netaji and at his patriotic fervour. On one side, the powerful Japanese Army that declared war against the two mightiest powers in the world Britain and America and reduced their power to ashes. On other side only three divisions of INA combatant forces. On one side, Japan occupying three fourths of the total area of Asia controlling the destiny of cores of people, on another side the Azad Hind Government functioning-and that too on the territory occupied by Japan on the strength of only three million Indians, and that too scattered all over East and South East Asia.

On one side, Japan moved fifteen divisions from its Headquarters in Rangoon to Indo-Burma frontiers to march to India, on another side the Supreme command. INA deployed two divisions to face onslaughts of enemy and to liberate the northeastern part of India, at the first outset. Japan's involvement in operation was, therefore, gigantic and stupendous and her military strategy allowed no room for experiments. The main thrust against enemy's position on the soil of India, especially in the north eastern zone was to be given by Japan's mechanised army and air force till INA was prepared to meet the challenge. From the military point of view and in the context of Japan's strength and involvement she insisted on a Japanese chairman in the council.

But Netaji would not yield. Soon after his arrival from Germany he sounded the Japanese High command on most vital issues and got assurance from Japan of all-out unconditional aid towards India's prosecution of war against Britain and he did not give any promise of military, economic or political concession to Japan in lieu of all her aid. And it was made emphatically clear when General Hideki Tojo, the Prime Minister of Japan declared, "The imperial Japanese Army will fight shoulder to shoulder with the Indian National Army under the leadership of Netaji Subhash Chandra Bose, on Indian soil". It was unequivocally clear.

When he met marshal Terauchi, the supreme commander of Japanese forces inland, air and sea, in East and South East Asia, Netaji made it clear that the main burden of liberating India through armed forces devolved on Indians and the Indian National Army and that any liberation of India secured through Japanese sacrifices was to him worse than slavery. The joint communique was issued to the effect that the INA soldier must form a spearhead of the advance into India and the Japanese soldier will advance as and when asked by the Commander of the Advance Headquarters of INA. All Japanese commanders were informed accordingly. In his special order of the day issued soon after assuming the office of Supreme Commander of the Indian National Army on August 25, 1943, Netaji said that he deemed it to be against the national honour of India that the soldiers of INA should stay behind in battles of India's independence, while the Japanese advanced into Indian territory. The first drop of blood to be shed on the sacred soil of India would be that of a soldier of the INA.

Now when the declared policy of Japan not to interfere into the vital problems arising out of campaign on Indian soil was there Netaji did not budge an inch and insisted on an Indian chairman in the proposed Indo-Japanese War Cooperation Council. The Azad Hind Government, Netaji said. Declared war against Britain and America and the Indian National Army was fighting the battles of India on Indian soil, under the order of the Government and naturally an Indian general should be the chairman of the council and conduct the battles for India's liberation with Japan as an ally.

But General Isoda, chief of the Hikari Kikan (Liaison Department), Major General Yamamoto, Col. Kogawa and Col. Kitabe were adamant in insisting a Japanese chairman. It was only when Netaji threatened that he would then withdraw from the movement and inform the Tokyo High Command and Marshal Terauchi that these officers of the Hikari Kikan came down and withdrew their suggestion for a Japanese chairman for the council. Netaji however, exercised tremendous self-restraint during those crucial moments and now took Japanese withdrawal of proposal with good grace and humour. The Japanese generals could see the mettle of a man who stood unruffled as a pillar of India's manhood not because of the enormity of men, money and materials at his disposal which was out of proportion while compared with those to be deployed at the mere bidding of the Japanese Military Authority but because of his inner faith in the soul of India and in her people in general and in the mettle of INA forces in particular.

Now the problem of the basis of cooperation and action between the Indian National Army and the Japanese Army in the campaign had to be solved. It was a gigantic task involving hundreds, of thousands of armed man belonging to INA and to Japanese army to be deployed to take offensive along the whole Indo-Burma border. This was thoroughly discussed between the Supreme Command, INA and General Kawabe, the commander-in-chief of the Japanese army. It was decided that the operation would resume as soon as Netaji ordered them to advance. The following basic guidelines were decided upon:

- A common strategy in the operation plan will be chalked out by the Commanders of the INA and Japanese Army Headquarters at Rangoon.
- The INA and Japanese army are allies and will enjoy equal status in all respects.
- The Command of INA forces and their units will remain in hands of INA Officers.
- The smallest unit of INA forces will be a battalion under an INA officer. INA forces should not be split up in small groups. All INA's units will be composite units and will not be attached to any Japanese formations.
- To maintain equal status of INA and Japanese army saluting was to be observed on a reciprocal basis. Junior officers of either army saluting the senior officer of the other army and officer of equal rank of both armies to salute at the same time.
- INA forces will be governed by INA Military Law and Army Act and the Japanese Headquarters will not be within its bounds to interfere in any way with its discipline and regulation. Total Mobilisation of men, money and materials on Indian soil will be conducted by the Provisional Government of Azad Hind.
- Territories liberated in Indian soil must be handed over to the INA for administration under the overall command of Major General Zamani Kiani the Divisional commander who will hand over the charge of administration of liberated areas to Major General A. C. Chatterjee, Governor designate of Liberated Areas and Leader of Azad Hind Dal.
- Dumps of arms, ammunitions, oil, stores, equipments, machineries and all war materials seized by the Japanese army must be handed over to Provisional Government of Azad Hind.
- Rule behaviour, looting and rape will not be tolerated. The commander-in-chief of Japanese forces accepted and appreciated the order of Netaji Subhash Chandra Bose to INA soldiers to shoot at sight any Indian or Japanese

found in looting or raping on Indian soil. The commander-in-chief, Burma Army, General Kawabe assured to issue similar orders to the Japanese Army.

- The only flag that would be permitted to fly over liberated areas is the Indian Tricolour — the Indian National Flag.

In arriving at the solution of fundamentals Netaji had to work ceaselessly to get over the strong opposition from the Hikari Kikan-the Liaison Department of the Japanese High Command.

Without budging an inch from the principle he over ruled the opposition of the General of the Hikari Kikan and his staff and directly negotiated with Marshal Terauchi, Marshal Sugiyama and General Kawabe the commander-in-chief of the Japanese Forces in Burma. On the question of equal status of INA with Japanese army the initial Japanese viewpoint that the latter being the senior army should have higher status, was rejected by Netaji.

So also the Japanese initial proposal on the question of officers holding the same rank in INA and Japanese army, that the Indian officers should salute first to Japanese officer, was vehemently opposed by Netaji.

On the Japanese proposal that small units or groups of INA soldiers be attached to larger Japanese formations, was not approved by Netaji for the simple reason that, INA soldiers must remain under the command of INA officers only and also that INA's solidarity should not be allowed to be disintegrated. On the question of military law and Army governing all combatant forces in East and South East Asia, General Kawabe at first proposed that the INA should be subject to Japanese military law just as all other allied armies, namely the Manchurian army, the China army, the Burmese army and the Thai army were subjected to.

Netaji treated the proposal with contempt and eventually succeeded through negotiations with the Japanese High Command in asserting that all combatant forces of the Azad Hind Government would be subjected to INA military law and Army Act.

Netaji made it clear to the Japanese High Command that it was India's war of Liberation and that the sacred burdens were to be shouldered by the Indian National Army. He was, therefore, continuously claiming that all war materials seized during the operation on Indian soil were the properties of the Azad Hind Government. The commander-in-chief of the Japanese army in Burma vehemently opposed the idea for military reasons. Netaji reminded that the Japanese army would fight shoulder to shoulder with INA, for India's independence which was the declared policy of Japan and not that the INA would fight shoulder to shoulder with Japan for the cause, Japan had to accede.

Regarding the governance of the Liberated Areas the Japanese High Command in Tokyo faced strong resentment from its combined armed forces in Burma on the Azad Hind Government's decision and directive delegate power (a) to Major General Zaman Kiani to control combined armed forces-INA and Japanese on Indian soil and (b) to Major General A. C. Chatterjee, to govern liberated areas as the head of Civil administration. Netaji was determined. Japan had to agree.

So the image of a resurgent India appeared before us — an India determined to wage war against British imperialism. A Free India was thus made conscious to shoulder the sacred burden — all by her sons and daughters with confidence and adherence to fundamentals so that Japanese imperialism could not infiltrate.

9

India of Netaji's Dreams

In India, now, after 63 years of independence, hundreds of problems have heaped up to cripple our national life. The poor have become poorer, while a handful of capitalist rich people have enormously inflated their earnings. Unemployment is steadily going up, health and education are far away from the reach of the common people. There is no indication of 'power' being handed over to the 'people'. The representatives of the national bourgeoisie capitalist class, with the patronage of the imperialist powers, are running the central administration, and as such, people's emancipation has not been achieved.

Beginning from the 1930s, Subhash Chandra Bose had been advocating from various platforms alternative means of socialist reconstruction, but our post-independence national leaders have never cared to follow them. From 1947 onwards India had gone through series of political experiments, but with no tangible result. Gandhian policy had failed.

Nehru's 'socialistic pattern of society' had also failed to bring solace to the toiling masses. Despite Indira Gandhi's series of 'nationalisation' programme and evoking 'Emergency' in the country, *'garibi'* (poverty) and unemployment, ill-health and illiteracy could not been eradicated. Rajiv Gandhi and Narshimha

Rao, aided with 'economic reforms' programme also failed to achieve results. Short spell regime of the United Front also didn't have the desired impact on our national Life. And the present NDA regime, headed by BJP, with the 'second generation reforms' has plunged the country in more socio-economic disasters and political crises.

The basic reason is that we are far from socialism. The ruling national bourgeoisie class, tied up with capitalist and imperialist forces, can not achieve socio-economic emancipation of the people. Against this background, people are showing their confidence in the ideals and programmes of Netaji Subhash Chandra Bose.

The people are having growing faith and conviction that for overcoming the problems of poverty-unemployment-illiteracy and disease, we must follow the path of socialist reconstruction as shown by Subhash Chandra Bose. Netaji has adequately expressed his socio-economic and political ideas for socialist reconstruction of the country in his various writings, speeches and discourses. We must study these documents which are quite relevant in the context of our present day national crisis.

Unique Reconstruction Programme

In his unique reconstruction programme, Netaji gave emphasis and priority on eradication of poverty and unemployment, illiteracy and disease, preceeded, of course, by a strong national defence system. According to him, these three priority areas constituted the most vital fundamental problems of the country. [Vide his Tokyo speech (1944) and Haripura speech (1938)]. He, therefore, wanted us to take effective measures to solve these three fundamental problems first. But, unfortunately, necessary attention has not been given to these problems on priority basis and hence, the basic needs of the people have not been satisfied. In 56 year rule the Governments have miserably failed to build and implement pro-people economy and planning.

In recent times the Nobel prize winner and renowned economist Amartya Sen has also said that for national development, first of all, we must introduce universal primary education and health-scheme. Subhash Chandra's thoughts are echoed through Sen's theory.

India's Reconstruction after Independence

After 'great escape' from India in January 1941, Netaji was in Germany for a considerable time where he organised the Indian Legion and was engaged in other preparatory work for his final war of independence from abroad. But even during these hectic days he was planning for India's reconstruction after independence. He asserted that for eradication of poverty and unemployment we urgently needed Industrialisation and scientific agriculture and that must be aided by the state. He wrote in an article, 'Free India and her problems', published in a German periodical in August 1942: 'India will therefore need industrialisation and scientific agriculture through state aid, if she has to serve the problem of poverty and unemployment.' Subhash Chandra further emphasised that, for successful implementation of his aforesaid three priority-based programmes we must increase our national production, particularly agricultural and industrial production, through modern scientific methods and arrange for their equitable social distribution. And more precisely, he wanted to develop this system of national production and distribution through socialist means.

Subhash Chandra declared very categorically that post-independence reconstruction of India could be achieved only through socialist means. His main objective was to establish socialism. Subhash told in his presidential address at the Haripura Congress session (1938): 'I have no doubt in my mind that our chief national problems relating to the eradication of poverty, illiteracy and disease, and to scientific production and distribution, can be effectively tackled only along socialistic lines.'

Incidentally, we may recall his observations on 'Science and Polities' made at the third general meeting of the Indian Science News Association at Calcutta on August 21, 1938. In reply to questions posed by Professor Meghnad Saha at the meeting, the then Congress President Subhash Chandra told: "Firstly, industrialisation is necessary for solving the problem of unemployment. Though scientific agriculture will increase the production of land, if food is to be given to every man and woman, a good portion of the population will have to be transferred from land to industry. Secondly, the rising generation are now thinking in terms of Socialism as the basis of national reconstruction and Socialism presupposes industrialisation.' In our present context, the term 'industry' has a wider connotation, which includes urban-based large scale industries, along with rural-based small scale and cottage industries, food-processing and other agro-based industries, etc. Moreover, we must realise the significance of Netaji's concept of industrialisation vis-a-vis socialism.

Socialist Thoughts

For furtherance of his socialist thoughts, Subhash Chandra wanted to form a National Planning Commission which would take care to formulate a comprehensive plan for post-independence national reconstruction. During the hectic days of Freedom Movement, Subhash Chandra had no doubt in his mind that India would achieve freedom shortly, and no imperialist power on earth could prevent it. He was, therefore, getting himself prepared with a draft plan as to how to reconstruct the country after attaining independence.

Subhash was the first national leader to form a National Planning Committee in 1938 while he was the President of the Indian National Congress. Even while he was vigorously engaged in his liberation struggle and his INA, he formed a separate 'reconstruction' department of the Provisional Government of Free India. As an ardent believer in socialism and planned economy, Netaji Subhash Chandra thus initiated the concept of Planning Commission in Indian politics. The concept of cooperative federalism based on principles of decentralisation and the endeavour to strengthen the local bodies by empowering the Panchayati Raj Institutions are in a way the legacy of the perceptions conceived by Netaji 65 years ago.

Tackling the Fundamental Problems

Incidentally, it may be mentioned that for tackling the three fundamental problems, as mentioned earlier, Netaji introduced two more important concepts in relation to his programme of national reconstruction which he explained in detail in his speech delivered before the students of Tokyo Imperial University in November, 1944. He mentioned in his speech that for tackling the three most important fundamental problems of India, viz. the problem of eradication of poverty and unemployment, illiteracy and disease, the responsibility must be taken by the State (in free India) and secondly, the methods for tackling these problems must be determined by the Indian conditions and in Indian way. He further explained the issue: 'Well, at present, public opinion in India is that we cannot leave it to private initiative to solve these national problems, especially the economic problem. If we leave it to private initiative to solve the problem of poverty and unemployment, for instance, it will probably take centuries.

Therefore, public opinion in India is in favour of some sort of socialist system, in which the initiative will not be left to private individuals, but the State will take over the responsibility for solving economic questions. Whether it is a question of industrialising the country or modernising agriculture, we want the State to step in and take over the responsibility and put through reforms within a short period, so that the Indian people could be put on their legs at a very early date.

'But in solving this problem, we want to work in our own way. We will, naturally, study experiments made in other countries ... but, after all, we have to solve our problems in an Indian way and under Indian conditions. Therefore, the system that we shall ultimately set up will be an Indian system to suit the needs of the Indian people.' [Tokyo speech, 1944]. But unfortunately, during the last five decades, this way of solving India's fundamental problems, as advocated by Netaji, has not been followed with proper planning and sincerity.

Moreover, it's a matter of concern that in recent times, public sector enterprises are being discouraged and closed and the private sector is given wider scope to operate even in areas of fundamental problems. An alarming policy of indiscriminate disinvestments and privatisation is being followed. Such a policy may benefit a limited section of the society, but the majority of the people will be plunged in more poverty. In accordance with the gravity of social needs and bigger public interest, it's now high time to demarcate the areas of public sector and private sector. Private sector can be allowed to operate in the economic field, say in the field of industry or agriculture or in the field of housing or infrastructure development, but they must work under the overall guidelines and policy framework of the state and national planning body. Private sector may also work in collaboration with public sector under the same policy framework. But for overall national interest, multinational companies cannot be generally encouraged to operate in Indian soil. It is a common experience for the developing countries that MNCs generally cause exploitation of the poor, weakening of national economy and uphold the interest of the neo-imperialist forces. Netaji time and again warned his countrymen against the evils of imperialism and possible activities of post-war neo-imperialist agencies.

Means of Eradication of Poverty

Subhash Chandra suggested in different contexts various means of eradication of poverty. The main facets of these suggestions are abolition of Zamindary system, radical land reforms, granting of agricultural loans and development of Cooperative Movement, increasing agricultural production by scientific methods, widespread industrial development plan under state ownership and state control, and at the same time, revival of cottage industries in necessary spheres, etc.

The relevant portion from Subhash Chandra's Haripura speech (1938) may be quoted in this context: Regarding reconstruction, our principal problem will be how to eradicate poverty from our country. That will require radical reform of our land system, including the abolition of landlordism. Agricultural indebtedness will have to be liquidated and provision made for cheap credit for the rural population. An extension of the Cooperative Movement will be necessary for the benefit of both producers and consumers. Agriculture will have to be put on a scientific basis with a view to increase the yield from the land.

To solve the economic problem, agricultural improvement will not be enough. A comprehensive scheme of industrial development under state ownership and control will be indispensable. A new industrial system will have to be built up in place of the old one, which has collapsed as a result of mass production abroad and alien rule at home. A Planning Commission will have to consider carefully and decide which of the home industries could be revived despite the competition of modern factories, and in which sphere large-scale production should be encouraged.

During the last five decades after independence all these means of reconstruction suggested by Subhash Chandra have not been followed by and large. Distribution of surplus land to landless, landownership rights to the tillers, recovery of vested fallow land and turning those to cultivable land, forest land to the landless poor and to develop social forestry and cultivation, etc. are some of the important facets of radical land reforms. This sort of radical land reforms have not been implemented throughout the whole country with due sincerity and urgency. Due to the central policy-makers' unholy compromise and alliance with the capitalists and landlords, the interests of the hungry poor millions have largely suffered.

Agriculture and Industrial Development

For the sake of pro-people agriculture and industrial developments, Subhash Chandra advocated state control and nationalisation. But he didn't stop at that point. He want further to make radical recommendations that all that we needed ultimately was the 'socialisation' of our means of agricultural and industrial production and distribution. He clearly stated in his Haripura speech (1938): 'The State, on the advice of Planning Commission, will have to adopt a comprehensive scheme for gradually socialising our entire agricultural and industrial system in the spheres of both production and distribution.' By virtue of his social and political foresight and intelligence, Subhash Chandra could realise that most of the beneficial effects of nationalisation might eventually be negatives due to crude intervention and control of bureaucrats.

But bureaucrats are not people's representatives, they have no commitments to the people. Hence, if needed, they do not hesitate to forego people's interest for the sake of their own personal benefits. Besides this, there comes the question of mental aptitude ... ardent sincerity to fulfil the targets — and unfortunately, the bureaucrats, in general are lacking in them. Eventually, the progress is slowed down, corruption prevails, and anti-people activities are accelerated. Subhash was aware of this character of bureaucracy.

Hence, he had apprehensions that nationalisation alone might not be able to bring the desired results. In fact, the experience of 56 years after independence has proved Subhash Chandra's apprehensions correct, that is why, Subhash Chandra rightly gave a call to 'change the composition and character of the bureaucracy' [Haripura speech, 1938].

Moreover, he wanted to lead the country towards 'socialisation' through a bold socialistic reconstruction programme. But, in fact, our national leaders did not follow him, and the country obviously didn't move on his line. In spite of nationalisation in the field of banking, insurance, a few heavy industries and others, mainly due to evils of bourgeois leadership and bureaucratic set-up, even after 56 years, the country is facing hundreds of acute problems ... and still now, millions of people are living below the poverty line. On the plea of this apparent failure of experiments with nationalisation, but obviously, ignoring the basic reasons behind, countrywide processes of denationalisation have now started.

The country has thus started moving again in backward direction. Series of disinvestments and privatisation have followed. The country is now being tied up with the reins of capitalist economy. In the midst of this difficult situation, the country again desires to seek solace and guidance in the planned socialistic reconstruction programme advocated by Netaji Subhash Chandra.

Incidentally, it may be mentioned that bureaucratic mentality or work may raise its head in different forms, but it, in each of its form, is harmful for the nation. As the administrative bureaucracy is harmful, so is equally harmful the party bureaucracy. That the party bureaucracy can occasionally be dangerously harmful for a nation, is quite very evident from the downfall of the Soviet Union. When the party in power becomes detached from the people and exploits the administration, there comes the possibility of such disastrous effects. It's now time for us to be cautious about this party bureaucracy. Subhash Chandra's concept of socialism can make us free from the evils of all bureaucratic set-ups.

Reconstruction and Socialisation

For implementation of Subhash Chandra's proposed programme of reconstruction and socialisation, we need, no doubt, extra capital. If we can go ahead with a well-planned, disciplined approach towards a well-defined goal of public welfare, we can solve the problem of capital by social utilisation of abundant resources that are available in a vast country like India. If we are sincere in our goal of raising the standard of living of millions of poor illiterate people, and if we never .deviate from this basic social objective the problem of capital can never stand in our way.

People's spontaneous support adds strength to people's welfare programmes. But during the last 56 years the bourgeois leadership lacked this will for sincere public welfare and as such, various capital-related problems arising out of the evils of capitalist system cropped up. Black money accumulated at the one end, and on the other hand, the poor became poorer.

Besides this general approach, Subhash Chandra gave some concrete suggestions for procuring extra capital. In his Haripura speech (1938), Subhash Chandra suggested that we can go for internal or external loans for the purpose or even we may take the course of inflation. To quote him: 'Extra capital will have to be procured for this, whether through internal or external loans or through inflation' [Haripura speech, 1938].

But these methods should be deeply scrutinised from all possible angles. In our present day circumstances, the country is so over burdened with huge quantity of internal and external debts, that these methods will not be feasible proposition.

Subhash Chandra agreed in principle to raise internal or external loans. But the main thing to be considered is, on what terms or from what sources or under what circumstances we should secure loans or take measures for inflation. Otherwise, there would be scope for confusion or wrong direction.

Our present day rulers have made our national economy crippled, dependent and anti-people by accepting external loans from imperialist and capitalist bodies (like IMF, World Bank or WTO) in their terms and conditions. That the country is now in a debt-trap, is a matter of serious concern. If we are clear in our objective and honest in our purpose, no vested interest can divert us to any anti-people wrong path. That is what Subhash taught us.

Bose's Political Vision and Objectives

That Subhash Chandra was very clear and transparent in his political vision and objectives, was evident from his political philosophy and a related statement which we may refer to here. The basic objective of his socialist thoughts was to improve the lot of millions of toiling masses of India, whom he called 'have-nots' and they are in majority of our population. Subhash Chandra wanted to improve their position at the cost of the 'haves' or the rich, who are minority in our society. Subhash argued: 'Moreover, if after the capture of political power, national reconstruction takes place on socialist line ... as I have no doubt it will ... it is the have-nots who will benefit at the expense of the haves and the Indian masses have to be classified among the have-nots', [Haripura Speech, 1938]. Ultimately, of course, Netaji aimed that there should be no have-nots in free India.

In this way, by defeating the capitalist system, patronised by imperialists, Subhash Chandra wanted to build up socialism in India. This was indeed a revolutionary idea. It is needless to mention that if the country proceeded in this way as advocated by Subhash Chandra, there would not have been any problem in respect of procuring capital for reconstruction work. But during the last 56 years' rule, the reverse has happened. Only 10 per cent of our population have grown rich, while the rest 90 per cent of our population have become poorer. The accumulated black money has started controlling the society and the State. It has so happened only because the country has not been led in Subhash' way. Unearthing of black money may be one of the means of regenerating our presently shattered economy.

Globalisation

In the name of 'globalisation', the present Indian policy is pushing the indigenous industry in sharp competition with the foreign industry of capitalist and imperialist countries, as a result of which the Indian industry and economy are on the brink of serious crises. Subhash Chandra warned the country long before ... 60 years ago — against the damaging effects of such unequal competition in industrial field. Subhash Chandra told: 'it is, of course, preposterous to permit foreigners in this country to compete with the nationals on equal terms, ... The right of the future Indian Parliament to differentiate or discriminate between nationals and non-nationals, whenever Indian interests require it, should remain intact and this we cannot sacrifice on any account.' Unfortunately, in free India many such rights are sacrificed in the interest of the neo-imperialist powers. When we are now swept away by the onslaught of globalisation and the country is on the verge of losing economic sovereignty, we remember how strongly Netaji advocated for national autonomy. In response to Prof. Meghnad Saha's query, he said: Though-from the industrial point of view the world is one unit, we should nevertheless aim at national autonomy, especially in the field of our principal needs and requirements.

Population Problem

Ever increasing population is undoubtedly a problem for successful implementation of reconstruction programme. Subhash Chandra had, therefore, rightly drawn our attention to the population problem long before. He was of the opinion that the trend of increasing population could create problem for any of our long-term programme. He explicitly told, 'I simply want to point out that where poverty, starvation and disease are stalling the land, we cannot afford to have our population mounting up by thirty millions during a single decade' [Haripura speech, 1938]. We have not been able to fully realise this truth even in 56 years; hence the problem goes on increasing. India's population was about 35 crores by the end of thirties, while currently the population of divided India has crossed 100 crores. We have failed so far to pay our due attention to the alarming aspects of this problem. The Government has failed to formulate a suitable national population policy. Population is the biggest asset of the country ... it is essential to utilise it properly. But if the situation so demands, it becomes imperative to restrict the population.

A New, Modern India

We must not forget another important aspect of Subhash Chandra's revolutionary reconstruction programme. Subhash Chandra wanted to build up a new modern India based on its earlier tradition and culture. He told before the students at Tokyo University: 'We want to build up a new and modern nation on the basis of our old culture and civilization'. In an earlier article also he asserted: 'India could contribute something to the common culture and civilization of humanity, in religion and philosophy, in architecture, in painting, dancing and music and in other arts and handicrafts, India would offer something unique to the world.'

In the October, 1935 issue of the journal 'Science and Culture', edited by Meghnad Saha, Subhash Chandra wrote in his article 'Some problems of nation-building' — that we must adopt modern science and culture in our work of nation-building. Neither the Gandhite opposition to modern industry, nor the orthodox leftists' opposition to computers or modem information technology is desirable. At the same time, we must not forget the past tradition and culture of India. Lessons from the aforesaid ideas of Subhash Chandra will no doubt help us in our task of nation-building.

Education: an Important Aspect

Education was also an important aspect of Subhash Chandra's socialistic reconstruction programme. He looked at Education on a national perspective. He said: 'through a common educational policy we shall have to foster a common spirit among the entire population' [Haripura speech, 1938]. But what about our present education system? It is discriminating in nature, offering vast opportunities to the rich and minimum to the poor, and thus creating a disparity in society, resulting in social imbalance right from the beginning.

Subhash Chandra deeply felt that education must develop a national spirit and patriotism amongst us right from our childhood. Children must be taught to love the country and render service to the common people. This sort of training would help to foster solidarity and harmony among the entire population. ['An Indian Pilgrim', S. C. Bose] Imparting such education is, therefore, very important with a view to nation-building. 'Man-making mission' propounded by Vivekananda and a vision of universality propagated by Rabindranath Tagore inspired Subhash Chandra to formulate such policy of education in free India.

We must also resist all sorts of attempts to commercialise and/or to communalise education. Education must not be allowed to be used as a commodity for making profits. A free and man-making education can strengthen the foundation of our nation.

Netaji also thought about other aspects of education. He suggested: 'experiments will have to be made for evolving a national system of education in accordance with the needs of the Indian people' ['Free India and her problems', Germany, August 1942]. Technical education and research should also be a priority issue for free India. Netaji said: 'We should also tackle the problems of technical education and technical research. So far as technical education is concerned, as in the case of Japanese students, our students should be sent abroad for training in accordance with a clear and definite plan so that as soon as they return home, they may proceed straightway to build up new industries.

'So far as technical research is concerned, we shall agree that it should be free of governmental control of every kind. It is only in this unfortunate country that government servants are entrusted with scientific research on receipt of princely salaries and we know very well what results have been obtained there from' ['Science and Polities' answers to questions posed by Prof. Meghnad Saha: August 21, 1938J].

Revolutionary Thoughts regarding overall Development of a United India

Of late, three very critical problems are bothering us most. These three problems are — firstly, regionalism and divisiveness; secondly, communalism and minority problems, and thirdly, problems of self-reliance for the backward, weaker and underdeveloped classes. By exploiting, distorting and instigating these three problems, many small or big parties have recently sprung up in Indian politics and are serving their self-interests, but basically they are retarding the progress of the country. Subhash Chandra had repeatedly warned us regarding these three problems and had expressed the necessity of solving them for proper reconstruction of the country.

Subhash Chandra's revolutionary thoughts regarding overall development of united India inspire us all the time. For a vast country like India having different castes, religions, languages and regional culture, Subhash Chandra wanted to strengthen the foundation of a strong central government, along with provincial or regional autonomy, in order to keep India united, and at the same time, ensuring regional development. He clarified his opinion in this respect: 'While unifying the country through a strong central government, we shall have to put all the minority communities, as well as the provinces at their ease, by allowing them a large measure of autonomy in cultural as well as governmental affairs' [Haripura speech, 1938]. During the last 50 years of national planning process, Subhash Chandra's ideal has not been followed ... hence, so many problems in this respect have cropped up throughout the country. There may be an apparent contradiction in the idea of a strong central government and, at the same time, regional autonomy, but a pragmatic political will and capability can make a harmony between the two. This has not been successfully achieved in India so far. Even during the last 56 years, a centre-state amicable relationship, a well-balanced good relationship built through a policy of equitable distribution of resources and other governmental rights and responsibilities — could not be achieved, and as such, regional and divisive forces are gradually raising their heads. We can make our country free from this vexed problem only by successful implementation of Subhash Chandra's ideas.

Fight against communalism and casteism is an integral part of Subhash Chandra's concept of socialism. He fought throughout his life against these two social monsters. When Subhash first gave this call for fight against discrimination on caste and creed, when he started to plead for socio-economic and educational development and self-reliance for the backward classes, at that time, many of today's so-called leaders of scheduled castes, tribes and backward classes could not be traced even. But during the last 50 years taking advantage of the Government's inaction and indifference in the matter, many divisive forces have come out in the open. We can get rid of such a situation only by following Subhash's way.

As Subhash Chandra fought against the capitalist and feudal forces, he also fought, particularly in view of Indian situation, against the divisive forces of casteism. He declared in his speech, at the London Conference in June, 1933: 'Free India will not be a land of capitalists, landlords and castes. Free India will be a social and political democracy'. [Presidential address at the Third Indian Political Conference, London: 10 June, 1933].

Netaji's concept about communalism was also very clear and deeply analytic. He was of the opinion that the problem of communalism was created — the Britishers used to nurse this discriminating policy in the interest of sustaining their rule in India. He said in Tokyo University in November 1944: 'You will find that outside, where there is no British influence, there are no differences among the Indian people. In the Indian Independence Movement in East Asia and in the Indian National Army there is no question of religion or caste or class. It is just in India where the British have influence and control that you will find these differences'. A few of the political parties also used to exploit this matter for satisfying their vested interests. Netaji believed that, once we could establish equality in true sense in socio-economic and political field, there would have no problem like minority-problem in our country. While presenting the picture of future free India as he dreamt of, he wrote: 'In the matter of political and economic rights there will be perfect equality among the whole population. When every individual has employment, food and education and has freedom in religious and cultural matters there will be no more any minority-problem in India' [The Indian Struggle, S. C. Bose].

Imperialism and Communalism

Netaji fought throughout his life against two sinister menace — one, imperialism, and the other, communalism, which he asserted, caused tremendous damage to India. During the dark days of 200 years of dependence, India was ruled and exploited by the British imperialism, and communalism ...as created, fomented and nursed by (lie Britishers — was one of their dirty weapons, which kept the people of India divided and weak as a consequence of their infighting. But the most alarming part of the whole story is this that, even after independence these two evil forces are still active in Indian peninsula and continue to damage the basic interest of the people and the country as a whole. Of course their apparent faces have changed, but their basic characters have remained unchanged. The principal leader of the world imperialism is now the USA and the communalism is now working through India's present ruling clique the BJP and its allies. Under the onslaught of this twin evil forces, India's prospect and sovereignty — both economic and geographical — are at stake. Although the days of imperialist colonies are over, neo-imperialism is now active through its various channels and agencies in the developing countries mainly aimed at economic exploitation. Agencies like IMF-WB-WTO on the one hand and the devastating policies of Liberalisation, Privatisation and Globalisation on the other hand are penetrating deep into the socio-economic fabrics of the developing countries putting them under the clout of growing poverty and unemployment. The establishment of WTO (World Trade Organisation) after the GATT (General Agreement on Tariffs and Trade) is a tool of the United States and other developed countries to interfere in the markets of Third World Countries in respect of trade and commerce, trade in services, patents, agriculture and all other economic issues. Socialism will be far away if we cannot combat these evil forces by our united fight against them. This must be our priority task to rebuild India in Netaji's Way.

Of course, Netaji could visualise it long before. While leading the INA in the final war of independence from abroad, Netaji wrote an open letter to Gandhiji sometime in 1944. Obviously, that was the time when the Second World War was heading for its final stage as the Anglo-American forces were fighting hard against the Axis Powers. During this critical juncture of time Netaji in his aforesaid letter made some historical comments, rather political forecast, about the emerging post-war World Power. Netaji said: 'Even if the Allies could somehow win the war, it will be United States of America, and not Britain, that will be top dog in future and it will mean that Britain will become a protege of the USA.'

Netaji further said in his letter about the war aims of the USA: I may say that the ruling clique at Washington is now dreaming of world domination. This ruling clique and its intellectual exponents, talk openly of the 'American Century', that is, in the present century the USA will dominate the world. In this ruling clique, there are extremists who go so far as to call Britain the 49th State of the USA.'

As we all know, Netaji's forecasts have been proved to be correct. The American imperialists are dominating the world since the post-war day. Their aggressive military powers, as well as economic ambitions are viciously spreading their tentacles over the hundreds of developing countries, and India is no exception.

After the end of Cold War the United States has embarked upon a course of global strategy. The foundation of the strategy is based on USA's imperialist interest all over the world. The USA, by using NATO, wages military actions against the poor countries to protect its global interest. By using IMF, World Bank and WTO the imperialists are interfering the internal affairs and sovereignty of poor nations.

The economic imperialism headed by USA in the name of Globalisation, Liberalisation and Privatisation is forcing the third world countries to evolve capitalist model of economy. While aspiring to rebuild India in Netaji's way, we must be firm and cautious to safeguard our country from the onslaught of the world imperialist and capitalist powers headed by the USA. We must remember Netaji's candid assertion: 'Ours is a struggle not only against British Imperialism, but against world imperialism as well' [Haripura speech, 1938].

Kabul Thesis

We find a comprehensive picture of Subhash Chandra's programme of freedom struggle and post-independence socialist reconstruction in his historical discourse 'Forward Bloc and its justification'. After secretly escaping from India, when he was absconding in Kabul and when danger and death were hunting him at every moment of his existence — then, at that critical juncture of his life. Subhash drafted this discourse in cool head (in January-February, 1941). In political circles, it is known as 'Kabul Thesis'. In his thesis, Subhash described his future plan of action and his objectives in the form of eight-point programme of his party Forward Bloc. This eight-point programme was summarised as follows:

- Complete national independence and uncompromising anti-imperialist struggle for attaining it.
- A thoroughly modern and socialist state.
- Scientific large-scale production for the economic regeneration of the country.
- Social ownership and control of both production and distribution.
- Freedom for the individual in the matter of religious worship.
- Equal rights for every individual.
- Linguistic and cultural autonomy for all sections of the Indian community.
- Application of the principles of equality and social justice in building up the New Order in Free India. In our determination and struggle for Rebuilding India in Netaji's way, we must keep in mind every point, every word of the aforesaid 8-point programme, and work accordingly. This programme is very relevant even today in our work for rebuilding India as per dreams of Netaji.

Bose's Relevance Today

India, as dreamt of by Netaji, is yet to be built. In a letter written to the revolutionary leader Barin Ghosh in 1930, Subhash had told about the aims and objects of his life and struggle as such: '...we do not want to emancipate the people merely from political bondage ... rather we want to free them from all restraint. The main objective of freedom struggle is to remove all the three types of restraint — political, economic and social restraint. Once we can remove all sorts of restraint, then only we can build a new society based on communism or Samyabad. The main objective of our freedom struggle is to build up 'a free and classless society'.

If we venture to rebuild India in Netaji's way, we must remember this main objective of his freedom struggle.

'There is no guarantee that our countrymen will be freed merely with the end of the British rule. After the removal of the foreign rulers, if power is vested in the hands of the local reactionary bourgeoisie clan, then the emancipation of the exploited poor people will not be achieved.' Netaji, with his political foresight and intelligence, didn't rule out one such possibility. In fact, it has exactly so happened in India.

Once it so happened, Netaji told, we would require a second revolution to free our people from the clutches of the reactionary national bourgeoisie. Netaji pronounced these words at a time in 1944 when the Indian National Army was engaged in their struggle for freedom. While teaching 'what is revolution', Netaji told his young trainees at the Cambay Swaraj Youth Training Camp on 25 April, 1944: 'If with the end of the British rule in India, power is vested in the hands of the Indians, but, in spite of that, the problems of poverty and unemployment, epidemics and death-rate still persist like before, and no adequate provisions are made for food for the hungry and education for the illiterate people, then our task would remain unfulfilled...

Our revolution would be completed only when we could build our new society based on truth and justice ... where every Indian would get his birthrights fulfilled ... If our revolution ends only after driving out the Britishers, then another revolution would be necessary for building up a new social order in India ... You can not retire from your work immediately after attaining India's independence only, as after fighting against the alien power, you have now the onerous task of saving the nation from the clutches of the reactionary forces in India.' History is the best witness, what Netaji pronounced, as stated above, have proved to be true in letter and spirit. We must, therefore, now make preparations for the second revolution which, in turn, would be our preparations for building up a new society ... or the New Order.

The aforesaid second revolution would obviously be a socialist revolution and as characterised by Netaji, it will be an 'Indian revolution in Indian way under Indian conditions.'

It is, thus, our firm conviction that to rebuild Indian in Netaji's way, we must strive to establish Socialism, and that, too, in an Indian way and under Indian conditions. Netaji unambiguously explained it in his speech at the Calcutta session of the All India Trade Union Congress on July 4, 1931: I have no doubt in my mind that salvation of India, as of the world, depends on Socialism. India should learn from and profit by the experience of other nations ... but India should be able to evolve her own methods in keeping with her own needs and her own environment. In applying any theory to practice, you can never rule out geography or history. If you attempt it, you are bound to fail. India should therefore, evolve her own form of socialism.' Netaji further clarified his idea of Socialism in his Presidential address at the conference of the All India Naujawan Bharat Sabha at Karachi on 5 April 1931 and also at the UP. Naujawan Bharat Sabha Conference held at Mathura on 26 May 1931.

While explaining his concept of Socialism, Netaji told that, our collective life must always be based on certain principles. According to him, there are five such principles, viz. Justice, Equality, Freedom, Discipline and Love; these are essential to form the basis of our collective life. Netaji adequately explained the significance of such principles in his aforesaid speeches at Karachi or Mathura. As for example, he said at Karachi (1931):

> There is hardly any necessity of arguing that all our affairs and relations should be guided by a sense of justice. In order to be just and impartial, we shall have to treat all men as equal. In order to make men equal we shall have to make them free. Bondage within the socio-economic or political system ... robs men of their freedom and gives rise to inequalities of various kinds. Therefore, in order to ensure Equality, we must get rid of bondage of every kind — social, economic and political — and we must become fully and wholly free. But freedom does not mean indiscipline or license. Freedom does not imply the absence of law. It only means the substitution of our own law and our own discipline in a place of an externally imposed law and discipline. Discipline imposed on us by ourselves is necessary not only when we have attained freedom, but is more necessary when we are struggling to achieve freedom. Therefore, discipline, whether for the individual or for society, is necessary as a basis of life. Lastly, all these fundamental principles, viz. Justice, Equality, Freedom and Discipline... presuppose or imply another higher principle, viz. Love. Unless we are inspired by a feeling of love for humanity we

> can neither be just towards all, nor treat men as Equal, nor feel called upon to suffer and sacrifice in the cause of freedom, nor enforce discipline of the right sort. These five principles, therefore, should in my opinion be the basis of our collective life. I shall go further and say that these principles constitute the essence of Socialism as I understand it, and the Socialism that I like to see established in India.

We must visualise this philosophy of Socialism as conceived by Netaji and we must go for this Socialism while rebuilding India in Netaji's way.

Netaji's Legacy

Netaji's Dream

Imphal, Manipur, and Moirang have nostalgic memories for all men and women who played their humble part in the INA under the leadership of Netaji Subhash Chandra Bose. Moirang the rare sanctity of being the hallowed spot where the immortal heroes of the INA hoisted the National Tricolour on the sacred soil of India for the first time after crossing the Burma border into India. Especially to all those who participated the Indian Independence Movement in East Asia. Moirang is a place of pilgrimage. It will remain a place of pilgrimage to all Indians and for ever. Moirang will go down in history as the spot where the dawn of India's Freedom came into view on the 14th April 1944.

On 21st October 1968, on the occasion of the celebration the Silver Jubilee of the Proclamation of the provisional Government of Azad Hind, Moirang witnessed an impressive ceremony to celebrate the Jubilee and to pay homage to the INA Martyrs, a Memorial to whom is fast taking shape in Moirang. Last year, on 23rd September our Prime Minister Shrimati Indira Gandhi came to Moirang and inaugurated the Museum wing of the INA Martyrs Memorial Hall. Our President, V. V. Giri, is expected to visit Moirang and install the life size statue of Netaji Subhash Chandra Bose, at the INA Martyrs Memorial site on 23rd January, 1971, on the occasion of the 75th Birth Anniversary of Netaji Subhash Chandra Bose.

When the battle for Imphal was at its height a quarter of a century age, news of its capture by the INA supported by the

Japanese forces was eagerly awaited every moment. But it was not to be. The odds against the INA proved formidable. After coming within striking distance of Imphal, the INA had to withdraw.

If Imphal had fallen to the INA, the course of history would have been changed. And Independence would have come to India even earlier than 15th August. 1947. Manipur would have been the first liberated territory administered by the Provisional Government of Azad Hind. Netaji had worked out the plan of administration to the minutest detail. A Governor designate had already been nominated for the liberated territories. The Azad Hind Dal had already been recruited and trained for reconstruction work. The Dal was composed of farmers, artisans, administrators, postmen and telegraphists, engineers and doctors.

These men were ready to follow the liberation forces to set up civil administration in areas vacated by the withdrawing British authorities. Normal civilian life would have been restored with the least dislocation. Temporary shelters would have been built with the least delay, cultivation of land would have been resumed quickly; water supply would have been ensured; medical relief would have been prompt. Money orders and other postal facilities would have been restored. Postage stamps and money order forms were ready; currency notes of the Azad Hind Government were also ready. There would have been no dislocation of normal life for civilians — for want of currency notes or postal stationary.

A full-fledged administration of the Provisional Government of Azad Hind on Indian soil would have been an accomplished fact as a result of meticulous advance planning by Netaji. That was the Dream of Subhash Chandra Bose. The dream did not become a reality. The dream was no less glorious, though it remained only a dream.

Those of us who had the rare good fortune and privilege of being closely associated with Netaji during the twenty five hectic, fateful months that he spearheaded the Independence Movement in East Asia, were fascinated by the charm and magnetism of the man. Love of the Motherland was a burning passion with him; his physical and moral courage was the highest order. His thoroughness was striking. From the moment the INA started advancing towards Imphal, Netaji began drawing up a Proclamation to the people of Manipur. He held a series of consultations with some citizens of Manipur who had crossed the Burma border and reached Rangoon. He wanted to understand the Mind of Manipur before drawing up the Proclamation. Once the proclamation was ready, he had it translated into Manipuri language by citizens of Manipur in the Rangoon camp.

He had an unshakeable faith in his destiny. He carried his life in the palm of his hand. Nobody could persuade him to take shelter when enemy bomber came overhead in swarms and rained bombs on Rangoon and other INA camping areas. When those near him begged of him to get into underground shelters at the height of the bombing, he would laugh off the suggestion and simply say: "The bomb to kill me has not yet been made."

His moral courage amazed even the Japanese. When news of reverse on the battlefronts began reaching Netaji at his headquarters, he was totally calm. He went ahead with his usual routine as if nothing untoward had happened. He never even for a moment lost his faith in the ultimate victory of his efforts. His self-confidence was of an infectious type. And the high-ranking Japanese civilian and military officers often wondered at this supreme self-assurance of Netaji.

The secret of Netaji's moral courage was his undying faith in God. He did not give a moment's thought to the immediate success or failure of his campaign for India's liberation from foreign rule. He concentrated all his thoughts and energies on the job in hand. He had knack of turning defeats into victories. When a small group of INA officers betrayed the cause and went over to the enemy, Netaji refused to be depressed by the betrayal. He used the betrayal as the occasion for a raging, tearing propaganda campaign to rouse the spirit of the entire INA personal to fever pitch, and made thoroughly sure that there would be no further desertions to the enemy.

When news of reverses began trickling from the battlefronts, Netaji took the civilians into confidence, and told them the unpleasant truth that the INA had failed to capture Imphal. At the same time he appealed to their sense of patriotism and urged them to support the INA with more men, more money, and more materials to attack Imphal ten times if necessary. Netaji's appeal had an electrifying effect. The civilians rose to the occasion and came forward to pour all they had into Netaji's war chest.

Netaji's finest hour was when news reached him that the Japanese had surrendered to the Anglo-Americans, and that the war was over. This meant an abrupt end to the INA fighting and a disastrous end to all his dreams. As he was upset only for a few moments. Then he recovered his composure and took supreme command of the entire situation, and issued a series of important orders to the civilian and military wings of the Movement in East Asia and told them in the smallest detail what was to be done by them to look after the entire civilian and military personal. Simultaneously, he held top level consultations with his own colleagues and with the Japanese military authorities as to his own future. He had to make the most momentous decisions about his own immediate plans. He had to take the ultimate decision on the fateful question as to whether he should stay in Singapore and allow himself to be taken prisoner by the Anglo-American forces returning as victors to Singapore and other areas.

In those dramatic few days after Japan's surrender, Netaji was extraordinarily cool and calm, and after listening patiently to all that his advisers had to say, finally decided to go on what he himself described as his "adventure into the unknown".

The life and achievements of Netaji Subhash Chandra Bose will always serve as a beacon light for the present and future generations of Indians who can draw inexhaustible inspiration from his patriotism, suffering, self sacrifice, and indomitable courage.

10

Netaji's Speeches

The Programme of Reconstruction

[*Speech at Haripura Session of Congress, February 1938*]

Mr. Chairman and Friends!

I am deeply sensible of the honour you have done me by electing me as the President of the Indian National Congress for the coming year. I am not so presumptuous as to think for one moment that I am in any way worthy of that great honour. I regard it as a mark of your generosity and as a tribute to the youths of our country, but for whose cumulative contribution to our national struggle, we would not be where we are today. It is with a sense of fear and trepidation that I mount the tribune which has hitherto been graced by the most illustrious sons and daughters of our motherland. Conscious as I am of my numerous limitations, I can only hope and pray that with your sympathy and support I may be able in some small measure to do justice to the high office which you have called upon me to fill.

At the outset, may I voice your feelings in placing on record our profound grief at the death of Shrimati Swaruprani Nehru, Acharya Jagadish Chandra Bose and Dr. Sarat Chandra Chatterji? Shrimati Swaruprani Nehru was to us not merely the worthy consort of Pandit Motilal and the revered mother of Pandit Jawaharlal Nehru. Her suffering, sacrifice and service in the cause of India's freedom were such as any individual could feel proud of. As compatriots we mourn her death and our hearts go out in sympathy to Pandit Nehru and other members of the bereaved family.

To Acharya Jagadish Chandra Bose India will always remain beholden for being the first to secure for her an honoured place in the modern scientific world. A nationalist to the core of his heart, Acharya Jagadish gave his life not merely to science, but to India as well. India knows it and is grateful for it. We convey our heartfelt sympathy to Lady Bose.

Through the untimely death of Dr. Sarat Chandra Chatterji, India has lost one of the brightest stars in her literary firmament. His name, for years a household word in Bengal, was not less known in the literary world of India. But if Sarat Babu was great as a litterateur, he was perhaps greater as a patriot. The Congress in Bengal is distinctly poorer today because of his death. We send our sincerest condolence to the members of his family.

Before I proceed further I should like to bow my head in homage to the memory of those who have laid down their lives in the service of the country since the Congress met last year at Faizpur. I should mention especially those who died in prison or in internment or soon after release from internment. I should refer in particular to Sjt. Harendra Munshi, a political prisoner in the Dacca Central Jail, who laid down his life the other day as a result of hungerstrike. My feelings are still too lacerated to permit me to say much on this subject. I shall only ask you if there is not 'something rotten in the state of Denmark' that such bright and promising souls as Jatin Das, Sardar Mahabir Singh, Ramkrishna Namadas, Mohit Mohan Maitra, Harendra Munshi and others should feel the urge not to live life but to end it.

When we take a bird's eye view of the entire panorama of human history, the first thing that strikes us is the rise and fall of empires. In the East as well as in the West, empires have invariably gone through a process of expansion and after reaching the zenith of prosperity, have gradually shrunk into insignificance and sometimes death. The Roman empire of the ancient times and the Turkish and Austro-Hungarian empires of the modern period are striking examples of this law. The empires in India — the Maurya, the Gupta and the Mogul empires - are no exceptions to this rule. In the face of these objective facts of history, can anyone be so bold as to maintain that there is in store a different fate for the British empire? That empire stands today at one of the crossroads of history. It will either go the way of other empires or it must transform itself into a federation of free nations. Either course is open to it. The Czarist empire collapsed in 1917 but of its debris sprang the Union of Soviet Socialist Republics. There is still time for Great Britain to take a leaf out of Russian history. Will she do so?

The British empire is a hybrid phenomenon in politics. It is a peculiar combination of self-governing countries, partially self-governing dependencies and autocratically governed colonies. Constitutional device and human ingenuity may bolster up this combination for a while, but not for ever. If the internal incongruities are not removed in good time, then quite apart from external pressure, the empire is sure to break down under its own strain. But can the British empire transform itself into a federation of free nations with one bold sweep? It is for the British people to answer this question.

One thing, however, is certain. This transformation will be possible only if the British people become free in their own homes; only if Great Britain becomes a socialist state. There is an inseparable connection between the capitalist ruling classes in Great Britain and the colonies abroad. As Lenin pointed out long ago, 'reaction in Great Britain is strengthened and fed by the enslavement of a number of nations'.

The British aristocracy and bourgeoisie exist primarily because there are colonies and overseas dependencies to exploit. The emancipation of the latter will undoubtedly strike at the very existence of the capitalist ruling classes in Great Britain and precipitate the establishment of a socialist regime in that country. It should, therefore, be clear that a socialist order in Great Britain is impossible of achievement without the liquidation of colonialism and that we who are fighting for the political freedom of India and other enslaved countries of the British empire are incidentally fighting for the economic emancipation of the British people as well.

It is well-known truism that every empire is based on the policy of divide and rule. But I doubt if any empire in the world has practised this policy so skilfully, systematically and ruthlessly as Great Britain. In accordance with the policy, before power was handed over to the Irish people, Ulster was separated from the rest of Ireland. Similarly, before any power is handed over to the Palestinians, the Jews will be separated from the Arabs. An internal partition is necessary in order to neutralise the transference of power. The same principle of partition appears in a different form in the new Indian Constitution. Here we find an attempt to separate the different communities and put them into watertight compartments. And in the Federal Scheme there is juxtaposition of autocratic princes and democratically elected representatives from British India. If the new Constitution is finally rejected, whether owing to the opposition of British India or owing to the refusal of the princes to joining it, I have no doubt that British ingenuity will seek some other constitutional device for partitioning India and thereby neutralising the transference of power to the Indian people. Therefore, any Constitution for India which emanates from Whitehall must be examined with the utmost care and caution.

The policy of divide and rule, though it has its obvious advantages, is by no means an unmixed blessing for the ruling power. As a matter of fact, it creates new problems and new embarrassments. Great Britain seems to be caught in the meshes of her own political dualism resulting from her policy of divide and rule. Will she please the Muslim or the Hindu in India? Will she favour the Arab or the Jew in Palestine; the Arab or the Kurd in Iraq? Will she side with the King or the Wafd in Egypt? The same dualism is visible outside the empire. In the case of Spain, British politicians are torn between such alternatives as Franco and the lawful government; and in the wider field of European politics, between France and Germany. The contradictions and inconsistencies in Britain's foreign policy are the direct outcome of the heterogeneous composition of her empire. The British Cabinet has to please the Jews because she cannot ignore Jewish high finance. On the other hand, the India Office and Foreign Office have to placate the Arabs because of imperial interests in the Near East and India. The only means whereby Great Britain can free herself from such contradictions and inconsistencies is by transforming the empire into a federation of free nations. If she could do that, she would be performing a miracle in history. But if she fails, she must reconcile herself to the gradual dismemberment of a vast empire where the sun is supposed not to set. Let the lesson of the Austro-Hungarian empire be not lost on the British people.

The British empire at the present moment is suffering from strain at a number of points. Within the empire, in the extreme West, there is Ireland and in the extreme East, India. In the middle lies Palestine with the adjoining countries of Egypt and Iraq. Outside the empire, there is the pressure exerted by Italy in the Mediterranean and Japan in the Far East, both of these countries being militant, aggressive and imperialist. Against this background of unrest stands Soviet Russia, whose very existence strikes terror into the heart of the ruling classes in every imperialist state. How long can the British empire withstand the cumulative effect of this pressure and strain?

Today, Britain can hardly call herself' the Mistress of the Seas. Her phenomenal rise in the 18th and 19th centuries was the result of her sea power. Her decline as an empire in the 20th century will be the outcome of the emergence of a new factor in world history — air force. It was due to this new factor, air force, that an impudent Italy could successfully challenge a fully mobilised British Navy in the Mediterranean. Britain can rearm on land, sea and air up to the utmost limit. Battleships may still stand up to bombing from the air, but air force as a powerful element in modern warfare has come to stay. Distances have been obliterated and despite all anti-aircraft defences, London lies at the mercy of any bombing squadron from a continental centre. In short, air force has revolutionised modern warfare, destroyed the insularity of Great Britain and rudely disturbed the balance of power in world politics. The clay feet of a gigantic empire now stand exposed as these have never been before.

Amid this interplay of world forces India emerges much stronger than she has ever been before. Ours is a vast country with a population of 350 millions. Our vastness in area and in population has hitherto been a source of weakness. It is today a source of strength if we can only stand united and boldly face our rulers. From the standpoint of Indian unity the first thing to remember is that the division between British India and the Indian states is an entirely artificial one. India is one and the hopes and aspirations of the people of British India and of the Indian states are identical. Our goal is that of an Independent India and in my view that goal can be attained only through a federal republic in which the provinces and the states will be willing partners.

The Congress has, time and again, offered its sympathy and moral support to the movement carried on by the states' subjects for the establishment of democratic government in what is known as Indian India. It may be that at this moment our hands are so full that the Congress is not in a position to do more for our compatriots in the states. But even today there is nothing to prevent individual Congressmen from actively espousing the cause of the states' subjects and participating in their struggle.

There are people in the Congress like myself who would like to see the Congress participating more actively in the movement of the states' subjects. I personally hope that in the near future it will be possible for the Indian National Congress to take a forward step and offer a helping hand to our fellow-fighters in the states. Let us not forget that they need our sympathy and our help.

Talking of Indian unity the next thing that strikes us is the problem of the minorities. The Congress has, from time to time, declared its policy on this question. The latest authoritative pronouncement made by the All India Congress Committee at its meeting in Calcutta in October, 1937, runs thus:

> The Congress has solemnly and repeatedly declared its policy in regard to the rights of the minorities in India and has stated that it considers it its duty to protect these rights and ensure the widest possible scope for the development of these minorities and their participation in the fullest measure in the political, economic and cultural life of the nation. The objective of the Congress is an independent and united India where no class or group or majority or minority may exploit another to its own advantage, and where all

the elements in the nation may cooperate together for the common good and the advancement of the people of India. The objective of unity and mutual cooperation in a common freedom does not mean the suppression in any way of the rich variety and cultural diversity of Indian life, which have to be preserved in order to give freedom and opportunity to the individual as well as to each group to develop unhindered according to its capacity and inclination.

In view, however, of attempts having been made to misinterpret the Congress policy in this regard, the All India Congress Committee desire to reiterate this policy. The Congress has included in its resolution on Fundamental Rights that:

i. Every citizen of India has the right of free expression of opinion, the right of free association and combination, and the right to assemble peacefully and without arms, for a purpose not opposed to law or morality;

ii. Every citizen shall enjoy freedom of conscience and the right freely to profess and practise his religion, subject to the public order and morality;

iii. The culture, language and script of the minorities and of the different linguistic areas shall be protected;

iv. All citizens are equal before the law, irrespective of religion, caste, creed or sex;

v. No disability attaches to any citizen by reason of his or her religion, caste, creed or sex, in regard to public employment, office of power or honour, and in the exercise of any trade or calling;

vi. All citizens have equal rights and duties in regard to wells, tanks, roads, schools and places of public resort, maintained out of state, or local funds, or dedicated by private persons for the use of the general public;

vii. The state shall observe neutrality in regard to all religions;

viii. The franchise shall be on the basis of universal adult suffrage;

ix. Every citizen is free to move throughout India and to stay and settle in any part thereof, to acquire property and to follow any trade or calling, and to be treated equally with regard to legal prosecution or protection in all parts of India. These clauses of the Fundamental Rights resolution make it clear that there should be no interference in matter of conscience, religion, or culture, and a minority is entitled to keep its personal law without any change in this respect being imposed by the majority.

> The position of the Congress in regard to the communal decision has been repeatedly made clear in Congress resolutions and finally in the Election. Manifesto issued last year. The Congress is opposed to this decision as it is anti-national, anti-democratic and is a barrier to Indian freedom and the development of Indian unity. Nevertheless, the Congress has declared that a change in or suppression of the Communal Decision should only be brought about by the mutual agreement of the parties concerned. The Congress has always welcomed and is prepared to take advantage of any opportunity to bring about such a change by mutual agreement.
>
> In all matters affecting the minorities in India, the Congress wishes to proceed by their cooperation and through their goodwill in a common undertaking and for the realisation of a common aim which is the freedom and betterment of all the people of India.

The time is opportune for renewing our efforts for the final solution of this problem. I believe I am voicing the feelings of all Congressmen when I say that we are eager to do our very best to arrive at an agreed solution, consistent with the fundamental principles of nationalism. It is not necessary for me to go into details as to the lines on which a solution should take place. Much useful ground has already been covered in past conferences and conversations. I shall merely add that only by emphasising our common interests, economic and political, can we cut across communal divisions and dissensions. A policy of live and let live in matters religious and an understanding in matters economic and political should be our objective. Though the Muslim problem looms large whenever we think of the question of the minorities and though we are anxious to settle this problem finally, I must say that the Congress is equally desirous of doing justice to other minorities and especially the so-called depressed classes whose number is a very large one. I would put it to the members of the minority communities in India to consider dispassionately if they have anything to fear when the Congress programme is put into operation. The Congress stands for the political and economic rights of the Indian people as a whole. If it succeeds in executing its programme, the minority communities would be benefited as much as any other section of the Indian population.

Moreover, if after the capture of political power, national reconstruction takes place on socialistic lines; as I have no doubt it will; it is the 'have-nots' who will benefit at the expense of the 'haves' and the Indian masses have to be classified among the 'have-nots'. There remains but one question which may be a source of anxiety to the minorities, viz., religion and that aspect of culture that is based on religion. On this question the Congress policy is one of live and let live; a policy of complete non-interference in matters of conscience, religion and culture as well as of cultural autonomy for the different linguistic areas.

The Muslims have, therefore, nothing to fear in the event of India winning her freedom; on the contrary, they have everything to gain. So far as the religious and social disabilities of the so-called depressed classes are concerned, it is well-known that during the last seventeen years the Congress has left no stone unturned in the effort to remove them, and I have no doubt that the day is not far off when such disabilities will be things of the past.

I shall now proceed to consider the method which the Congress should pursue in the years to come as well as its role in the national struggle. I believe more than ever that the method should be Satyagraha or non-violent noncooperation in the widest sense of the term, including civil disobedience. It would not be correct to call our method passive resistance. Satyagraha, as I understand it, is not merely passive resistance but active resistance as well, though that activity must be of a nonviolent character. It is necessary to remind our countrymen that Satyagraha or non-violent non-cooperation may have to be resorted to again. The acceptance of office in the provinces as an experimental measure should not lead us to think that our future activity is to be confined within the limits of strict constitutionalism. There is every possibility that a determined opposition to the forcible inauguration of Federation may land us in another big campaign of civil disobedience.

In our struggle for independence we may adopt either of two alternatives. We may continue our fight until we have our full freedom and in the meantime decline to use any power that we may capture while on the march. We may, on the other hand, go on consolidating our position while we continue our struggle for Purna Swaraj or complete independence. From the point of view of principle, both the alternatives are equally acceptable and a priori considerations need not worry us. But we should consider very carefully at every stage as to which alternative would be more conducive to our national advancement.

In either case, the ultimate stage in our progress will be the severance of the British connection. When that severance takes place and there is no trace left of British domination, we shall be in a position to determine our future relations with Great Britain through a treaty of alliance voluntarily entered into by both parties. What out future relations with Great Britain will or should be, it is too early to say. That will depend to a large extent on the attitude of the British people themselves. On this point I have been greatly impressed by the attitude of President de Valera. Like the President of Eire, I should also say that we have no enmity towards the British people. We are fighting Great Britain and we want the fullest liberty to determine our future relations with her. But once we have real self-determination, there is no reason why we should not enter into the most cordial relations with the British people.

I am afraid there is a lack of clarity in the minds of many Congressmen as to the role of the Congress in the history of our national struggle. I know that there are friends who think that after freedom is won, the Congress Party having achieved its objective, should wither away. Such a conception is entirely erroneous. The party that wins freedom for India should be also the party that will put into effect the entire programme of post-war reconstruction. Only those who have won power can handle it properly. If other people are pitchforked into seats of power which they were not responsible for capturing, they will lack that strength, confidence and idealism which is indispensable for revolutionary reconstruction. It is this which accounts for the difference in the record of the Congress and non-Congress ministries in the very narrow sphere of Provincial Autonomy.

No, there can be no question of the Congress Party withering away after political freedom has been won. On the contrary, the Party will have to take over power, assume responsibility for administration and put through its programme of reconstruction. Only then will it fulfil its role. If it were forcibly to liquidate itself, chaos would follow. Looking at post-war Europe we find that only in those countries has there been orderly and continuous progress where the party which seized power undertook the work of reconstruction.

I know that it will be argued that the continuance of a party in such circumstances, standing behind the state, will convert that state into a totalitarian one; but I cannot admit the charge. The state will possibly become a totalitarian one, if there be only one party as in countries like Russia, Germany and Italy. But there is no reason why other parties should be banned. Moreover, the party itself will have a democratic basis, unlike, for instance, the Nazi Party which is based on the 'leader principle'. The existence of more than one party and the democratic basis of the Congress Party will prevent the future Indian state becoming a totalitarian one. Further, the democratic basis of the party will ensure that leaders are not thrust upon the people from above, but are elected from below.

Though it may be somewhat premature to give a detailed plan of reconstruction, we might as well consider some of the principles according to which our future social reconstruction should take place. I have no doubt in my mind that our chief national problems relating to the eradication of poverty, illiteracy and disease and to scientific production and distribution can be effectively tackled only along socialistic lines. The very first thing which our future national government will have to do, would be to set up a commission for drawing up a comprehensive plan of reconstruction. This plan will have two parts; an immediate programme and a long-period programme.

In drawing up the first part, the immediate objectives which will have to be kept in view will be three-fold; first, to prepare the country for self-sacrifice; secondly, to unify India; and thirdly, to give scope for local and cultural autonomy. The second and third objectives may appear to be contradictory, but they are not really so. Whatever political talent or genius we may possess as a people, will have to be used in reconciling these two objectives. We shall have to unify the country so that we may be able to hold India against any foreign invasion. While unifying the country through a strong central government, we shall have to put all the minority communities as well as the provinces at their ease, by allowing them a large measure of autonomy in cultural as well as governmental affairs.

Special efforts will be needed to keep our people together when the load of foreign domination is removed, because alien rule has demoralised and disorganised us to a degree. To promote national unity we shall have to develop our *lingua franca* and a common script. Further, with the help of such modern scientific contrivances as aeroplanes, telephone, radio, films, television, etc., we shall have to bring the different parts of India closer to one another and through a common educational policy we shall have to foster a common spirit among the entire population. So far as our lingua franca is concerned, I am inclined to think that the distinction between Hindi and Urdu is an artificial one.

The most natural lingua franca would be a mixture of the two, such as is spoken in daily life in large portions of the country and this common language may be written in either of the two scripts - Nagari or Urdu. I am aware that there are people in India who strongly favour either of the two scripts to the exclusion of the other. Our policy, however, should not be one of exclusion. We should allow the fullest latitude to use either script. At the same time, I am inclined to think that the ultimate solution, and the best solution would be the adoption of a script that would bring us into line with the rest of the world. Perhaps, some of our countrymen will gape with horror when they hear of the adoption of the Roman script, but I would beg them to consider this problem from the scientific and historical point of view. If we do that, we shall realise at once that there is nothing sacrosanct in a script.

The Nagari script, as we know it today, has passed through several phases of evolution. Besides, most of the major provinces of India have their own script and there is the Urdu script which is used largely by the Urdu-speaking public in India and by both Muslims and Hindus in provinces like the Punjab and Sindh. In view of such diversity, the choice of a uniform script for the whole of India should be made in a thoroughly scientific and impartial spirit, free from bias of every kind. I confess that there was a time when I felt that it would be anti-national to adopt a foreign script.

But my visit to Turkey in 1934 was responsible for converting me. I then realised for the first time what a great advantage it was to have the same script as the rest of the world. So far as our masses are concerned, since more than 90 per cent are illiterate and are not familiar with any script, it will not matter to them which script we introduce when they are educated. The Roman script will, moreover, facilitate their learning a European language. I am quite aware how unpopular the immediate adoption of the Roman script would be in our country. Nevertheless, I would beg my countrymen to consider what would be the wisest solution in the long run.

With regard to the long-period programme for a Free India, the first problem to tackle is that of our increasing population. I do not desire to go into the theoretical question as to whether India is overpopulated or not. I simply want to point out that where poverty, starvation and disease are stalking the land, we cannot afford to have our population mounting up by thirty million during a single decade.

If the population goes up by leaps and bounds, as it has done in the recent past, our plans are likely to fall through. It will, therefore, be desirable to restrict our population until we are able to feed, clothe and educate those who already exist. It is not necessary at this stage to prescribe the methods that should be adopted to prevent a further increase in population, but I would urge that public attention be drawn to this question.

Regarding reconstruction, our principal problem will be how to eradicate poverty from our country. That will require a radical reform of our land system, including the abolition of landlordism. Agricultural indebtedness will have to be liquidated and provision made for cheap credit for the rural population. An extension of the cooperative movement will be necessary for the benefit of both producers and consumers. Agriculture will have to be put on a scientific basis with a view to increasing the yield from the land.

To solve the economic problem agricultural improvement will not be enough. A comprehensive scheme of industrial development under state ownerships and state control will be indispensable. A new industrial system will have to be built up in place of the old one which has collapsed as a result of mass production abroad and alien rule at home. The planning commission will have to carefully consider and decide which of the home industries could be revived despite the competition of modern factories and in which sphere large scale production should be encouraged.

However much we may dislike modern industrialism and condemn the evils which follow in its train, we cannot go back to the pre-industrial era, even if we desire to do so. It is well, therefore, that we should reconcile ourselves to industrialisation and devise means to minimise its evils and at the same time explore the possibilities of reviving cottage industries where there is a possibility of their surviving the inevitable competition of factories. In a country like India, there will be plenty of room for cottage industries, especially in the case of industries including handspinning and handweaving allied to agriculture.

Last but not the least, the state on the advice of a planning commission, will have to adopt a comprehensive scheme for gradually socialising our entire agricultural and industrial system in the spheres of both production and appropriation. Extra capital will have to be procured for this, whether through internal or external loans or through inflation.

Opposing or resisting the provincial part of the Constitution will be hardly possible now, since the Congress Party has accepted office in seven out of eleven provinces. All that could be done would be to strengthen and consolidate the Congress as a result of it. I am one of those who were not in favour of taking office — not because there was something inherently wrong in doing so, not because no good could come out of that policy, but because it was apprehended that the evil effects of office acceptance would outweigh the good. Today I can only hope that my forebodings were unfounded.

How can we strengthen and consolidate the Congress while our ministers are in office? The first thing to do is to change the composition and character of the bureaucracy. If this is not done, the Congress Party may come to grief. In every country, the ministers come and go, but the steel frame of the permanent services remains. If that is not altered in composition and character, the governmental party and its cabinet are likely to prove ineffective in putting their principles into practice. This is what happened in the case of the Social Democratic Party in postwar Germany and perhaps in the case of the Labour Party in Great Britain in 1924 and 1929.

It is the permanent services who really rule in every country. In India they have been created by the British and in the higher ranks they are largely British in composition. Their outlook and mentality are in most cases neither Indian nor national and a national policy cannot be executed until the permanent services become national in outlook and mentality. The difficulty, of course, will be that the higher ranks of the permanent services being, under the Statute, directly under the Secretary of State for India and not under the Provincial Government, it will not be easy to alter their composition.

Secondly, the Congress ministers in the different provinces should, while they are in office, introduce schemes of reconstruction in the spheres of education, health, prohibition, prison reforms, irrigation, industry, land reform, workers' welfare etc. In this matter, attempts should be made to have as far as possible, a uniform policy for the whole of India. This uniformity could be brought about in either of two ways. The Congress ministers in the different provinces could themselves come together; as the Labour Ministers did in October, 1937, in Calcutta; and draw up a uniform programme. Over and above this, the Congress Working Committee, which is the supreme executive of the Congress could lend a helping hand by giving directions to the different departments of the Congress-controlled provincial governments in the light of such advice as it may get from its own experts.

This will mean that the members of the Congress Working Committee should be conversant with the problems that come within the purview of the Congress governments in the provinces. It is not intended that they should go into the details of administration. All that is needed is that they should have a general understanding of the different problems so that they could lay down the broad lines of policy. In this respect, the Congress Working Committee could do much more than it has hitherto done and unless it does so, I do not see how that body can keep an effective control over the different Congress ministries.

At this stage I should like to say something more about the role of the Congress Working Committee. This Committee, in my judgement, is not merely the directing brain of the national army of fighters for freedom. It is also the Shadow Cabinet of Independent India and it should function accordingly. This is not an invention of my own.

It is the role which has been assigned to similar bodies in other countries that have fought for their national emancipation. I am one of those who think in terms of a Free India; who visualise a national government in this country within the brief span of our own life. It is consequently natural for us to urge that the Working Committee should feel and function as the Shadow Cabinet of a Free India. This is what President de Valera's Republican Government did when it was fighting the British Government and was on the run. And this is what the Executive of the Wafd Party in Egypt did before it got into office. The members of the Working Committee while carrying on their day to day work should accordingly study the problems they will have to tackle in the event of their capturing political power.

More important than the question of the proper working of the Congress Governments is the immediate problem of how to oppose the inauguration of the federal part of the Constitution. The Congress attitude towards the proposed Federal Scheme has been clearly stated in the resolution adopted by the "Working Committee at Wardha on February 4, 1938, which will be placed before this Congress" after the Subjects Committee has considered it. That resolution says:

The Congress has rejected the new Constitution and declared that a Constitution for India which can be accepted by the people must be based on Independence and can only be framed by the people themselves by means of a Constituent Assembly without the interference by any foreign authority. Adhering to this policy of rejection, the Congress has, however, permitted the formation in provinces of Congress Ministries with a view to strengthening the nation in its struggle for Independence. In regard to the proposed Federation, no such consideration applies even provisionally, or for a period, and the imposition of this Federation, will do grave injuries to India and tighten the bonds which hold her under the subjection of an imperialist domination. This scheme of Federation excludes from the sphere of responsibility the vital function of a government.

The Congress is not opposed to the idea of Federation but a real Federation must, even apart from the question of responsibility, consist of free units, enjoying more or less the same measure of freedom and civil liberty and representation by a democratic process of election. Indian states participating in the Federation should approximate to the provinces in the establishment of representative institutions, responsible government, civil liberties and the method of election to the Federal House. Otherwise Federation as it is now contemplated will, instead of building Indian unity, encourage separatist tendencies and involve the states in internal and external conflict.

The Congress, therefore, reiterates its condemnation of the proposed scheme and calls upon Provincial and Local Congress Committees and the people generally as well as Provincial Governments and Ministries to prevent its inauguration. In the event of an attempt being made to impose it, despite the declared will of the people, such an attempt must be combated in every way and the Provincial Government and Ministries must refuse to cooperate with it.

In case such a contingency arises, the AICC is authorised and directed to determine the line of action to be pursued in this regard.

I should like to add some more arguments to explain our attitude of uncompromising hostility towards the proposed Federation. One of the most objectionable features of the Federal Scheme relates to the commercial and financial safeguards in the new Constitution. Not only will the people continue to be deprived of any power over defence or foreign policy, but the major portion of the expenditure will also be entirely out of popular control. According to the budget of the Central Government for the year 1937-38, the army expenditure comes to 44.61 crores of rupees (£ 33.46 million) out of a total expenditure of 77.90 crores of rupees (£ 58.42 million); that is, roughly 57 per cent of the total expenditure of the Central Government.

It appears that the reserved side of Federal Government which will be controlled by the Governor-General will handle about 80 per cent of the Federal expenditure. Moreover, bodies like the Reserve Bank and the Federal Railways Authority are already created or will be created which will work as *imperium in imperio* uncontrolled by a Federal Legislature. The Legislature will be deprived of the powers it possesses at present to direct and influence railway policy, and it will not have any voice in determining the currency and exchange policy of the country which has a vital bearing on its economic development.

The fact that external affairs will be a reserved subject under the Federal Government will prejudicially affect the freedom of the Indian Legislature to conclude trade agreements and will seriously restrict, in effect, fiscal autonomy. The Federal Government will not be under any constitutional obligation to place such trade agreements before the Legislature for their ratification, even as they decline at present to give an undertaking to place the Indo-British Trade Agreement before the Indian Legislative Assembly.

The so-called fiscal autonomy convention will have no meaning unless it is stipulated that no trade agreement on behalf of India shall be signed by any party without its ratification by the Indian Legislature. In this connection, I should like to state that I am definitely of opinion that India should enter into bilateral trade agreements with countries like Germany, Czechoslovakia, Italy and the United States of America with whom she had close trade relations in the past. But under the new Constitution, it will not be within the power of the Federal Legislature to force the Federal Government to enter into such bilateral trade agreements.

The iniquitous and inequitable commercial safeguards embodied in the Act will make it impossible for any effective measure to be adopted in order to protect and promote Indian national industries especially where they might, as they often do, conflict with British commercial or industrial interests. In addition to the Governor General's special responsibility to see that provisions with regard to discrimination, as laid down in the Act, are duly carried out, it is also his duty to prevent any action which would subject British goods imported into India to any kind of discriminatory or penal treatment.

A careful study of these stringent and wide provisions will show that India can adopt no measures against British competition which the Governor-General cannot, in effect, stultify or veto, whether in the legislative or in the administrative sphere. It is, of course, preposterous to permit foreigners in this country to compete with the nationals on equal terms and there can be no genuine Swaraj if India is to be denied the power to devise and adopt a national economic policy including the right, if her interests so require, of differentiating between nationals and non-nationals.

In a famous article in Young India, under the caption 'The Giant and the Dwarf' written soon after the conclusion of the Gandhi-Irwin Pact in 1931, Mahatma Gandhi declared plainly that "to talk of no discrimination between Indian interests and English or European, is to perpetuate Indian haritage. What is equality of rights between a giant and a dwarf?" Even the meagre powers enjoyed by the Central Legislature at present to enact a measure like the reservation of the Indian coastal trade for Indian-owned and Indian-managed vessels has been taken away under the so-called reformed Constitution. Shipping is a vital industry which is essential for defensive as well as for economic purposes, but all the accepted and legitimate methods of developing this key industry including those adopted even by several British

Dominions are henceforth rendered impossible for India. To justify such limitations on our sovereignty on the ground of 'reciprocity' and 'partnership' is literally to add insult to injury.

The right of the future Indian Parliament to differentiate or discriminate between nationals and non-nationals, whenever Indian interests require it, should remain intact and this right we cannot sacrifice on any account. I would like in this connection to cite the Irish parallel. The Irish Nationality and Citizenship Act of 1935 provides for a distinct Irish citizenship in connection with the electoral system, entry into public life, merchant shipping law, aircraft, as also in connection with special privileges which it thought proper to reserve for Irish nationals, such as those conferred through measures for assisting Irish industry. Irish citizenship, in other words, is distinct from British, which cannot claim equal rights in the State of Eire (or Ireland) on the basis of British citizenship, which is not recognised there. I feel that India must similarly seek to develop her own distinct nationality and establish a citizenship of her own.

While on the question of fiscal autonomy and commercial safeguards, I might refer briefly to the need of an active foreign trade policy for India. India's foreign trade should be viewed not in a haphazard or piecemeal manner as is often done in order to provide some immediate or temporary benefit to British industry, but in a comprehensive manner so as to coordinate India's economic development with its export trade on the one hand and its external obligation on the other.

The very nature of India's export trade makes it essential that it should not have any restrictive agreement with England such as would jeopardise its trade with the various non-empire countries which have been in several respects its best customers, or such as would tend to weaken India's bargaining power vis-a-vis other countries. It is unfortunate that the protected negotiations for an Indo-British Trade Agreement are still proceeding, while the Ottawa Agreement, even after the expiry of its notice period and despite the decision of the Legislative Assembly to terminate it, still continues, and along with the differential duties on British steel and textiles, the said Ottawa Agreement secures the prevailing advantages for British industries. There is no doubt that under the existing political conditions, any trade agreement between England and India is bound to be of an unequal character because our present political relationship would weigh the scales heavily in favour of England. There is also no doubt that the British preferential system is political in origin and before we permit non-Indian vested interests to be established or consolidated in this country under the shelter of a trade agreement, we should be careful as to its political repercussions and economic consequences. I trust that the present Indo-British Trade negotiations will not be allowed to impede the conclusion of bilateral trade agreements with other countries whenever possible and that no such trade agreement will be signed by the Government of India unless it is ratified by the Indian Legislature.

From the above, it will be quite clear that there is no analogy between the powers of the Provincial Ministries and those of the proposed Federal Ministry. Moreover, the composition of the Federal Legislature is reactionary to a degree. The total population of the Indian states is roughly 24 per cent of that of the whole of India. Nevertheless, the Rulers of the States, not their subjects, have been given 33 per cent of the seats in the Lower House and 40 per cent in the Upper House of the Federal Legislature.

In these circumstances, there is no possibility, in my opinion, of the Congress altering its attitude towards the Federal Scheme at any time. On our success in resisting the imposition of Federation by the British Government will depend our immediate political future. We have to fight Federation by all legitimate and peaceful means; not merely along constitutional lines; and in the last resort, we may have to resort to mass civil disobedience which is the ultimate sanction we have in our hands. There can be little doubt that in the event of such a campaign being started in the future, the movement will not be confined to British India but will spread among the states' subjects.

To put up an effective fight in the near future, it is necessary to put our own house in order. The awakening among our masses during the last few years has been so tremendous that new problems have arisen concerning our party organisation. Meetings attended by fifty thousand men and women are a usual occurrence nowadays. It is sometimes found that to control such meetings and demonstrations, our machinery is not adequate. Apart from these passing demonstrations, there is the bigger problem of mobilising this phenomenal mass energy and enthusiasm and directing them along proper lines. But have we got a well-disciplined Volunteer Corps for this purpose? Have we got a cadre of officers for our national service? Do we provide any training for our budding leaders, for our promising young workers?

The answers to these questions are too patent to need elaboration. We have not yet provided all these requirements of a modern political party, but it is high time that we did. A disciplined Volunteer Corps manned by trained officers is exceedingly necessary. Moreover, education and training should be provided for our political workers so that we may produce a better type of leaders in future.

This sort of training is provided by political parties in Britain through Summer Schools and other institutions; and is a speciality in totalitarian states. With all respect to our workers who have played a glorious part in our struggle, I must confess that there is room for more talent in our party. This defect can be made up partly by recruiting promising young men for the Congress and partly by providing education and training for those whom we already have. Everybody must have observed how some European countries have been dealing with this problem. Though our ideals and methods of training are quite different from theirs, it will be admitted on all hands that a thorough scientific training is a requisite for our workers. Further, an institution like the Labour Service Corps of the Nazis deserves careful study and, with suitable modification may prove beneficial to India.

While dealing with the question of enforcing discipline within our own party, we have to consider a problem which has been causing worry and embarrassment to many of us. I am referring to organisations like the Trade Union Congress and the Kisan Sabhas and their relations with the Indian National Congress. There are two opposing schools of thought on this question — those who condemn any organisations that are outside the Congress and those who advocate them. My own view is that we cannot abolish such organisations by ignoring or condemning them. They exist as objective facts and since they have come into existence and show no signs of liquidating themselves, it should be manifest that there is a historical necessity behind them. Moreover, such organisations are to be found in other countries. I am afraid that whether we like it or not, we have to reconcile ourselves to their existence.

The only question is how the Congress should treat them. Obviously, such organisations should not appear as a challenge to the National Congress which is the organ of mass struggle for capturing political power. They should, therefore, be inspired by Congress ideals and methods and work in close cooperation with the Congress. To ensure this, Congress workers should in large numbers participate in trade union and peasant organisations. From my own experience of trade union work I feel that this could easily be done without landing oneself in conflict or inconsistency. Cooperation between the Congress and the other two organisations could be facilitated if the latter deal primarily with the economic grievances of the workers and peasants and treat the Congress as a common platform for all those who strive for the political emancipation of their country.

This brings us to the vexed problem of the collective affiliation of workers' and peasants' organisations of the Congress. Personally, I hold the view that the day will come when we shall have to grant this affiliation in order to bring all progressive and anti-imperialist organisations under the influence and control of the Congress. There will, of course, be difference of opinion as to the manner and the extent to which this affiliation should be given and the character and stability of such organisations will have to be examined before affiliation could be agreed to.

In Russia, the united front of the Soviets of workers, peasants and soldiers played a dominant part in the October Revolution; but, on the contrary, in Great Britain we find that the British Trade Union Congress exerts a moderating influence on the National Executive of the Labour Party. In India, we shall have to consider carefully what sort of influence organisations like the Trade Union Congress and the Kisan Sabhas will exert on the Indian National Congress in the event of affiliation being granted and we should not forget that there is the possibility that the former may not have a radical outlook if their immediate economic grievances are not involved. In any case, quite apart from the question of collective affiliation, there should be the closest cooperation between the National Congress and other anti-imperialist organisations and this object would be facilitated by the latter adopting the principles and methods of the former.

There has been a great deal of controversy over the question of forming a party, like the Congress Socialist Party, within the Congress. I hold no brief for the Congress Socialist Party and I am not a member of it. Nevertheless, I must say that I have been in agreement with its general principles and policy from the very beginning. In the first place, it is desirable for the leftist elements to be consolidated into one party.

Secondly, a leftist bloc can have a *raison d'etre* only if it is socialist in character. There are friends who object to such a bloc being called a party, but to my mind it is quite immaterial whether you call that bloc a group, league or party. Within the limits prescribed by the Constitution of the Indian National Congress, it is quite possible for a leftist bloc to have a socialist programme, in which case it can be very well called a group, league or party. But the role of the Congress Socialist Party, or any other party of the same sort, should be that of a left-wing group. Socialism is not an immediate problem for us — nevertheless, socialist propaganda is necessary to prepare the country for socialism when political freedom has been won. And that propaganda can be conducted only by a party like the Congress Socialist Party, which stands for and believes in socialism.

There is one problem in which I have been taking a deep personal interest for some years and in connection with which I should like to make my submission; I mean the question of a foreign policy for India and of developing international contacts. I attach great importance to this work because I believe that in the years to come, international development will favour our struggle in India. But we must have a correct appreciation of the world situation at every stage and should know how to take advantage of it. The lesson of Egypt stands before us as an example. Egypt won her Treaty of Alliance with Great Britain without firing a shot, simply because she knew how to take advantage of the Anglo-Italian tension in the Mediterranean.

In connection with our foreign policy, the first suggestion that I have to make is that we should not be influenced by the internal politics of any country or the form of its state. We shall find in every country men and women who will sympathise with Indian freedom, no matter what their own political views may be. In this matter we should take a leaf out of Soviet diplomacy. Though Soviet Russia is a communist state, her diplomats have not hesitated to make alliances with non-socialist states and have not declined sympathy or support coming from any quarter. We should, therefore, aim at developing a nucleus of men and women in every country who feel sympathetic towards India.

To create and develop such a nucleus, propaganda through the foreign press, through Indian-made films and through art exhibitions would be helpful. The Chinese, for example, have made themselves exceedingly popular in Europe through their art exhibitions. Above all, personal contacts are necessary. Without such personal contacts it would be difficult to make India popular in other countries. Indian students abroad could also help in this work, provided we in India look to their needs and requirements. There should be closer contact between Indian students abroad and the Indian National Congress at home. If we could send out cultural and educational films made in India, I am sure that India and her culture would become known and appreciated by people abroad. Such films would prove exceedingly useful to Indian students and Indian residents in other countries, who at present are like our non-official ambassadors.

I do not like the word propaganda; there is an air of falsity about it. But I insist that we should make India and her culture known to the world. I say this because I am aware that such efforts will be welcomed in every country in Europe and America. If we go ahead with this work, we shall be preparing the basis for our future embassies and legations in different lands. We should not neglect Great Britain either. We have even in that country a small but influential group of men and women who are genuinely sympathetic towards Indian aspirations. Among the rising generation and students, in particular, interest in and sympathy for India is rapidly on the increase. One has only to visit the universities of Great Britain to realise that.

To carry on this work effectively, the Indian National Congress should have its trusted agents in Europe, Asia, Africa and in North, Central and South America. It is a pity that we have so far neglected Central and South America where there is profound interest in India. The Congress should be assisted in this work of developing international contact by cultural organisations in India, working in the field of international culture and by the Indian Chambers of Commerce working in the sphere of international commerce. Further, Indians should make it a point to attend every international congress or conference — participation in such conferences is a very useful and healthy form of propaganda for India.

While talking of international contacts, I should remove a misgiving which may be present in some minds. Developing international contacts does not mean intriguing against the British Government. We need not go in for such intrigues and all our methods should be aboveboard. The propaganda that goes on against India all over the world is to the effect that India is an uncivilised country and it is inferred therefrom that the British are needed in order to civilise us. As a reply, we have only to let the world know what we are and what our culture is like. If we can do that, we shall create such a volume of international sympathy in our favour that India's case will become irresistible before the bar of world opinion.

I should not forget to refer to the problems, the difficulties and the trials which face our countrymen in different parts of Asia and Africa — notably in Zanzibar, Kenya, South Africa, Malaya and Ceylon. The Congress has always taken the keenest interest in their affairs and will continue to do so in future. If we have not been able to do more for them it is only because we are still slaves at home. A free India will be a healthy and potent factor in world politics and will be able to look after the interests of its nationals abroad.

I must in this connection stress the desirability and necessity of developing closer cultural relations with our neighbours, viz., Persia, Afghanistan, Nepal, China, Burma, Siam, Malay States, East Indies and Ceylon. It would be good for both parties if they knew more of us and we knew more of them. With Burma and

Ceylon, in particular, we should have the most intimate cultural intercourse, in view of our age-long contacts.

Friends, I am sorry I have taken more of your time than I had intended at first, but I am now nearing the end of my address. There is one important matter — the burning topic of the day; to which I should now draw your attention; the question of the release of detainees and political prisoners. The recent hungerstrikes have brought this question to the forefront and have focused public attention on it. I believe that I am voicing the feelings of at least the rank and file of the Congress when I say that everything humanly possible should be done to expedite release. So far as the Congress ministries are concerned, it would be well to note that the record of some of them has not come up to public expectation. The sooner they satisfy the public demand, the better it will be for the Congress and for the people who are suffering in provinces ruled by non-Congress ministries. It is not necessary for me to labour this point and I fervently hope that in the immediate future, the public will have nothing to complain of so far as the record of the Congress ministries on this point is concerned.

It is not only the detainees and political prisoners in jail and detention who have their tale of woe. The lot of those who have been released is sometimes no better. They often return home in shattered health, victims of fell diseases like tuberculosis. Grim starvation stares them in the face and they are greeted, not with the smiles but with the tears of near and dear ones. Have we no duty to those who have given of their best in the service of their country and have received nothing but poverty and sorrow in return? Let us, therefore, send our heartfelt sympathy to all those who have suffered for the crime of loving their country and let us all contribute our humble mite towards the alleviation of their misery.

Friends, one word more and I have done. We are faced with a serious situation today. Inside the Congress there are differences between the right and the left which it would be futile to ignore. Outside, there is the challenge of British Imperialism which we are called upon to face. What shall we do in this crisis? Need I say that we have to stand foursquare against all the storms that may beset our path and be impervious to all the designs that our rulers may employ? The Congress today is the one supreme organ of mass struggle. It may have its right bloc and its left; but it is the , common platform for all anti-imperialist organisations striving for Indian emancipation. Let us, therefore, rally the whole country, under the banner of the Indian National Congress. I would appeal specially to the leftist groups in the country to pool all their/ strength and their resources for democratising the Congress and reorganising it on the broadest anti-imperialist basis. In making this appeal, I am greatly encouraged by the attitude of the leaders of the British Communist Party whose general policy with regard to India seems to me to be in keeping with that of the Indian National Congress.

In conclusion, I shall voice your feelings by saying that all India fervently hopes and prays that Mahatma Gandhi may be spared to our nation for many years to come. India cannot afford to lose him and certainly not at this hour. We need him to keep our people united. We need him to keep our struggle free from bitterness and hatred. We need him for the cause of Indian Independence. What is more — we need him for the cause of humanity. Ours is a struggle not only against British Imperialism but against world Imperialism as well, of which the former is the keystone. We are, therefore, fighting not for the cause of India alone but of humanity as well. India freed means humanity saved.

Bande Mataram

The Fall of Singapore

[*First Broadcast, 19th February 1941*]

This is Subhash Chandra Bose speaking to you over the Azad Hind Radio.

For about a year I have waited in silence and patience for the march of events and now that the hour has struck, I come forward to speak.

The fall of Singapore means the collapse of British Empire, the end of iniquitous regime which it has symbolised and the dawn of a new era in Indian history. The Indian people who have long suffered from the humiliation of a foreign yoke and have been ruined spiritually, culturally, politically and economically while under British domination must now offer their humble thanks to the Almighty for the auspicious event which bears for India the promise of life and freedom.

British Imperialism has in modern history been the most diabolical enemy of freedom and the most formidable obstacle to progress. Because of it, a very large section of mankind has been kept enslaved and in India alone, about one-fifth of the human race has been ruthlessly suppressed and persecuted. For other nations, British Imperialism may be the enemy of today, but for India, it is the eternal foe. Between these two others can be neither peace nor compromise. And the enemies of British Imperialism are today the natural allies of India - just as the allies of British Imperialism are today our natural enemies.

The outside world hears from time to time voices coming from India, claiming to speak either in the name of Indian National Congress or of the Indian people. But these voices are coming through the channels of British propaganda and nobody should make the fatal mistake of regarding them as representative of Free India. As is natural in a land that has been under foreign domination, the British oppressors have endeavoured to create divisions among the Indian people. As a consequence thereof, we find in India those who openly support British Imperialism. There are others who, whether intentionally or unintentionally, help the British cause while often camouflaging their real motives by talking of cooperation with China, Russia and other Allies of England. There is, however, the vast majority of the Indian people who will have no compromise with British imperialism but will fight on till full independence is achieved. Owing to war-time conditions prevailing in India, the voice of these freedom-loving Indians cannot cross the frontiers of that country, but we who have fought for more than two decades for our national emancipation, know exactly what the vast majority of our country men think and feel today.

Standing at one of the cross-roads of world-history, I solemnly declare on behalf of all freedom-loving Indians in India and abroad that we shall continue to fight British Imperialism till India is once again the mistress of her own destiny. During this struggle and in the reconstruction that will follow, we shall heartily cooperate with all those who will help us in overthrowing the common enemy. I am confident that in this sacred struggle, the vast majority of the Indian will be with us. No manoeuvre, intrigue or conspiracy on the part of the agents of Anglo-America Imperialism, however prominent they may be and to whichever nationality they may belong, can throw dust in the eyes of the Indian people or swerve them from the path of patriotic duty. The hour of India's salvation is at hand. India will now rise and break the chains of servitude that have bound her so long. Through India's liberation will Asia and the world move forward towards the larger goal of human emancipation.

We will not Cease Fighting until Mother India is Free

[Broadcast over Azad Hind Radio from Germany on 11th March 1942]

For some time I have watched the changes in the world calmly and quietly. The fall of Singapore is a prelude to the fall of British Empire. A new era is setting in. By enslaving us, the British have entirely ruined our morality and our finances. We bow our heads before God, who has granted us such an auspicious occasion for freeing India. In this age there is no greater enemy of freedom and progress than Britain. Now is the time to wake up from your slumber. The end of British domination will mean the end of a tyrannous regime, and the beginning of a new life in the history of India. The British have heaped indignities and humiliations upon us. Again we thank God for giving us this auspicious opportunity. Today many nations of the world are the enemies of Britain. The friends of Britain are our enemies.

The Indian National Congress claims to guide the nation. But its half-hearted measure have encouraged British leaders to continue to follow the old and hackeyed course, namely, of making promises without meaning to fulfil them. I also know that there are such people in India who are anxious to preserve the British Empire. The majority of Indians do not want either British rule or their economic system.

We will not cease fighting until Mother India is free.

In the world is dawning a new age. A true patriot says that his own fate must be decided by himself. We are ready to cooperate with any nations that will help us in regaining our independence. I hope that all my Indian brothers and sisters will help me in this war against the British. Even with her cunning, and under-hand policy, Britain cannot fall India, neither can she stop Indians from cherishing their ideal of nationalism. India has decided to fight for her freedom. She will not only free herself, but will free Asia and even the whole world.

To Delhi, to Delhi

[Speech at a military review of the Indian National Army, July 5, 1943]

SOLDIERS of India's Army of Liberation!

Today is the proudest day of my life. Today it has pleased Providence to give me the unique privilege and honour of announcing to the whole world that India's Army of Liberation has come into being. This army has now been drawn up in military formation on the battlefield of Singapore, which was once the bulwark of the British Empire.

This is not only the Army that will emancipate India from the British yoke, it is also the Army that will hereafter create the future national army of Free India. Every Indian must feel proud that this Army, his own Army, has been organised entirely under Indian leadership and that when the historic moment arrives, under Indian leadership it will go to battle.

There are people who thought at one time that the Empire on which the sun did not set was an everlasting empire. No such thought ever troubled me. History had taught me that every empire has its inevitable decline and collapse. Moreover I had seen with my own eyes, cities and fortresses that were once the bulwarks but which became the graveyards of by-gone empires. Standing today on the graveyard of the British Empire, even a child is convinced that the almighty British Empire is already a thing of the past.

When France declared war on Germany in 1939 and the campaign began, there was but one cry which rose from the lips of German soldiers — "To Paris, To Paris!" When the Brave soldiers of Nippon set out on their march in December 1941 there was but one cry which rose from their lips — "To Singapore, to Singapore!" Comrades! Soldiers! Let your battle-cry be — "To-Delhi To Delhi!" How many of us will individually survive this war of freedom, I do not know. But I do know this, that we shall ultimately win and our task will not end until our surviving heroes hold the victory parade on another graveyard of the British Empire, the Lal Qila or Red Fortress of ancient Delhi.

Throughout my public career, I have always felt that though India is otherwise ripe for independence in every way, she has lacked one thing, namely an army of liberation. George Washington of America could fight and win freedom, because he had his army. Garibaldi could liberate Italy, because he had his armed volunteers behind him. It is your privilege and honour to be the first to come forward and organise India's national army. By doing so, you have removed the last obstacle in our path to freedom. Be happy and proud that you are the pioneers, the vanguard, in such a noble cause.

Let me remind you that you have a two-fold task to perform. With the force of arms and at the cost of your blood you will have to win liberty. Then, when India is free, you will have to organise the permanent army of Free India, whose task it will be to preserve our liberty for all time. We must build up our national defence on such an unshakable foundation that never again in our history shall we lose our freedom.

As soldiers, you will always have to cherish and live up to the three-ideals of faithfulness, duty and sacrifice. Soldiers who always remain faithful to their nation, who are always prepared to sacrifice their lives, are invincible. If you, too, want to be invincible, engrave these three ideals in the innermost core of your hearts.

A true soldier needs both military and spiritual training. You must, all of you, so train yourselves and your comrades that every soldier will have unbounded confidence in himself, will be conscious of being immensely superior to the enemy, will be fearless of death, and will have sufficient initiative to act on his own in any critical situation should the need arise. During the course of the present war, you have seen with your own eyes what wonders scientific training, coupled with courage, fearlessness and dynamism, can achieve. Learn all that you can from this example, and build up for Mother India an absolutely first-class modern army.

To those of you who are officers, I should like to say that your responsibility is a heavy one. Though the responsibility of an officer in every army in this world is indeed great, it is far greater in your case. Because of our political enslavement, we have no tradition like that of Mukden, Port Arthur or Sedan to inspire us. We have to unlearn some of the things that the British taught us and we have to learn much that they did not teach. Nevertheless. I am confident that you will rise to the occasion and fulfil the task that your countrymen have thrown on your brave soldiers. Remember always that officers can make or unmake an army. Remember, too, that the British have suffered defeats on so many fronts largely because of worthless officers. And remember also that out of your ranks will be born the future General Staff of the Army of Free India.

To all of you I should like to say that in the course of this war you will have to acquire the experience and achieve the success which alone can build up a national tradition for our Army. An army that has no tradition of courage, fearlessness and invincibility cannot hold its own in a struggle with a powerful enemy.

Comrades! You have voluntarily accepted a mission that is the noblest that the human mind can conceive of. For the fulfilment of such a mission no sacrifice is too great, not even the sacrifice of one's life. You are today the custodians of India's national honour and the embodiment of India's hopes and aspirations. So conduct yourself that your countrymen may bless you and posterity may be proud of you.

I have said that today is the proudest day of my life. For an enslaved people, there can be no greater pride, no higher honour, than to be the first soldier in the army of liberation. But this honour carries with it a corresponding responsibility and I am deeply conscious of it. I assure you that I shall be with you in darkness and in sunshine, in sorrow and in joy, in suffering and in victory. For the present, I can offer you nothing except hunger, thirst, privation, forced marches and death. But if you follow me in life and in death, as I am confident you will, I shall lead you to victory and freedom. It does not matter who among us will live to see India free. It is enough that India shall be free and that we shall give our all to make her free. May God now bless our Army and grant us victory in the coming fight!

Inquilab Zindabad! Azad Hind Zindabad!

On Assuming Direct Command of INA

[Order of the Day, August 26 1943]

In the interest of the Indian Independence Movement and of the Azad Hind Fauj, I have taken over the direct command of our Army from this day.

This is for me a matter of joy and pride, because for an Indian there can be no greater honour than to be Commander of India's Army of Liberation. But I am conscious of the magnitude of the task that I have undertaken and I am weighed down with a sense of responsibility. I pray that God may give me the necessary strength to fulfil my duty to Indians, under all circumstances, however difficult or trying they may be.

I regard myself as the servant of the 38 crores of my countrymen, who profess different religious faiths. I am determined to discharge my duties in such a manner that the interests of these 38 crores may be safe in my hands and every single Indian will have reason to put complete faith in me. It is only on the basis of undiluted nationalism and perfect justice and impartiality that India's Army of Liberation can be built up.

In the coming struggle or the emancipation of our motherland, for the establishment of a Government of Free India based on the goodwill of 38 crores of Indians and for the creation of a permanent army which will guarantee Indian independence for all times, the Azad Hind Fauj has a vital role to play. To fulfil this role we must weld ourselves into an army that will have only one goal, namely the freedom of Indians, and only one will, namely to do or die in the cause of India's freedom. When we stand, the Azad Hind Fauj has to be like a wall of granite; when we march, the Azad Hind Fauj has to be like a steamroller.

Our task is not an easy one; the war will be long and hard, but I have complete faith in the justice and invincibility of our cause. Thirty-eight crores of human beings, who form about one-fifth of the human race, have a right to be free and they are now ready to pay the price of freedom. There is consequently no power on earth that can deprive us of our birthright of liberty any longer.

Comrades, officers and men! With your unstinted support and unflinching loyalty, the Azad Hind Fauj will become the instrument of India's liberation. Ultimately victory will certainly be ours, I assure you.

With the slogan 'Onward to Delhi' on our lips, let us continue to fight till our National Flag flies over the Viceroy's House in New Delhi, and the Azad Hind Fauj holds its victory parade inside the ancient Red Fortress of the Indian metropolis.

Give Me Blood! I Promise You Freedom!!

[At a rally of Indians in Burma, July 4, 1944. This was the statement he made at the great rally where he was elected with acclaim as the leader of the Freedom Movement in East Asia. The speech infused new life to a movement which had been weakened by internal dissentions].

Friends! Twelve months ago a new programme of 'total mobilisation' or 'maximum sacrifice' was placed before Indians in East Asia. Today I shall give you an account of our achievements during the past year and shall place before you our demands for the coming year. But, before I do so, I want you to realise once again what a golden opportunity we have for winning freedom.

The British are engaged in a worldwide struggle and in the course of this struggle they have suffered defeat after defeat on so many fronts. The enemy having been thus considerably weakened, our fight for liberty has become very much easier than it was five years ago. Such a rare and God-given opportunity comes once in a century. That is why we have sworn to fully utilise this opportunity for liberating our motherland from the British yoke.

I am so very hopeful and optimistic about the outcome of our struggle, because I do not rely merely on the efforts of three million Indians in East Asia. There is a gigantic movement going on inside India and millions of our countrymen are prepared for maximum suffering and sacrifice in order to achieve liberty.

Unfortunately, ever since the great fight of 1857, our countrymen are disarmed, whereas the enemy is armed to the teeth. Without arms and without a modern army, it is impossible for a disarmed people to win freedom in this modern age. Through the grace of Providence and through the help of generous Nippon, it has become possible for Indians in East Asia to get arms to build up a modern army. Moreover, Indians in East Asia are united to a man in the endeavour to win freedom and all the religious and other differences that the British tried to engineer inside India, simply do not exist in East Asia. Consequently, we have now an ideal combination of circumstances favouring the success of our struggle- and all that is wanted is that Indians should themselves come forward to pay the price of liberty. According to the programme of 'total mobilisation', I demanded of you men, money and materials. Regarding men, I am glad to tell you that I have obtained sufficient recruits already. Recruits have come to us from every corner of east Asia- from China, Japan, Indo-China, Philippines, Java, Borneo, Celebes, Sumatra, Malaya, Thailand and Burma...

You must continue the mobilisation of men, money and materials with greater vigour and energy, in particular, the problem of supplies and transport has to be solved satisfactorily.

We require more men and women of all categories for administration and reconstruction in liberated areas. We must be prepared for a situation in which the enemy will ruthlessly apply the scorched earth policy, before withdrawing from a particular area and will also force the civilian population to evacuate as was attempted in Burma.

The most important of all is the problem of sending reinforcements in men and in supplies to the fighting fronts. If we do not do so, we cannot hope to maintain our success at the fronts. Nor can we hope to penetrate deeper into India.

Those of you who will continue to work on the Home Front should never forget that East Asia — and particularly Burma — from our base for the war of liberation. If this base is not strong, our fighting forces can never be victorious. Remember that this is a 'total war' — and not merely a war between two armies. That is why for a full one year I have been laying so much stress on 'total mobilisation' in the East.

There is another reason why I want you to look after the Home Front properly. During the coming months I and my colleagues on the War Committee of the Cabinet desire to devote our whole attention to the fighting front — and also to the task of working up the revolution inside India. Consequently, we want to be fully assured that the work at the base will go on smoothly and uninterruptedly even in our absence.

Friends, one year ago, when I made certain demands of you, I told you that if you give me 'total mobilisation', I would give you a 'second front'. I have redeemed that pledge. The first phase of our campaign is over. Our victorious troops, fighting side by side with Nipponese troops, have pushed back the enemy and are now fighting bravely on the sacred soil of our dear motherland. Gird up your loins for the task that now lies ahead. I had asked you for men, money and materials. I have got them in generous measure. Now I demand more of you. Men, money and materials cannot by themselves bring victory or freedom. We must have the motive-power that will inspire us to brave deeds and heroic exploits.

It will be a fatal mistake for you to wish to live and see India free simply because victory is now within reach. No one here should have the desire to live to enjoy freedom. A long fight is still in front of us.

We should have but one desire today — the desire to die so that India may live — the desire to face a martyr's death, so that the path to freedom may be paved with the martyr's blood.

Friend's! my comrades in the War of Liberation! Today I demand of you one thing, above all. I demand of you blood. It is blood alone that can avenge the blood that the enemy has spilt. It is blood alone that can pay the price of freedom. Give me blood and I promise you freedom.

Why INA withdrew?

[On August 13, 1944. When the Imphal expedition failed largely because of the failure of the Japanese military supplies to the front and the complete dominations the British and American forces had over the skies of Burma, Netaji had to explain that this was not the end of the war. It was a setback but not the final defeat].

We started the operations too late. The monsoon was disadvantageous to us. Our roads were submerged. River traffic had to be against the current. Against this, the enemy had first-class roads. Our only chance was to take Imphal before the rains started; and we would have succeeded if we had more air support and if the enemy forces in Imphal had not special orders to make a stand to the last man. If we had started in January, we would have succeeded. In all sectors, till the rains began, we either held the enemy or advanced. In the Arakan Sector, the enemy was held; In the Kaladan Sector, we routed the enemy and advanced; In Tiddim, we advanced; In Palel and Kohima also, we advanced; In the Haka Sector, we held them — and all this in spite of the numerical superiority that the enemy had, plus equipment and rations.

When the rains came, we had to postpone the general assault on Imphal. The enemy was able to send mechanised divisions and thus was able to retake the Kohima-Imphal Road. The question then arose: where should we hold the line? There were two courses open: either to hold on to the Bishenpur-Palel Line and not allow the enemy to advance; or to fall back and hold a more advantageous position.

What are the lessons we have learnt from the campaign? We have received our baptism by fire. A body of ex-civilians, who were ordered to withdraw, and with fixed bayonets they charged the enemy. They came back victorious.

Our troops have gained much confidence. We have learnt that the Indian troops with the enemy are willing to come over. We must now make arrangements to take them over. We have learnt the tactics of the enemy. We have captured enemy documents. The experience gained by our Commanders has been invaluable. Before the campaign started, the Japanese had no confidence in our troops and wanted to break them up into batches attached to the Japanese Army. I wanted a front to be given to our men and this was ultimately given.

We have also learnt our defects. Transport and supply were defective owing to the difficult terrain. We had no frontline propaganda. Though we had prepared personnel for this, we could not use them owing to lack of transport. Henceforth, each unit of the INA will have a propaganda unit attached to it. We wanted loudspeakers but the Japanese failed to supply them to us. We are now making our own.

India will be Free

[Message of August 17, 1945, to Indiano in East Asia, retranslated from the Tamil version published by Swatantra India, Singapore].

Brothers and Sisters! A great chapter in the history of India's freedom struggle has come to a close now. India's sons and daughters living in East Asia have secured a permanent place in this chapter.

By contributing men, money and supplies to the struggle for Indian independence, you have set up a shining example of patriotism and sacrifice. I can never forget your generous and enthusiastic response to my call of Total Mobilisation. Like a perennial spring you sent your sons and daughters to the Azad Hind Fauj and Jhansi Rani Regiment. You gave generous donations in cash and kind to the war fund of the Provisional Government of Azad Hind. In short, you have carried out your duty as the real sons and daughters of India. I am more aggrieved than you by the fact that your sufferings and sacrifices have not yielded immediate results.

Neverthless they have not gone waste, because they have paved the path of deliverance of our motherland and will be a perpetual source of inspiration to Indians living all over the world. The future will bless you and will speak with pride of your sacrifices at the altar of Indian independence and of your solid achievements.

At this unprecedented juncture in our history I have a word for you. Do not be disheartened by our temporary defeat; be cheerful and optimistic. Above all, never lose your faith in the destiny of India. There is no power on earth which can keep India in bondage. India will be free and, that too, soon. JAI HIND!

11

Golden Words of Netaji

- "You give me your blood and I will give you Independence!"
- "One individual may die for an idea; but that idea will, after his death, incarnate itself in a thousand lives. That is how the wheel of evolution moves on and the ideas and dreams of one nation are bequeathed to the next."
- "Freedom is not given, it is taken."
- "As soldiers, you will always have to cherish and live up to the three ideals of faithfulness, duty and sacrifice. Soldiers who always remain faithful to their nation, who are always prepared to sacrifice their lives, are invincible. If you, too, want to be invincible, engrave these three ideals in the innermost core of your hearts."
- "Gird up your loins for the task that now lies ahead. I had asked you for men, money and materials. I have got them in generous measure. Now I demand more of you. Men, money and materials cannot by themselves bring victory or freedom. We must have the motive-power that will inspire us to brave deeds and heroic exploits."
- "I have no doubt in my mind that our chief national problems relating to the eradication of poverty, illiteracy

and disease and the scientific production and distribution can be tackled only along socialistic lines."

- "Nationalism is inspired by the highest ideals of the human race, satyam [the true], shivam [the god], sundaram [the beautiful]. Nationalism in India has ... roused the creative faculties which for centuries had been lying dormant in our people."
- "It is our duty to pay for our liberty with our own blood. The freedom that we shall win through our sacrifice and exertions, we shall be able to preserve with our own strength."
- "No real change in history has ever been achieved by discussions."
- "We should have but one desire today? The desire to die so that India may live? The desire to face a martyr's death, so that the path to freedom may be paved with the martyr's blood."

12

Subhash Chandra Bose's Life at a Glance

1897: He was born in a Bengali family in the year 1897. His early education was at Ravenshaw Collegiate School in Calcutta and Fitzwilliam College at Cambridge University. Subhash Chandra Bose was a great Indian freedom fighter and was greatly interested in joining Indian Freedom Movement.

April 14, 1906: Shri Subhash Chandra Bose made Vande Mataram the song of his Indian National Army and it was regularly broadcast from his Singapore radio station. A procession of patriots was canned at Calcutta due to recitation of Vande Mataram. Maharishi Arvind, who was also in the procession, was injured in the canning. Maharishi translated into English the Vande Mataram song.

1909: Netaji Subhash Chandra Bose came to Uttarpara once and gave his political speech. A heritage building is under renovation process to keep the memory of this great freedom fighter.

1910: Jawaharlal Nehru and Subhash Chandra Bose led the Freedom Movement in which commoners actively participated.

1921: Subhash Chandra Bose was deeply disturbed by the Jallianwalla Bagh massacre, and left his Civil Services apprenticeship midway to return to India in 1921. After returning to India Netaji Subhash Chandra Bose came under the influence of Mahatma Gandhi and joined the Indian National Congress. On Gandhiji's instructions, he started working under Deshbandhu Chittaranjan Das, whom he later acknowledged his political guru.

1923: Appointed editor of Forward Bloc.

October 22, 1933: The mortal remains of Vithhalbhai were sent to Bombay from Geneva, where he died on October 22, 1933, by Netaji Subhash Chandra Bose, who was at his bedside till the end.

1938: He was elected President of the Indian Congress Party and presided over the Haripura Session. He was re-elected the next year and presided over the Tripuri Session. He resigned from the presidency on 28 April 1939.

Mar 7, 1938: Subhash Chandra Bose was on the Time cover. Not that Time really loved Netaji, in fact Time used a lot of pejoratives for him all the time and his Indian National Army.

May 3, 1939: Forward Bloc was formed on 3 May 1939 by Netaji Subhash Chandra Bose who resigned from the Congress Party. During Second World War, Netaji Subhash Chandra Bose led the Indian National Army against the British colonialists. The British outlawed the Forward Bloc and ransacked their offices. After the war, AIFB was reorganised. Early there was a split in the Bloc, leading to the existence of FB (Ruiker) and FB (Marxist).

June 22, 1940: Subhash Chandra Bose came to see Savarkar. Savarkar told Bose, "Why do you waste time in your movement to remove the monument to 'Black Hole of Calcutta'?"

1941: Assassination Attempts. In 1941, when the British learned that Bose had sought the support of the Axis Powers, they ordered their agents to assassinate Bose.

2 November 1941: Opened the Free India Centre in Berlin.

4 July 1943: Became leader of the Indian Independence League at a formal ceremony in Singapore.

5 July 1943: Renamed the Indian National Army as Azad Hind Fauj or the "Free India Army".

August 25, 1943: On 25 August, 1943, the day Netaji formally assumed command of the Indian National Army, he remarked: "With the slogan 'Onwards to Delhi' (Dilli Chalo) on our lips, let us continue to labour and fight till our national flag flies over the Viceroy's House in New Delhi." 'Dilli Chalo' became an inspiring slogan for all patriots.

December 30, 1943: The Andaman islands were occupied by Japan during World War II. The islands were nominally put under the authority of the Arzi Hukumat-e-Azad Hind (Provisional Government of Free India) headed by Netaji Subhash Chandra Bose. Netaji visited the islands during the war, and renamed them as *Shaheed* (Martyr) and *Swaraj* (Self-rule).

July 4, 1944: Subhash Chandra Bose spoke his most famous quote. As part of a motivational speech for the Indian National Army, he urged the people of India to join him in his fight for independence against the British government. Spoken in Hindi, his words were highly evocative — "Give me blood, and I shall give you freedom." India, an independent nation.

August 18, 1945: Raja Habibur Rehman Khan was the only Indian accompanying Subhash Chandra Bose and thus the only Indian witness at the time of the alleged death of Subhash Chandra Bose in a plane crash in Taihoku on 18 August 1945. Raja Habibur Rehman Khan was taken prisoner by allied forces and at the end repatriated to India. Several committees have been set up by the Government of India to probe into this matter.

Bibliography

Anton Pelinka: *Renee Schell, New Brunswick,* Transaction Publishers, Rutgers University Press, New Jersey, 2003.

Anuj Dhar: *Back from Dead: Inside the Subhas Bose Mystery,* Manas Publications, New Delhi, 2005.

Ashman, Sam: *India: Imperialism, Partition and Resistance,* International Socialism, 1997.

Bix, Herbert: *Hirohito and the Making of Modern Japan,* Perennial, 2001.

Bose, Subhas Chandra: *Netaji Subhas Chandra Bose: Correspondence and Selected Documents, 1930-1942,* Inter-India, New Delhi, 1992.

Bose, Sugata: *The New Cambridge History of India: Peasant Labour and Colonial Capital: Rural Bengal Since 1770,* Cambridge University Press, Cambridge, 1993.

Brothers Against the Raj: *A Biography of Indian Nationalists Sarat and Subhas Chandra Bose,* Princeton University Press, London, 1990.

Brown, Giles: *The Hindu Conspiracy, 1914-1917, The Pacific Historical Review,* University of California Press, 1948.

Butow, Robert J. C.: *Japan's Decision to Surrender,* Stanford University Press, 1954.

Chandler, Malcolm, Wright, John: *Modern World History,* Heinemann Educational Publishers, 2001.

Chandra, Bipan, Mridula Mukherjee, Aditya Mukherjee, Sucheta Mahajan, Panikkar, K. N.: *India's Struggle for Independence,* Penguin Books, New Delhi, 1989.

Chopra, Pram Nath: *A Comprehensive History of Modern India,* Sterling Publishing, 2003.

Collett, Nigel: *The Butcher of Amritsar: General Reginald Dyer,* Hambledon and London, 2007.

Collins, Larry, Lapierre, Dominique: *Freedom at Midnight,* HarperCollins, London, 1997.

Cook, Haruko Taya, Theodore Cook, F.: *Japan at War: An Oral History,* New Press, 1992.

Dower, John: *Embracing Defeat: Japan in the Wake of World War II,* W. W. Norton and Company Inc., 1999.

Feifer, George: *The Battle of Okinawa: The Blood and the Bomb,* The Lyons Press, Guilford, 2001.

Ford, Daniel: *The Last Raid,* Air&Space Smithsonian, 1995.

Forest, G. W.: *The Indian Mutiny 1857-1858,* Low Price Publications, Delhi, 2000.

Frank, Richard, B.: *Downfall: the End of the Imperial Japanese Empire,* Penguin, New York, 1999.

Fraser, Thomas, G.: *Germany and Indian Revolution, 1914-18: Journal of Contemporary History,* Sage Publications, 1977.

Gandhi, Mohandas: *An Autobiography: The Story of My Experiments With Truth,* Beacon Press, Boston, 1993.

Hasegawa, Tsuyoshi: *Racing the Enemy: Stalin, Truman and the Surrender of Japan,* Harvard University Press, 2005.

Hoover, Karl: *The Hindu Conspiracy in California, 1913-1918, German Studies Review,* German Studies Association, 1985.

Hopkirk, Peter: *Like Hidden Fire: The Plot to Bring Down the British Empire,* Kodansha Globe, 1997.

Hoyt, Edwin, P.: *Japan's War: The Great Pacific Conflict,* Cooper Square Press, New York, 1986.

James, Lawrence: *The Rise and Fall of the British Empire,* Macmillan, 1997.

John Murray: *Burma: The Forgotten War/Jon Latimer,* London, 2004.

Joyce, Lebra, C.: *Japanese-trained Armies in Southeast Asia: Independence and Volunteer Forces in World War II,* Columbia University Press, New York, 1977.

Kuhlmann, Jan: *Subhas Chandra Bose und die Indienpolitik der Achsenmächte,* Hans Schiler, Berlin, 2003.

Leonard, Gordon, A.: *Brothers Against the Raj — A biography of Indian Nationalists Sarat and Subhas Chandra Bose,* Princeton University Press, New York, 1990.

Lost Hero: *A Biography of Subhas Bose/Mihir Bose,* Quartet Books, London, 1982.

Lovett, Sir Verney: *A History of the Indian Nationalist Movement,* Frederick A. Stokes Company, New York, 1920.

Majumdar, R. C.: *History of the Freedom Movement in India.*

Nehru, Jawaharlal: *Discovery of India,* Oxford University Press, Delhi, 1989.

Nirad, Chaudhuri, C.: *Subhas Chandra Bose-His Legacy and Legend,* Pacific Affairs, 1953.

Palo Alto: *The Pacific War Research Society, Japan's Longest Day.* California: Kodansha International, 1968.

Peter Fay, W.: *The Forgotten Army: India's Armed Struggle for Independence, 1942-1945,* University of Michigan Press, 1993.

Philip Mason: *A Matter of Honour: An Account of the Indian Army,* Officers and Men.

Popplewell, Richard J.: *Intelligence and Imperial Defence: British Intelligence and the Defence of the Indian Empire 1904-1924,* Routledge, 1995.

Ravindra Kumar: *Correspondence and Selected Documents, 1930-1942/Subhas Chandra Bose,* Inter-India, New Delhi, 1992.

Reynolds, Clark, G.: *The Fast Carriers: The Forging of an Air Navy,* McGraw-Hill Book Company, Sydney, 1968.

Romen Bose: *A Will for Freedom: Subhas Chandra Bose and the Indian Independence Movement in Southeast Asia,* V. J. Times, Singapore, 1993.

Sarkar, B. K.: *Political Science Quarterly,* The Acedemy of Political Science, 1921.

Sarkar, Sumit: *Modern India: 1885-1947,* Macmillan, Madras, 1983.

Seal, Anil: *Emergence of Indian Nationalism: Competition and Collaboration in the Later Nineteenth Century,* Cambridge U.P., London, 1968.

Seth, Vikram: *Two Lives,* Brown, London, 2005.

Shah, Nasra M.: *An Overview of Present and Future Emigration Dynamics in South Asia,* International Migration Quarterly Review, 1994.

Sisir Bose, K.: *International Netaji Seminar,* Netaji Research Bureau, India, 1973.

Sisir K. Bose and Sugata Bose: *The Essential Writings of Netaji Subhas Chandra Bose,* Oxford University Press, Delhi, 1997.

————: *Indian Pilgrim: An Unfinished Autobiography/Subhas Chandra Bose,* Oxford University Press, Calcutta, 1997.

————: *Letters to Emilie Schenkl, 1934-1942/Subhash Chandra Bose,* Permanent Black, New Delhi, 2004.

————: *The Indian Struggle, 1920-1942/Subhas Chandra Bose,* Oxford University Press, Calcutta, 1997.

————: *Netaji and India's Freedom: Proceedings of the International Netaji Seminar,* International Netaji Seminar, India, 1973.

Skates, John Ray: *The Invasion of Japan: Alternative to the Bomb,* University of South Carolina Press, Columbia, 1994.

Smith, John B., Malcolm McConnell: *The Last Mission: The Secret Story of World War II's Final Battle,* Broadway Books, New York, 2002.

Sofri, Gianni: *Gandhi and India: A Century in Focus,* The Windrush Press, Gloucestershire, 1999.

Spector, Ronald, H.: *Eagle Against The Sun,* Vintage, 1985.

Springing Tiger: *Subhash Chandra Bose / Hugh Toye*, Cassell, London, 1959.

Strachan, Hew: *The First World War, Volume I: To Arms*, Oxford University Press, USA, 2001.

Subhas Chandra Bose: *A Biography/Marshall J. Getz*, McFarland & Co., USA, 2002.

The Springing Tiger: *Subhash Chandra Bose, Hugh Toye*, Cassell, London, 1959.

Tinker, Hugh: *India in the First World War and after Journal of Contemporary History, 1918-19: From War to Peace*, Sage Publications, 1968.

Wainstock, Dennis: *The Decision to Drop the Atomic Bomb*, Greenwood Publishing Group, 1996.

Weinberg, Gerhard, L.: *A World at Arms: A Global History of World War II*, Cambridge University Press, 1999.

Weintraub, Stanley: *The Last Great Victory: the End of World War II*, Dutton Adult, 1995.

Zollner, Hans-Bernd: *Der Feind Meines Feindes ist Mein Freund – Subhas Chandra Bose und das Zeitgenössische Deutschland unter dem Nationalsozialismus 1933-1943*, LIT Verlag, Hamburg, 2000.

Index

❑❑❑